THE BETTER ANGEL

ALSO BY ROY MORRIS, JR.
Sheridan: The Life and Wars of General Phil Sheridan
Ambrose Bierce: Alone in Bad Company
The Devil's Dictionary (editor)

The Better Angel

WALT WHITMAN
IN THE CIVIL WAR

Roy Morris, Jr.

OXFORD
UNIVERSITY PRESS

2000

OXFORD
UNIVERSITY PRESS

Oxford   New York

Athens   Auckland   Bangkok   Bogotá   Buenos Aires   Calcutta
Cape Town   Chennai   Dar es Salaam   Delhi   Florence   Hong Kong   Istanbul
Karachi   Kuala Lumpur   Madrid   Melbourne   Mexico City   Mumbai
Nairobi   Paris   São Paulo   Singapore   Taipei   Tokyo   Toronto   Warsaw

and associated companies in

Berlin   Ibadan

Copyright © 2000 by Roy Morris, Jr.

Published by Oxford University Press, Inc.
198 Madison Avenue, New York, New York 10016

Oxford is a registered trademark of Oxford University Press

Library of Congress Cataloging-in-Publication Data
Morris, Roy.
The better angel : Walt Whitman in the Civil War / Roy Morris, Jr.
        p.   cm.
Includes bibliographical references and index.
ISBN 0-19-512482-0
1. Whitman, Walt, 1819–1892.
2. Whitman, Walt, 1819–1892—Views on war.
3. United States—History—Civil War, 1861–1865—War work.
4. Poets, American—19th century—Biography.   I. Title.
PS3232.M67 2000
811'.3—dc21
[B]
99-086210

Book design by Adam B. Bohannon

1 3 5 7 9 0 8 6 4 2
Printed in the United States of America
on acid-free paper

For Leslie, with love
"You had me at 'Hello.'"

CONTENTS

ACKNOWLEDGMENTS

Walt Whitman has never lacked for biographers, beginning with his friend John Burroughs in 1867 and continuing through the millennium. Until now, however, no one has seen fit to devote more than a passing chapter, at best, to Whitman's Civil War years, a time that the poet himself considered "the greatest privilege and satisfaction" of his life. With this book I hope to redress that somewhat surprising historical imbalance and to put, whenever possible, a human face on a most inhuman tragedy.

To all those earlier biographers I offer my thanks. I would like to cite particularly the work of the late George L. Sixbey, whose pioneering doctoral dissertation, "Walt Whitman's Middle Years: 1860–1867," is an invaluable guide to Whitman's often murky existence in the years immediately preceding the Civil War. Thanks also to my agent, Tom Wallace, for his kindness and encouragement; to my editor, Peter Ginna, for his patience, tact, and insightful advice; to my father-in-law, G. Burton Pierce, for his unfailing generosity; and to my wife, Leslie, for teaching me each day for the past twenty years how to be a better person. I don't know how well the lessons have taken, but I couldn't have asked for a more willing—or winning—teacher.

THE BETTER ANGEL

The Medicine
of Daily Affection

The Civil War saved Walt Whitman. *Saved* was his word, and like all great poets, Whitman chose his language carefully. To save is "to deliver from sin; to rescue or deliver from danger or harm; to preserve or guard from injury, destruction, or loss." In Whitman's mind, the war did all those things for him personally, even as it also saved the Union itself, delivering it from the sin of slavery, rescuing it from the danger of secession, and preserving it from political destruction. That the nation's salvation brought with it a staggering cost in ruined lives and spiritual devastation, Whitman did not—indeed could not—dispute. But unlike many intellectuals, then and later, he never doubted that the cost had been worth it. How could he, since his own psychic identification with the Union was so complete and unwavering that to have questioned its preservation would have meant questioning his very existence? The republic lived within Walt Whitman as surely as Walt Whitman lived within the republic.

Of the comparative handful of American writers who personally witnessed the Civil War, Whitman was the unlikeliest candidate to become its recorder. Not only was he nearly forty-two years old when the war began, but he was also a poet, a philosopher, a freethinker, a bohemian, a mystic, a near Quaker, and a homosexual. Yet despite the fact that he never saw a battle and only briefly visited the front, his intimate involvement with the aftermath of battles—the bruised and broken young men who filled the military hospitals, the convalescent camps, and the cemeteries—ensured his importance as a wartime witness. Indeed, so closely did Whitman become associated with the war that his friend William D. O'Connor repeatedly urged him to write a book about his experiences, predicting accurately that "no history of our times would ever be written without it. . . . [I]t would itself be history."[1]

There were some, to be sure, who did not believe that Whitman had earned the right to chronicle the war. Union Army veteran Thomas Wentworth Higginson, for one, openly accused him of cowardice for not picking up a musket and joining the ranks. The charge was as specious as it was unfair. No one who knew the bluff, companionable Whitman could ever imagine him in the role of a soldier. He said so himself: "I had my temptations, but they were not strong enough to tempt. I could never think of myself as firing a gun or drawing a sword on another man." His young disciple John Burroughs was even more adamant. "Think of belittling him because he did not enlist as a soldier," Burroughs complained. "Could there be anything more shocking and incongruous than Whitman killing people? One would as soon expect Jesus Christ to go to war."[2]

His lack of military experience, however, did not prevent Whitman from serving the Union cause as wholeheartedly as Higginson or any other frontline soldier. From December 1862 until well after the war was over, he personally visited tens of thousands of hurt, lonely, and scared young men in the hospitals in and around Washington, bringing them the ineffable but not inconsiderable gift of his magnetic, consoling presence. In the process, he lost forever his own good health, beginning a long decline that would leave him increasingly enfeebled for the rest of his life. To his credit, he never regretted his wartime service, or what it had cost him personally. "I only gave myself," he told a friend. "I got the boys."[3]

And more to the point, they got him. Whitman entered the rank, fever-ridden hospitals in the nation's capital like a literal breath of fresh air, bringing with him a knapsack full of humble but much-appreciated gifts: fruit, candy, clothing, tobacco, books, magazines, pencils, and paper. His long white beard, wine-colored suit, and bulging bag of presents gave him a decided resemblance to Santa Claus, and the wounded soldiers, many of them still in their teens, called after him plaintively at the end of each visit: "Walt, Walt, come again!" Except for a six-month period in late 1864 when he was forced to return home to Brooklyn to regain his health, he did come again, scarcely missing a day on his self-appointed rounds. "Walt Whitman, Soldiers' Missionary," he styled himself proudly on the front of his notebook.[4]

A few of the more punctilious members of the United States

Sanitary Commission complained openly about his informal status, his unconventional religious beliefs, and his unpredictable habit of coming and going as he saw fit. Whitman paid them little mind. "As to the Sanitary commissions & the like," he said, "I am sick of them all . . . you ought to see the way the men as they lie helpless in bed turn their faces from the sight of these Agents, Chaplains, &c . . . they seem to me always a set of foxes & wolves." Unlike them, he gave no lectures, handed out no tracts, and prayed no prayers for the immortal souls of white-faced boys writhing on their beds. Instead, he simply sat and listened. That was what they needed most, more than any medicine, and Whitman sensed it instinctively. "I supply often to some of these dear suffering boys in my presence & magnetism that which doctors nor medicines nor skills nor any routine assistance can give," he wrote. "I can testify that friendship has literally cured a fever, and the medicine of daily affection, a bad wound."[5]

In return, the soldiers gave Whitman their love, friendship, and eternal gratitude. Through their humble, uncomplaining valor, they also gave him back his country—which is to say, himself. He began the Civil War in a deep depression, a crumbling *kosmos* whose noble dreams of glory, for himself and his nation, were fast disappearing in an aimless round of bohemian posturing, late-night roistering, and homosexual cruising. He ended the war as "the Good Gray Poet," a beloved, almost mystical figure who personally embodied for millions of Americans a democratic ideal of sharing and brotherhood that remains undimmed nearly a century and a half later.

Despite the myriad horrors of the hospitals—the blood, the

pus, the suffering, and the death—Whitman looked back on the Civil War years as the most fulfilling period of his life. Those darkest of all American days were lit by the courage and sacrifice of thousands of young men, Union and Confederate, who proved on the temples of their own bodies that they cared about a cause more than they cared about themselves. Walt Whitman, in turn, cared about them. "The dead, the dead, the dead, *our* dead," he mourned. And despite his famous caveat that "the real war will never get in the books," some few of those lost young men did get into his books. Their names are there for all to read: John Holmes, Oscar Wilber, Erastus Haskell, Thomas Haley, Lewy Brown, Stewart Glover, Johnny Mahay, Frank Irwin, Thomas Sawyer—just a handful of the thousands of soldiers whose lives he touched, however fleetingly, as he made his rounds. Half a decade before the war, in *Leaves of Grass*, he had written: "I am the man, I suffer'd, I was there." After the Civil War, he could truly say that he had lived those words. More than that, he had lived his ideals. If he was not literally an angel—and he never claimed he was—he was a more than passable substitute.[6]

CHAPTER ONE

New York Stagnation

An uncharacteristically quiet—some said sullen—crowd of thirty thousand New Yorkers clogged the streets around the ornate Astor House on the west side of Broadway on the afternoon of Tuesday, February 19, 1861. They were there to see, if not necessarily to cheer, the president-elect of the United States, then en route from his home in Springfield, Illinois, to Washington, D.C., to take up the reins of an increasingly fractious and runaway nation. Shortly before 4 P.M., a procession of horse-drawn carriages arrived at the front entrance of the hotel, which was located diagonally across the street from P. T. Barnum's American Museum. As Abraham Lincoln climbed out of his carriage, an uneasy silence filled the air. Given the circumstances, he must have felt a little like one of the Great Humbug's prize exhibits.[1]

New York as a whole was cool toward Lincoln. In the

presidential election the past November, the city had given the Republican nominee a mere 35 percent of its votes. Since then, an increasingly emboldened Mayor Fernando Wood, himself a Tammany Hall Democrat, had begun recommending publicly that New York secede from the Union and transform itself into a new city-state, somewhat clumsily named Tri-Insula, with himself presumably serving as doge. Secession was on every-one's minds just then. The day before Lincoln's arrival, former U.S. senator Jefferson Davis of Mississippi had taken his own oath of office in Montgomery, Alabama, as president of the nascent Confederate States of America. Already, seven deep South states had seceded; more were expected to follow any day. Decades of worsening intersectional strife, culminating in the savage guerrilla war between pro- and antislavery supporters in "Bleeding Kansas" and John Brown's abortive raid at Harpers Ferry, Virginia, had led to the formation of the Republican party and Lincoln's bitterly divisive election with a scant mi-nority of the popular vote. After years of self-righteous postur-ing, political demagoguing, and outright lying by Northern ab-olitionists and Southern fire-eaters, the nation as a whole was looking straight down the barrel of a ruinous civil war.[2]

Marooned atop a stage in the massive traffic jam around the Astor House that afternoon was a forty-one-year-old Brooklyn-ite as troubled in his way as the nation itself. Walt Whitman — former carpenter, former printer, former schoolteacher, former newspaper editor, former novelist, former political activist, and, as it sometimes seemed, former poet — was becalmed in his own "horrible sloughs." Six years after his astonishing poetic debut, *Leaves of Grass*, had seemed to presage, as Ralph Waldo Emerson told him, "the beginning of a great career," Whitman was locked in the grip of a spiraling depression. His low spirits were occasioned more or less equally by the loss of his job as editor of the *Brooklyn Daily Times*, the mixed reception of his latest book of poetry, the ongoing burdens of his troubled and troublesome family, the bankruptcy of his Boston-based publishers, and the end of an unhappy love affair with a young man several years his junior. He was currently spending most of his days like today, riding alongside New York's hard-bitten stagecoach drivers as they made their way through the city's teeming streets. His nights were spent at Pfaff's beer cellar in Greenwich Village, drinking, talking, and swapping barbs with the tavern's self-styled bohemians. Far from being poised on the brink of a great career, Whitman increasingly felt stranded in a personal and professional dead end, caught in a vortex of "quicksand years that whirl me I know not whither."[3]

Whitman's depression mirrored the mood of anxious Americans everywhere concerning the future — if any — of their imperiled republic. Always politically sensitive, he understood only too well the likely consequences of Lincoln's election and the failure of political leaders on both sides of the Mason-Dixon line to resolve their differences peaceably. In a prescient passage in *Leaves of Grass* he had tried almost physically to hold the states together by force of will:

States!
Were you looking to be held together by the lawyers?
By an agreement on a paper? Or by arms?
Away!

I arrive, bringing these, beyond all the forces of courts and
    arms,
These! to hold you together as firmly as the earth itself is
    held together.[4]

Against the rising tide of sectionalism, Whitman urged "a
new friendship" between the states, "indifferent of place" and
woven together by an overarching affection. "Those who love
each other," he insisted, "shall be invincible." Ironically, Abraham Lincoln, the one individual charged with holding the states
together politically as Whitman had tried to do poetically,
would say much the same thing at his upcoming inauguration.
In *Leaves of Grass*, Whitman had promised that "affection shall
solve every one of the problems of freedom." Lincoln, who in
his own way was also a poet, would put it slightly differently
in his first inaugural address. "We are not enemies, but friends,"
he would say, directing his speech to the unhappy South. "We
must not be enemies. Though passion may have strained, it
must not break our bonds of affection. The mystic chords of
memory, stretching from every battlefield, and patriot grave, to
every living heart and hearthstone, all over this broad land, will
yet swell the chorus of the Union, when again touched, as surely
they will be, by the better angels of our nature."[5]

Few individuals had heard those chords as long or as often
as Whitman himself. From the time of his birth at West Hills,
Long Island, on May 31, 1819, he had absorbed the American
democratic experience in all its boisterous variety. His ancestors
were English and Dutch immigrants, stolid farmers and canny
horse traders who during the Revolutionary War had thrown

in their lot with the patriots. His paternal grandmother had told him hair-raising stories of British atrocities during the military occupation of Long Island; his grand-uncle had been killed at the Battle of Brooklyn. As a boy, Whitman had found the washed-up bones of some of the twelve thousand American prisoners of war who had died in the rotting prison ships in Brooklyn's Wallabout Bay; and years later, as editor of the *Brooklyn Daily Eagle*, he had successfully led a public campaign to raise a monument to the borough's martyred dead. As a child of six, he had been lifted into the arms of the Marquis de La-fayette during the old hero's triumphant return to America. He had seen President Andrew Jackson parading down Fulton Street in a white beaver hat, and as an office boy he had per-sonally delivered legal papers to the fallen dynast Aaron Burr. American history, particularly the revolution, lived vividly in his imagination, engendering an almost religious devotion to the Union. In his own household, three of his brothers were named after presidents: George Washington, Thomas Jefferson, and Andrew Jackson. His father was an acquaintance of Thomas Paine.[6]

Whitman's intense love of country was reflected in his art. *Leaves of Grass* was not simply a book of poetry, it was a work-ing manifesto for a new American religion based upon "the su-premacy of Individuality"—and Whitman himself was nothing if not an individual. His groundbreaking poetry, with its frank discussion of sex, bodily functions, and sweaty quotidian life, together with his carefully cultivated image as a rough-and-ready man of the people, openly challenged accepted norms of behavior. His "barbaric yawp" was a new kind of language, the *lingua franca* of the common man, transmitting its revolutionary message of self-liberation and personal worth to people across all strata of society. The all-including "I" of "Song of Myself," the longest poem in *Leaves of Grass* and the first great poem in the American vernacular, was not simply "Walt Whitman, an American" but men and women everywhere, particularly those of his native country. "I celebrate myself and sing myself," he said in the poem's famous opening lines, "and what I assume you shall assume, for every atom belonging to me as good belongs to you." He heard America singing, he said, in the humble voices of her workers, the unheralded farmers, sailors, storekeepers, and mechanics who quietly transacted the daily business of the republic. To their rough voices he lent his own:

> Take my leaves America, take them South and take them
> North,
> Make welcome for them everywhere, for they are your own
> offspring,
> Surround them East and West, for they would surround
> you,
> And you precedents, connect lovingly with them, for they
> connect lovingly with you.[7]

At the time of Lincoln's New York visit, Whitman was contemplating a national tour of his own to broadcast his vision of a cohesive country, "strong, limber, just, open-mouthed, American-blooded, full of pride, full of ease, of passionate friendliness." He was too late. The nation was indeed full of passion and pride, but by early 1861 it was far from friendly. Lincoln's journey to the capital seemed more like a foray into enemy territory than a triumphant political victory march. A covey of bodyguards, including future Union generals John Pope, Edwin Sumner, and David Hunter and private detective Allan Pinkerton, shadowed the president-elect every step of the way. Armed guards patrolled each bridge and overpass, suspiciously eyeing the welcoming crowds, and spare locomotives were parked ahead of time in all of the cities that Lincoln was scheduled to visit, ready to spirit him away instantly at the first sign of trouble. Even with such extraordinary precautions, a bomb was discovered under Lincoln's seat on his private train, and a sinister gang of toughs called the Blood Tubs was said to be plotting his immediate assassination. Whitman was not the only one who worried, when Lincoln stepped out of his carriage at the Astor House, that "many an assassin's knife and pistol lurk'd in hip or breast-pocket there, ready, as soon as break and riot came."[8]

There was no riot that day in New York, merely an anticlimactic "dumb-show" in which Lincoln and the assembled crowd looked at each other with silent curiosity. Whitman, atop his stagecoach, had "a capital view of it all, and especially of Mr. Lincoln, his look and gait—his perfect composure and coolness—his unusual and uncouth height, his dress of complete black, stovepipe hat push'd back on the head, dark-brown complexion, seam'd and wrinkled yet canny-looking face, black, bushy head of hair, disproportionately long neck, and his hands held behind him as he stood observing the people." Whitman felt that it would take four different sorts of genius—Plutarch, Aeschylus, Michaelangelo, and Rabelais—to truly sketch Lincoln's portrait. Somewhat surprisingly, he failed to realize that he had already taken the new president's measure himself, six years earlier, in his unpublished essay, "The Eighteenth Presidency!".[9]

Written against the backdrop of the dispiriting 1856 presidential campaign between Democratic nominee James Buchanan, the American (Know-Nothing) party's Millard Fillmore, and the Republican party's first standard-bearer, John C. Frémont, "The Eighteenth Presidency!" was an impassioned appeal to the idealized workingmen and women of the nation. These open-hearted laborers Whitman contrasted favorably to the corrupt politicians then in power, the "limber-tongued lawyers, very fluent but empty, feeble old men, professional politicians, dandies, dyspeptics, and so forth," who controlled the nation's destiny. Their ranks included a dizzying array of malefactors: "robbers, pimps . . . malignants, conspirators, murderers . . . infidels, disunionists, terrorists, mail-riflers, slave-catchers . . . body-snatchers . . . monte-dealers, duelists, carriers of concealed weapons, blind men, deaf men, pimpled men, scarred inside with the vile disorder, gaudy outside with gold chains made from the people's money and the harlot's money twisted together . . . the lousy combings and born freedom sellers of the earth." At the head of the whole unsavory combination, Whitman charged, sat the president of the United States, Franklin Pierce, who "eats dirt and excrement for his daily meals."[10]

Against such a malodorous combination, the poet yearned

for a "Redeemer President" who would come out of the West, "some heroic, shrewd, fully-informed, healthy-bodied, middle-aged, beard-faced American blacksmith or boatman . . . dressed in a clean suit of working attire, and with the tan all over his face, breast, and arms." This was a remarkably accurate, if incomplete, description of Lincoln himself, written a good two years before Whitman or most of the nation had ever heard of him, and nearly five years before the poet first laid eyes on the president-elect in front of the Astor House. "I would certainly vote for that sort of man," Whitman had promised, and four years later he did just that. It remained to be seen if the majority of the country, which had not voted for Lincoln, would react as favorably when he finally took office.[11]

The slashing poem "Respondez!", written the same year as "The Eighteenth Presidency!", offered little hope for optimism. In its almost hysterical linking of public and private corruption, the poem recalls the darkest passages in *Timon of Athens*, depicting a depraved, demoralized society led by "murderers, bigots, fools, unclean persons." The poem posits a nightmare world in which the worst people dominate the best, a godless society governed by "money, business, imports, exports, custom, authority, precedents, pallor, dyspepsia, smut, ignorance, unbelief." Traditional roles are grotesquely reversed: judges trade places with criminals, jailers with prisoners, masters with slaves. The highest ideals of American life—freedom, democracy, and equality—are replaced by "management, caste, comparison." Wholesome sexuality has become the province of "she-harlots and he-harlots." All the cardinal virtues have been lost:

Let freedom prove no man's inalienable right! every one
   who can tyrannize, let him tyrannize to his satisfaction!
Let none but infidels be countenanced!
Let the eminence of meanness, treachery, sarcasm, hate,
   greed, indecency, impotence, lust, be taken for granted
   above all![12]

In their bitterness and cynicism, "The Eighteenth Presidency!" and "Respondez!" are light-years removed from the utopian expansionism of *Leaves of Grass* (even the exclamation points in the titles reveal a desperate stridency). Whitman himself, in the half-decade since their composition, had undergone a similar transformation. Gone was the gladsome, celebratory poet of the open road; he had been replaced by a detached, world-weary onlooker who had taken to spending much of his time indoors in a vaultlike tavern inhabited by some distinctly unquiet ghosts.

Whitman had begun going to Pfaff's beer cellar, at 653 Broadway, in the summer of 1859, soon after he lost his job as editor of the *Brooklyn Daily Times*. Pfaff's had become the nightly meeting place for an ever-changing group of poets, artists, journalists, critics, actors, agents, and assorted hangers-on, united only by their artistic pretensions and their *épater les bourgeois* approach to life. Chief among them was Henry Clapp, the acid-tongued editor of the *Saturday Press*, a New York weekly whose literary prestige was exceeded only by its fiscal fragility. Clapp had been to Paris in the 1840s and witnessed the birth of *la vie de bohème*. He had returned to America determined to establish a New World beachhead for modish artistes. Pfaff's, conveniently located just down the street from the New York Free Love League (which he also frequented), was Clapp's chosen staging ground. The beer was cold, the sausages and potato pancakes were tasty, and the wine cellar was considered one of the finest in the city.[13]

With his short stature, high-pitched voice, grizzled beard, and ever-present pipe, Clapp looked a little like a down-on-his-luck leprechaun. A reporter for the *New York Leader* described him in appropriately continental terms as "a queer fellow—a character. He is a born Yankee; speaks French like a native; plays poker like a Western man; drinks like a fish, smokes like a Dutchman; is as full of dainty conceits as a Spanish or Italian poet, is as rough in his manners as a Russian or a Russian bear." No one was safe from Clapp's sharp tongue. Fellow editor Horace Greeley was "a self-made man that worships his creator." William Dean Howells and Nathaniel Hawthorne were "a couple of shysters." A certain local clergyman was "awaiting a vacancy in the Trinity." Wall Street, with its howling and screeching traders, was "Caterwaul Street," and the United States Treasury was said to be changing its motto from "In God We Trust" to "In Gold We Trust." One of his favorite bits of advice was: "Never tell secrets to your relatives. Blood will tell."[14]

For all his sniping, Clapp had a generous side, and he was one of Whitman's earliest and strongest supporters, at a time when the poet needed all the friends he could get. Years later, Whitman would tell his young disciple Horace Traubel: "I don't know if you have ever realized . . . what it means to be a horror in the sight of the people about you: but there was a time when

I felt it to the full—when the enemy—and nearly all were the enemy then—wanted for nothing better or more than simply, without remorse, to crush me, to brush me, without compunction or mercy . . . to do anything, everything, to rid themselves of me."[15]

Clapp was different. He recognized Whitman's poetic genius—many did not—and he also saw the poet's symbolic value as an avatar of the rising new bohemian. As the reigning "King of Bohemia," Clapp enthusiastically welcomed Whitman into Pfaff's inner circle; more important, he gave him a public forum for his work, however sporadic it would prove to be in the years preceding the Civil War. He published favorable—and sometimes unfavorable—reviews of Whitman's work, free advertisements for *Leaves of Grass*, parodies written in the Whitman style, and snippets of what could only be called press agentry, such as the November 12, 1859, announcement that "whoever wishes to see a perfect likeness of Walter Whitman should go to Root's Gallery, No. 363 Broadway." It was with a deep sense of gratitude that Whitman told Traubel, late in life, that "Henry Clapp stepped out from the crowd of hooters—was my friend, a much needed ally at that time. . . . My own history could not be written with Henry left out. I mean it—that is not an extravagant statement."[16]

Clapp was the acknowledged ringleader at Pfaff's, but he was far from alone in his subterranean kingdom. Sitting at the head of a long, low table strategically placed at the far end of the cellar, he presided over a raucous gathering of the city's most outrageous, if not always most talented, literati. Among the regulars were Artemus Ward, the western comedian and friend of

Mark Twain; future novelist Thomas Bailey Aldrich; Irish-born short-story writer Fitz-James O'Brien; poet-humorist George Arnold; drama critic Edward G. P. Wilkins; drug addict-turned-author Fitz-Hugh Ludlow; *New York Times* journalist John Swinton; Polish expatriate Count Adam Gurowski; and travel writer and poet Bayard Taylor.

Adding immeasurably to the beauty and tumult of the surroundings were two remarkable women: Ada Clare and Adah Isaacs Menken. Clare, whose real name was Jane McElheney, was a Charleston, South Carolina, beauty who had relocated to New York as a girl of nineteen to become an actress. Her professional debut in *The Hunchback* was a disaster; critics found her arms too thin and her voice too shrill. Undismayed, she turned to poetry as her creative outlet, publishing a number of confessional lyrics on the subject of lost love. It was a topic she knew painfully well—her seduction and jilting by concert pianist Louis Gottschalk was a famous scandal, producing an out-of-wedlock child with whom she traveled openly, signing hotel guestbooks with a defiant flourish, "Miss Clare and Son."[17]

Sharing Clare's bad luck with men was her fellow-Southerner Menken. The New Orleans–born Menken was the more successful actress, largely because of her well-rounded figure, which she showed to good effect in the Broadway melodrama *Mazeppa*, in which she wore flesh-colored tights and rode off into the sunset on the back of a "fiery steed." But despite being widely acclaimed as "the most perfectly developed woman in the world," Menken also had trouble holding onto men. She was married four times, and her second husband, heavyweight boxing champion John "the Benicia Boy" Heenan, publicly disowned both her and their son, denying unchivalrously that he and Menken had ever been married in the first place.[18]

Despite, or perhaps because of, his comparative immunity to the two Ada(h)s' potent sexual charms, Whitman got along well with the distaff bohemians. He encouraged their writing, listened sympathetically to their romantic travails, and in general acted the role of a literal Dutch uncle. Menken in turn fulsomely praised Whitman as a great philosopher, "centuries ahead of his contemporaries," and predicted that one day he would have marble statues erected in his honor. "It is very curious that the girls have been my sturdiest defenders," Whitman mused later. "Some would say they were girls little to my credit, but I disagree with them there." After Clare's grisly death from hydrophobia at the age of thirty-eight—she was bitten through the nose by her theatrical agent's rabid lapdog—he went out of his way to mourn "poor, poor Ada Clare," whose uncoventional lifestyle, he said, had been "gay, easy, sunny, free, loose, but not ungood." As for Menken, he returned her good will by standing best man at her penultimate wedding.[19]

Whitman's relations with the male bohemians were not always as smooth. Reflecting, perhaps, his depressed, disordered state, the usually good-natured poet quarreled openly, and at times physically, with the men at Pfaff's. He derided the foppish drama critic Wilkins for being "sickish, dressy, Frenchy." When Aldrich published a book of poems titled *The Bells*, Whitman told him cuttingly, "Yes, Tom, I like your *tinkles*: I like them very well." William Winter earned his lasting enmity for characterizing *Leaves of Grass* as "odiferous." Whitman, in turn, characterized Winter as "a dried up cadaverous schoolmaster," and years later still remembered him hotly as "little Willy Winter, miserable cuss!" It was all part of the backbiting repartee common to literary gatherings everywhere—not even Whitman was immune from scorn. One night, he told Traubel, he was forced to listen helplessly while someone at the table gave a burlesque reading of *Leaves of Grass*, "the strokes bright, witty, unsparing." According to the poet, he had been untroubled by the teasing— "I was inclined to let them be amused." He was decidedly not so inclined when, shortly after the beginning of the Civil War, would-be humorist George Arnold rose to his feet and proposed a mock toast: "Success to Southern arms!" Whitman, ever the patriot, jumped up and denounced the toast in loud, angry terms. The embarrassing scene ended with the two men scuffling briefly and Arnold giving Whitman's beard a vigorous parting tug.[20]

In a poem fragment from the period, Whitman pointedly associates the underground tavern with a burial vault:

> The vault at Pfaff's where the drinkers and laughers meet to
>   eat and drink and carouse
> While on the walk immediately overhead pass the myriad
>   feet of Broadway
> As the dead in their graves are underfoot hidden
> And the living pass over them, recking not of them,
> Laugh on laughers!
> Drink on drinkers!
> Bandy the jest!
> Toss the theme from one to another!
>
>   · · ·

The lights beam in the first vault—but the other is entirely
    dark.[21]

The poem was written on the back of some notes that Whitman had made on the occasion of the two-hundredth anniversary of the Presbyterian church at Jamaica, Long Island. The
Reverend James M. Macdonald, rededicating the church, had
taken as his text the well-known passage from Ecclesiastes: "One
generation passeth away, and another generation cometh: but
the earth abideth forever." As generations go, the bohemians at
Pfaff's passed away more swiftly than most. Ned Wilkins, the
group's reigning Beau Brummell, died in 1861 of tuberculosis
contracted, fittingly enough, in a damp garret. The brawny and
brawling Irishman Fitz-James O'Brien, an early volunteer to the
Union cause, died of tetanus on April 6, 1862, the result of a
fatal bullet wound suffered in a twilight encounter with Confederate cavalry leader Turner Ashby on a disputed Virginia
backroad. O'Brien and Aldrich had both applied for a position on Brigadier General Frederick Lander's staff, prompting
Clapp to comment drily that "Aldrich was shot in O'Brien's
shoulder."[22]

Next to die was George Arnold, who passed away from pa-
ralysis in November 1865. Seven months later, Artemus Ward
died of tuberculosis in England at the early age of thirty-three.
Fitz-Hugh Ludlow died in Geneva in 1870; and Ada Clare met
her horrific fate in 1874. In 1877 Edmund Stedman, another
regular, found a list he had made in 1860 of a party at the tavern.
Of the fourteen names on the list, nine were dead, including
Clapp, who drank himself to death in April 1875. The *New York*

Daily Graphic, in a caustic obituary headlined "A Bohemian's Checkered Life," postured disapprovingly: "There has rarely been a more pathetic picture than this poor old man presented, reduced to rags, consumed by a horrible thirst, and utterly without hope for this world or the next."[23]

However fractious and doom-laden the crowd at Pfaff's proved to be, it nevertheless represented a welcome change from Whitman's worrisome family life. Ever pressed for money, the family was forced to rent out the top part of its Brooklyn house and live in the basement—Whitman was spending an inordinate amount of time underground, just then. Besides Walt and his mother, Louisa, the crowd at 106 North Portland Avenue included Whitman's crippled and retarded brother, Eddy, "a poor, stunted boy" prone to "infernal, damnable fits"; older brother Jesse, an ex-sailor who had begun exhibiting the erractic behavior and violent mood swings of tertiary syphilis, contracted on shore from an Irish prostitute; young brother George, a comparatively normal if unimaginative carpenter; and Walt's favorite brother, Jeff, along with Jeff's wife, Mattie, and their baby daughter, Mannahatta. Nearby lived another brother, Andrew, a tubercular alcoholic, his slatternly wife, Nancy, and their two neglected sons, Jimmy and Georgy (a third son, Andrew, would be run over and killed a few years later while playing unwatched on a Brooklyn street). Married sister Hannah had moved to Vermont, but she still managed to keep the family in constant turmoil with her plaintive letters home describing her alleged mistreatment at the hands of her husband, landscape artist Charles Heyde.[24]

Life in the Whitman household was an emotional rollercoaster. Mrs. Whitman suffered from a number of real or imagined physical complaints, which she never hesitated to share with Walt, her most sympathetic listener. The severely handicapped Eddy had the mind of a child but the appetite, quite literally, of a horse—he had to be watched at mealtimes, or else he would continue eating until he passed out. Jesse, between benders, would periodically threaten his mother, brothers, or sisters-in-law with a chair; at other times he would sit silently beside his infant niece, rocking her cradle back and forth for hours. Andrew and his wife stopped by frequently to cadge money and drop off their barely housebroken sons; George and Jeff argued; Mannahatta cried; and Hannah's latest domestic crisis was loudly debated around the dinner table. Small wonder that Walt spent as little time as possible in the bosom of his family, or that he preferred the company of two-fisted stagecoach drivers or Greenwich Village aesthetes to his own importunate flesh and blood.[25]

More or less by default, Walt had become the family's chief breadwinner, an unwelcome and uncongenial role that added immeasurably to the poet's cup of woe. After losing his job as editor of the *Daily Times*—supposedly for writing editorials advocating the licensing of prostitutes and the rights of unmarried women to experiment with sex—Whitman earned a precarious six or seven dollars a week writing filler for other local newspapers. He also received occasional royalties on the sale of *Leaves of Grass*, a third edition of which appeared in 1860. Still, it was a pinched, penurious existence, and there is more than a trace of desperation in a note that he scribbled to himself at the time: "It is time now to *stir* first for *Money* enough to live and provide

for *M*—*to stir*—first write stories, and get out of this Slough."
(*M* presumably was his mother.)[26]

But finances alone were not the only source of Whitman's
depression. Besides struggling with money matters, he was also
struggling with his sexuality. He had always been attracted to
young men—a recent biographer, David S. Reynolds, has even
suggested that, as young Long Island schoolteacher, Whitman
was tarred, feathered, and run out of town on a rail after being
accused of inappropriate relations with one of his students—
and in late 1859 he unburdened himself of his romantic concerns
in a painfully revealing cluster of poems entitled "Calamus,"
after the phallic and upthrusting plant of the same name. The
poems, he said, were "fit to be perused during the days of the
approach of Death." Like Shakespeare's dark sonnets, they re-
count a middle-aged poet's unrequited love for a beautiful
young man:

> For an athlete is enamour'd of me, and I of him,
> But toward him there is something fierce and terrible in
>   me eligible to burst forth,
> I dare not tell him it in words, not even in these songs.[27]

In poem after poem Whitman confesses a deep sense of
shame for his inmost desires:

> Beneath this impassive face the hot fires of hell continually
>   burn—within me the lurid smutch and the smoke;
> Not a crime can be named but I have it in me waiting to
>   break forth,

Lusts and wickedness are acceptable to me,
I walk with delinquents with passionate love.[28]

The poet's misgivings seem to have been well-founded, as he ruefully recounts in "Hours Continuing Long," where he declares himself "discouraged, distracted—for the one I cannot content myself without, soon I saw him content himself without me." And in the same poem he wonders aloud:

Is there even one other like me—distracted—his friend, his
    lover, lost to him?
Is he too as I am now? Does he still rise in the morning,
    dejected, thinking who is lost to him? and at night,
    awaking, think who is lost?[29]

At length, Whitman poignantly declares, "I loved a certain person ardently and my love was not return'd." The lover in question may have been Fred Vaughan, a young Brooklyn cabbie who shared Whitman's Classon Avenue home during the three-year period between 1856 and 1859 when Walt temporarily lived apart from his family. The two probably met at Pfaff's, but they also frequented Whitman's regular haunts along the ferry docks and lumberyards. The underlying cause of their breakup may have been Vaughan's own conflicted sexuality. In recently unearthed letters, Vaughan frets continually about being dishonest to himself, his family, and his friends; and a dozen years after his parting with Whitman, he somewhat wonderingly finds himself possessed of a wife and four children. At any rate,

Vaughan was neither the first nor the last young man whom Whitman would lose to marriage, and the relationship had been over for at least two years before Vaughan married in May 1862.[30]

Whoever the lost lover may have been, the "Calamus" poems display a constant longing for reconnection, and following the end of his painful affair Whitman began a compulsive quest for a new lover, or lovers, among the assorted stage drivers, ferryboat pilots, soldiers, sailors, firemen, wharf rats, runaways, drifters, and juvenile deliquents who comprised the flip side of his more rarefied friendships. His notebooks from the time contain multitudinous names and physical descriptions of the young men he encountered on his restless rounds. George Marler, a "candy butcher" from Ohio, was "a large-nosed tallish fellow"; Mark Graynor, a plumber, was "young, 5 ft 7 in, black moustache"; an ex-boxer named Philip was "tallish, black-eyed, brownish, sharp-faced, with a suspicion of squint in his eyes — reckless." Nineteen-year-old David Wilson, a blacksmith, was taken home by Whitman to spend the night, as was Daniel Spencer, a "somewhat feminine" stage driver who "had never been in a fight — and did not drink at all."[31]

This is not to suggest that all — or perhaps any — of the young men became physically intimate with Whitman. But the sheer numbers and variety would seem to imply that, if nothing else, the poet was drifting aimlessly through what he termed a "city of orgies," where strangers' "frequent and swift flash of eyes [offer] me love." This longing is made manifest in another poem, "To a Stranger":

Passing stranger! you do not know how longingly I look
  upon you,
You must be he I was seeking, or she I was seeking,
  (it comes to me as of a dream,)
I have somewhere surely lived a life of joy with you,

. . .

I am to wait, I do not doubt I am to meet you again,
I am to see to it that I do not lose you.[32]

And in "What Think You I Take My Pen in Hand?", the
poet tosses a wistful glance at

. . . two simple men I saw to-day on the pier in the midst
  of the crowd, parting the parting of dear friends,
The one to remain hung on the other's neck and passion-
  ately kiss'd him,
While the one to depart tightly prest the one to remain in
  his arms.[33]

A Brooklyn ferryboat pilot named Thomas Gere left behind
a vivid description of Whitman at the time. "He was quite six
feet in height, with the frame of a gladiator, a flowing gray
beard mingled with the hairs on his broad, slightly bared chest,"
Gere recalled. "In his well-laundered, checked shirt-sleeves, with
trousers frequently pushed into his boot-legs, his fine head covered with an immense slouched black or light felt hat." Other
ferry passengers, Gere told Whitman, surmised that he was a
retired ship's captain, an actor, an army officer, a clergyman, or

a smuggler. One even whispered that Whitman was crazy, a suggestion that made the poet laugh until he cried. Another ferry pilot, John Y. Bauldsir, remembered Whitman colloquially as "a fine, strappin' fellow, tall, broad-shouldered, and straight. He had a kind word for everybody and from everybody, for everybody liked him."[34]

Nowhere was this liking more evident than between Whitman and the "strange, quick-eyed, wondrous race" of stage drivers with whom he spent most of his daylight hours. The men who drove the clattering wooden omnibuses up and down Broadway were a distinctive, colorful lot; they sported names like Broadway Jack, Balky Bill, Yellow Joe, and Old Elephant. Most had come to Manhattan from the countryside, and their homespun ways and muscular, suntanned looks appealed to Whitman on various levels. He was never happier than when riding alongside the drivers on their daily rounds, swapping yarns and trading confidences in the brisk open air while the New York traffic swirled around them. These men, too, went into his notebooks. James Doyle had a "coarse pleasing smiling round face" with hardly any chin. George Wright was "tallish, thinnish, brunette," with a "black moustache & oily, labial way of talking." Glouscester, England, native Vincent Reynolds was "round, plump, red-haired"; Barney Riley was a "stout, plump Irish boy." Thomas Cummings, "aged about 34," was "smallish sized, brown beard"; and twenty-three-year-old James Sloan was a "plain, homely American."[35]

Whitman rode with everyone—besides the company, it was also a good way to travel for free from the Brooklyn ferryboat terminus to Pfaff's uptown—and in return he helped the drivers collect their fares, handle their horses, and pass the tedious, wearying hours. So closely associated was Whitman with the stage drivers of the time that the fastidious New England poet, James Russell Lowell, warned a foreign visitor against looking up the author of *Leaves of Grass*. "Whitman," said Lowell, "is a rowdy, a New York tough, a loafer, a frequenter of low places, a friend of cab drivers." Walt, of course, would have been delighted by the description.[36]

Like many physical occupations in nineteenth-century America, driving a New York stage was always dangerous and often deadly. Collisions with other stages, private coaches, brewery wagons, horseback riders, and unwary pedestrians could send drivers pitching headfirst under their rigs, to be trampled by their horses' hooves or crushed beneath their wooden wheels. Roving gangs of street toughs with such fearsome and well-deserved names as the Plug Uglies, the Roach Guards, and the Dead Rabbits might yank them off their seats and beat them insensible at the slightest provocation. Violent altercations with other drivers were commonplace, and disputes were often settled with knives, rocks, whips, and guns. Nor were accidents and arguments the drivers' only job-related perils. Exposure to the elements, as well as constantly breathing in the pungent mixture of dried horse manure, pig slop, rotting garbage, and human sewage running in the streets, weakened the drivers' resistance to disease and left them susceptible to the various scourges of the time, particularly those affecting the respiratory tract.

Sick and injured drivers were taken routinely to Broadway Hospital, at the corner of Broadway and Pearl Street. With his

habitual kindness and comradely concern, Whitman soon became a fixture at the drivers' bedsides and a favorite of the hospital doctors and staff. In a series of articles in the *New York
Leader*, he chronicled the men's precarious medical conditions:
"There they are, many pining and wasting week after week with
painful and incurable diseases—burning fevers, racking rheumatism, erysipelas, palsy, consumption, pneumonia, and all the
long list; many brought in from sudden accidents, resulting in
amputation, often followed by death." In 1861 alone, he wrote,
the hospital had received 358 fever cases, 205 rheumatism cases,
95 typhoid cases, 62 bronchitis cases, 167 consumption cases, 131
measles cases, 79 delirium tremens cases, 49 pneumonia cases,
35 dysentery cases, 120 ulcer cases, 62 gunshot wounds, 261 fractured bones, 62 gunshot wounds, and 6 opium overdoses. Reflecting the daily perils of the working class, the hospital that
year recorded 24 deaths from stabs or gunshot wounds, 82 from
falls, 14 from railroad accidents, 22 from burns and scaldings,
and 8 from being run over by stages or other vehicles. Life on
the streets of New York, in the true Hobbesian sense, was often
nasty, brutish, and short.[37]

In one article, Whitman made a tour of hospital wards. Each
ward contained twenty-four beds along the walls, with a card
posted above each one listing the patient, his disease, and the
recommended treatment. "What a volume of meaning, what a
tragic poem there is in every one of those sick wards," Whitman
wrote. Here he found stage driver Charles Green, who had been
run over on Fourth Avenue. One of Green's legs was broken,
the other badly mashed, and he had been confined to the hospital for five weeks with his leg in a box. In the cot beside him

was Frank Osborne, a young fireman who had been knocked down while running to a fire and suffered a broken collarbone and several fractured ribs. Another patient had gotten his hand caught in a steam engine, losing two fingers. In the next bed over lay a foundry worker who had been struck on the head by a hammer and was not expected to live. And in the corner bed was "poor James Watson . . . three weeks ago a picture of athletic manly health, size and good looks." The twenty-six-year-old Watson had been thrown from a railroad car at Jersey City and suffered "a frightful wound" and a broken ankle. The surgeons had decided not to amputate the foot, and Watson had subsequently contracted a fatal fever. Another ward contained a young medical student who had broken his back while foolishly trying to perform a headstand on a wobbly table.[38]

Particularly upsetting to Whitman, the son of an alcoholic, were the delirium tremens sufferers. One "brown-faced, middle-aged Hercules of a fellow," a sailor whose sinewy arms were covered with tattoos, had been on a week-long bust, drinking three-cent brandy. For fifty hours, the man told Whitman, "he had been attacked, covered, pulled at, buffeted, &c., by swarms of grinning monkeys and apes, who put him to every conceivable torture and annoyance. Then he had the company of a large, fierce, black dog, that amused itself by incessantly springing at him and biting him, first on one spot, and then another; and then crowds of infuriated men and women would chase him and belabor him with cudgels, and pull his hair." Another man "labor[ed] under the idea that there was a beautiful, angelic lady floating up in the air, over his bed, reaching down to him a glass of liquor. He mounted on a table to take it, and the attendants had to pull him down."[39]

There was, in fact, a real-life counterpart to the rummy's "angelic lady" at the hospital, and Whitman soon made her acquaintance. "There is a lady comes from time to time," he reported in the *Leader*. "She brings illustrated and other papers, books of stories, little comforts in the way of eating and drinking, shirts, gowns, handkerchiefs, &c. I dare not mention her name, but she is beautiful. . . . She is clearly averse to the eclat of good works, and sometimes, to avoid show, sends her gifts by a servant." Who the mysterious angel was, and how well Whitman knew her, is a matter of continuing speculation. She may have been the New York stage actress Ellen Grey, a blonde-haired, blue-eyed beauty whom he had first seen perform at the Bowery Theatre in 1857 and whose photograph he kept tacked above his mantle as an old man, describing her to Horace Traubel as "an old sweetheart of mine." Or she may have been the ever-venturesome Ada Clare, whose name, as Whitman biographer Jerome Loving has pointed out, closely echoes the nom de plume of a woman signing herself "Ellen Eyre" who wrote a mysterious letter to Whitman at the same time that his article appeared concerning the "benevolent lady" of the hospital.[40]

The letter, hand-delivered to Whitman at Pfaff's by the lady's servant, is strongly suggestive. It seems to hint, however indirectly, that she and the poet had enjoyed some sort of sexual encounter. "My Dear Mr. Whitman," she wrote, "I fear you took me last night for a female privateer. It is true that I was sailing under false colors—but the flag I assure you covered nothing piratical although I would joyfully have made your heart a captive." She went on to confess "the fancy I had long nourished for you . . . the unknown mine of latent affection a man may have unconsciously inspired in a woman's breast. . . . My social position enjoins precaution and mystery. . . . I preserve my incognito, yet mystery lends an ineffable charm to love and when a woman is bent upon the gratification of her inclinations she is pardonable if she still spreads the veil of decorum over her actions."[41]

Decorous or not, Miss Eyre was defiantly unrepentant about her actions. "I can see no vice in that generous sympathy with which we share our caprices with those who have inspired us with tenderness. I trust you will think well enough of me soon to renew the pleasure you afforded me last p.m. and I therefore write to remind you that there is a sensible head as well as a sympathetic heart, both of which would gladly evolve with warmth for your diversion and comfort. You have already my whereabouts and my hours. It shall only depend on you to make them yours and me the happiest of women."[42]

There is no indication that Whitman ever took up Miss Eyre's frankly sexual invitation. The only other mention of the fascinating episode comes in Whitman's notebook citation for July 8, 1862: "Frank Sweezey (July 8, '62) 5th Ave. Brown face, large features, black moustache (is the one I told the whole story to about Ellen Eyre)—talks very little." By then, Whitman seemed more interested in the dark-complected Sweezey than the swashbuckling Miss Eyre.[43]

At any rate, Whitman's visits to the Broadway Hospital were less important for his possible romantic interludes than for the grounding experience they gave him in medicine. The hard-pressed doctors, no less than the patients, welcomed his regular bedside visits. The chief surgeon at the facility, Dr. D. B. St. John Roosa, recalled Whitman's effect on him and the other members of his staff. "We young men were often very tired," Roosa wrote, "for our labor was arduous, day and night, and Walt Whitman interested us, and his presence was always restful. He seemed to live above the ordinary affairs of life."[44]

The doctors gave Whitman the run of the hospital, and he happily poked around every nook and cranny with his customary childlike curiosity. The pathological museum, with its horrific collection of excised tumors, scrofulous limbs, gallstones, kidney stones, and assorted other bodily extrusions, held a certain morbid fascination. So, too, did the operations, some of which Whitman attended personally. He looked on with near-professional aplomb as doctors amputated one man's foot: "The bones of the foot forward were all amputated, and then the flap of the heel brought around and left to make a cushion to walk upon." He observed gallbladder surgery on a young fireman named James Kelly. "The patient was thoroughly chloroformed, and the operation, as near as I could judge, was admirably put through. The calculus (stone) extracted at last by Dr. Peters with a gentle but firm hand, holding a pair of nippers, seemed to be larger than the end joint of my thumb, and round as a cherry." And he witnessed the curious case of a woman who somehow had dislocated her own jaw by "gaping." The woman "was etherized; the jaw was then pressed in a proper manner, and put back in its connections, almost in an instant. The poor woman was then brought to, with as good a jaw as ever, and went away rejoicing." Not everyone shared Whitman's strong stomach. English novelist Anthony Trollope, who also visited the hospital at the time, fainted dead away during a tour of the wards.[45]

Occasionally, Whitman brought the off-duty doctors to Pfaff's for late-afternoon sandwiches and beer. At that time of day the tavern's bohemian clientele typically was off doing other things, and the two groups never interacted. Roosa, in fact, got the false impression that Whitman "had no intimate acquaintance with other literary New Yorkers of that time [and] was not generally considered a literary man." Later, when the poet gave Roosa a copy of *Leaves of Grass*, the doctor had to confess "that I did not understand them then, any more than I understand the character of the man who wrote them." Roosa often wondered what the "gentle and refined" Whitman saw in the burly stage drivers he visited at the hospital, although he freely admitted that "no one could see him sitting by the beside of a suffering stage driver without learning that he had a sincere and profound sympathy for this order of men."[46]

The doctors would have felt more affinity for another group of Whitman's friends, a loose gathering of young men about town dubbed the Fred Gray Association after the group's leader, physician's son Frederick Schiller Gray. Along with Gray and his brother, Nat, the group included another doctor's son, Charles Chauncey, well-to-do athlete Charles Kingsley, and Hugo Fritsch, the son of an Austrian diplomat. With both these groups Whitman mingled freely and easily, but he went to some pains to keep them from meeting each other—a function perhaps of his homosexual closeting. And when, by chance, Boston novelist John Townsend Trowbridge encountered Whitman reading proofs at his publisher's printing office "with a lank, unwholesome-looking lad at his elbow, listlessly watching him," the poet immediately sent the boy away and explained with some embarrassment that "he is a friendless boy I found at my boarding place. I am trying to cheer him up and strengthen him with my magneticism."[47]

For all the breadth and variety of his friendships, Whitman was essentially a lonely man. He crowded his hours with superficial camaraderie, but there was always at his core a hesitancy, a reluctance to reach out emotionally to others. Even close friends such as the naturalist John Burroughs sensed a fundamental reticence behind his apparent bonhomie. "He seems always to have been a sort of visitor in life," Burroughs noted perceptively. English admirer Edward Carpenter, calling on Whitman late in life, found in the poet a surprising "reserve and sadness . . . a sense of remoteness and inaccessibility." Whitman himself said as much, complaining to another friend, would-be biographer Richard Bucke: "I am by no means the benevolent, equable, happy creature you portray." He had made that clear in *Leaves of Grass*:

> Trippers and askers surround me,
> People I meet, the effect upon me of my early life or the
>   ward and city I live in, or the nation,
> The latest dates, discoveries, inventions, societies, authors
>   old and new,

My dinner, dress, associates, looks, compliments, dues,
The real or fancied indifference of some man or woman
   I love,

      . . .

These come to me days and nights and go from me again,
But they are not the Me myself.[48]

Whether by choice or by chance, Whitman was alone on the evening of April 12, 1861. He had been to the New York Academy of Music on Fourteenth Street to see a performance of Verdi's opera *A Masked Ball*—Lincoln had attended the same opera two months earlier on his passage through the city. Walking down Broadway to catch the ferry home to Brooklyn, he suddenly heard "the loud cries of the newsboys, who came presently tearing and yelling up the street, rushing from side to side even more furiously than usual." Buying a newspaper, he crossed over to the streetlamps in front of the Metropolitan Hotel, where he and a gathering crowd listened silently while someone read aloud the dire news from South Carolina: Rebel forces had fired on Fort Sumter. The Civil War had begun.[49]

Whitman's first reaction to the news was anger; he slammed his fist to the pavement as he walked away. Three days later, upon reflection, he characteristically sought to personalize the crisis: "I have this hour, this day, resolved to inaugurate for myself a pure, perfect, sweet, cleanblooded robust body by ignoring all drinks but water and pure milk—and all fat meats, late suppers—a great body—a purged, cleansed, spiritualized, invigorated body." He may have briefly considered enlisting in the Union Army—the note on nutrition followed by one day

Lincoln's call for seventy-five thousand volunteers to put down the rebellion—but if that was the case, he quickly got over the notion. His brother George had no such reservations; he enlisted immediately in the 13th New York State Militia and marched off to safeguard the nation's capital, parading gaily down Broadway with his newfound comrades, "all provided," Walt observed, "with pieces of rope, conspicuously tied to their musket barrels, with which to bring back each man a prisoner from the audacious South, to be led on a noose, on our men's early and triumphant return!"[50]

No one expected the war to last very long. A brief rattling of sabers, it was thought, would frighten the recalcitrant Confederates into surrendering, or else a quick, decisive clash of arms would show them the grievous error of their ways. The mayor of Brooklyn airily assured Whitman that "the Southern fire-eaters would . . . be at once so effectually squelch'd, we would never hear of secession again." Soon Walt was informing George: "All of us here think the rebellion as good as broke—no matter if the war does continue for some months yet." George felt the same way. "Mother you need not worry about me at all as I am not in want of anything and I dont believe we shal see any fighting at all," he wrote from camp.[51]

Three days later, the Confederate Army surprised the Federal forces along Bull Run creek at Manassas, Virginia. The ensuing rout sent the inexperienced Union troops streaming back into Washington, humbled and humiliated. Whitman, 235 miles away in Brooklyn, imaginatively relived the battle's final moments, when "the national forces . . . exploded in a panic and fled from the field. . . . Where are your banners and your bands of music and your ropes to bring back your prisoners? Well, there isn't a band playing, and there isn't a flag but clings ashamed and lank to its staff." In Whitman's retelling, drawn from various newspaper accounts, the demoralized mob of soldiers poured into the capital, mingling with an equally terrified crowd of "citizens, darkies, clerks . . . lookers-on, women in the windows." Southern sympathizers laughed in their faces, while a few industrious Union supporters set up tables on the sidewalks and handed out bread and coffee to openly weeping soldiers. It was, said Whitman, "one bitter, bitter hour—perhaps proud America will never again know such an hour."[52]

He was wrong there—the country would know many such hours, and worse, in the next four years. For the time being, he turned his hand to producing an unsubtle but effective recruiting poem, "Beat! Beat! Drums!":

Beat! beat! drums!—blow! bugles! blow!
Through the windows—through doors—burst like a ruthless force,
Into the solemn church, and scatter the congregation,
Into the school where the scholar is studying;
Leave not the bridegroom quiet—no happiness must he have now with his bride,
Nor the peaceful farmer any peace, ploughing his field or gathering his grain,
So fierce you whirr and pound you drums—so shrill you bugles blow.[53]

Whitman read his poem aloud to the languorous bohemians at Pfaff's, and it was published more or less simultaneously in the *Boston Evening Transcript*, the *New York Leader*, and *Harper's Weekly*. James Russell Lowell, no Whitman admirer, rejected three other poems for *The Atlantic Monthly* for the odd reason that "we could not possibly use [them] before their interest, — which is of the present—would have passed." There was no chance of that. The war inexorably gained momentum as the year wore on, a "hurrying, crashing, sad, distracted year." It was, Whitman wrote, a year that was fit not for

> . . . some pale poetling seated at a desk lisping cadenzas
>   piano,
> But as a strong man, erect, clothed in blue clothes, advanc-
>   ing, carrying a rifle on your shoulder,
> With a well-gristled body and sunburnt face and hands,
>   with a knife in the belt at your side.[54]

A second jingoistic poem, "First O Songs for a Prelude," praises New Yorkers for their swift response to the crisis:

> (O superb! O Manhattan, my own, my peerless!
> O strongest you in the hour of danger, in crisis! O truer
>   than steel!)
> How you sprang—how you threw off the costumes of
>   peace with indifferent hand,
> How your soft opera-music changed, and the drum and
>   fife were heard in their stead,

How you led to the war, (that shall serve for our prelude,
  songs of soldiers,)
How Manhattan drum-taps led.[55]

And later in the poem, Whitman exclaims:

War! an arm'd race is advancing! the welcome for battle,
  no turning away;

War! be it weeks, months, or years, an arm'd race is advancing to welcome it.[56]

It is doubtful that Whitman fully realized—who did?—the
terrible consequences of the rush to war. Years later, he would
look back with chagrin on his naive patriotism:

Arous'd and angry, I'd thought to beat the alarum, and
  urge relentless war,
But soon my fingers fail'd me, my face droop'd and I resign'd myself,
To sit by the wounded and soothe them, or silently watch
  the dead.[57]

Now when he went to the Broadway Hospital, it was filled
with sick soldiers from the volunteer regiments passing through
the city on their way to the front—the hospital received seventy-
five cents a day for each soldier it treated. Their plangent expressions haunted Whitman: "I have many hours afterwards, in
far different scenes, had the pale faces, the look of death, the

appealing eyes, come curiously of a sudden, plainly before me." Touched, he began spending his Sundays with the soldiers, two-thirds of whom suffered from measles, which in the first months of the war was both epidemic and deadly to the thousands of country-bred young men who had left home for the first time. Most of the soldiers had no relatives in New York, and Whitman took it upon himself to rally their spirits, "just to help cheer and change a little the monotony of their sickness and confinement—and indeed, just as much, too, for the melancholy entertainment and friendly interest and sympathy, I found aroused in myself toward and among the men." It was good training for what was to come.[58]

In the autumn of 1861, George Whitman returned home, his initial enlistment over, and immediately joined the 51st New York Volunteers for another three years or the duration of the war. It was the beginning of a remarkable military odyssey that would take him on more than twenty thousand miles of marches, twenty-one battles, innumerable skirmishes, the inside of a Rebel prison, and a steady round of promotions from private to major. At home, brother Jesse took work at the Brooklyn Navy Yard, and even poor tubercular Andrew enlisted briefly in the Union Army. Jeff was temporarily exempted by dint of his marriage, and he later paid a draft bounty of four hundred dollars to stay that way. Meanwhile, Walt remained strangely abstracted, scratching out a series of potboiling articles on the flora and fauna of old-time Brooklyn and vacationing on Long Island with a laughing group of young men and women.

The war, however, would not go away, and Whitman continued his hospital visits and his weekend saunters to Fort

Greene, where he collected firsthand accounts of the distant fighting. In late September 1862, he spent an evening at Pfaff's with Fred Gray, who was serving on the staff of Brigadier General William F. Smith, and heard "a fearful account" of the just concluded Battle of Antietam. George Whitman had been there, too, and had taken part in the famous fighting around Burnside's Bridge on September 17. "The way we showered the lead across that creek was noboddys buisness," he wrote proudly. The day after the battle, the bloodiest single day in American history, Whitman heard from stage driver James Sloan that a mutual friend, William Giggee, had been killed at Antietam. "Arthur took him in his arms, and he died in about an hour and a half—Arthur buried him himself—he dug his grave." The war was hitting close to home.[59]

In mid-December 1862, it showed up abruptly on the Whitmans' own doorstep. From George's letters, they knew him to be in camp near Fredericksburg, Virginia, where, he reported optimistically, "I hardly think there will be a fight." George was a better soldier than prognosticator. Major General Ambrose Burnside, late of Antietam bridge-taking fame, had assumed command of the Union Army of the Potomac, and despite his own well-founded doubts about his suitability as a leader, he had been given to understand that President Lincoln expected quick, decisive results. The horribly mismanaged Battle of Fredericksburg, on December 13, 1862, produced results all right, but they were not the sort that Lincoln expected. Thirteen thousand Union soldiers were killed or wounded in a daylong frontal attack on entrenched Confederate positions on Marye's Heights. Lengthy casualty lists began appearing in Northern newspapers. The Whitmans, like other families with men in the war, scanned the lists with mounting dread.[60]

Walt was home with his mother on the morning of December 16, when the *New York Tribune* carried another list of regimental casualties. Among those cited for the 51st New York was "First Lieutenant G. W. Whitmore [sic], Company D." There was no description of the type or severity of George's wounds, but Walt had seen enough operations at Broadway Hospital to fear the worst. Hurriedly packing a few clothes, some notebooks, and fifty dollars in cash from Mrs. Whitman's scanty nest egg, he left within the hour for Washington. Except as a visitor, he would never again return to Brooklyn. His "New York stagnation," he told Ralph Waldo Emerson two weeks later, was over. The rest of his life, although he did not yet know it, had already begun.[61]

CHAPTER TWO

A Sight in Camp

Determined to find his brother — dead or alive — Whitman plunged headlong into the maelstrom of war. In the confused aftermath of Fredericksburg, thousands of similarly frantic relatives had embarked for the front, thronging railroad stations and riverboat docks from Maine to Wisconsin. His own three-day journey, Whitman told his mother, entailed "the greatest suffering I ever experienced in my life." He crowded aboard a ferry to Manhattan, took a second across the Hudson River to New Jersey, and caught the night train to Philadelphia. Pressing his way through a mob of fellow travelers, he had his pocket picked while changing trains, and he arrived in Washington without a penny to his name. "Any pickpocket who failed to avail himself of such opportunities as Walt offered, with his loose baggy trousers and no suspenders, would have been a disgrace to his profession," one of his friends observed drolly.[1]

It was anything but an auspicious beginning to Whitman's new life, and his first view of the nation's capital did little to elevate his sagging spirits. Senator George Randolph's fabled "city of magnificent distances" had become a teeming jumble of close-pressed squalor. The unfinished dome of the Capital, which Lincoln wanted capped as a way of demonstrating the national will, might just as easily have symbolized a dying country's decline and fall. Ugly black scaffolding squatted atop the cast-iron shell like a giant, malevolent bird of prey, looking down on a city that almost overnight had become the most heavily fortified place in the world. Below, white marble office buildings bobbed uneasily on a sea of brown, dusty streets jammed with the ceaseless traffic of soldiers and civilians, wagons and carriages, horses and riders, and an untended menagerie of cows, chickens, goats, and pigs. A fetid canal bordered the northern edge of the mall, floating with dead cats, broken whiskey bottles, and rotting garbage. Ramshackle livery stables, saloons, and brothels jostled for space alongside such well-appointed landmarks as Willard's Hotel. The truncated shaft of Washington's monument, still less than a third of its projected height, looked more like a failing factory's idle smokestack than a soaring tribute to the Father of His Country. And on the east portico of the Capitol, amid the litter of unraised pillars and discarded bricks, sculptor Horatio Greenough's much derided statue of George Washington as Jupiter sat bare chested and forlorn like a fallen Titan.

Whitman, at any rate, had little time for sightseeing. Hungry, exhausted, and increasingly footsore, he trudged dispiritedly from hospital to hospital, hoping to find his wounded brother.

There were dozens of facilities to choose from. The largest, Armory Square, through some inexplicable lapse of medical logic, backed up against the stagnant canal. Others were scattered throughout the city and strewn about the surrounding hills. Whitman looked in on them all, worriedly scanning the upraised faces for a glimpse of George's familiar visage. After two fruitless days of constant searching, "walking all day and night, unable to ride, trying to get information, trying to get access to big people," Walt was at his wit's end. "I could not get the least clue to anything," he complained to his mother.[2]

Finally, he managed to locate someone he knew, his former Boston publisher, Charles W. Eldridge, who had gone bankrupt after publishing the third edition of *Leaves of Grass* and now was working as a clerk in the army paymaster's office. Eldridge and a second Boston acquaintance, antislavery novelist William D. O'Connor, loaned the frazzled poet a little money and, more important, gave him some much needed moral support. From his superior, Major Lyman S. Hapgood, Eldridge secured a pass for Whitman on the regular army train from Aquia Landing to Falmouth, Virginia, where George's regiment was recuperating after the battle. Whitman left his carpetbag at O'Connor's L Street home and set out immediately for the front, still not knowing whether his brother was dead or alive.[3]

George, as it happened, was very much alive—in fact, he was in capital spirits. Not only had he survived the terrible battle with merely a scratch but his new promotion to captain had just come through. "Remember your galliant Son is a Capting," he wrote to his mother with more pride than grammar. A shell fragment had cut a gash through his cheek—"You could stick a splint through into the mouth," Walt would observe a few days later—but it did not seem to bother the imperturbable George. By then he was a much traveled veteran, having "seen the elephant," as the soldiers put it, from Roanoke Island, North Carolina, to Antietam, Maryland, and the Virginia battlefields at Cedar Mountain, Second Manassas, Chantilly, and Fredericksburg. Along the way he had acquired a certain gift for understatement that was entirely at odds with his brother's famously expansive style. Of his regiment's bloody repulse at Fredericksburg, George noted matter-of-factly that "the Regt. struggled on to the front, and opened fire and kept it up until they expended their 60 rounds of ammunition, and there we laid down, as fresh troops came in and relieved us, but as it was getting late in the afternoon it was thought best to leave the regt where it was until dark as it was much safer there. . . . As soon as it was dark we went back to our old place by the bank of the river."[4]

It is a bit of a stretch to compare such barely literate prose to that of Ernest Hemingway, as one hyperbolic Whitman biographer has done, but the unadorned quality of George's writing does bespeak a veteran soldier's authentic experience; it is the voice of a man who does not need to pose. Years later, when Walt read his brother's diary, he proudly proclaimed it "a perfect poem of the war" and unabashedly placed its author among "a newer larger race of human giants." Interestingly, George did not note Walt's arrival in either his diary or his letters home. Perhaps his two years of campaigning had allowed him a broader perspective on family life—he no longer lived in his mother's basement. Or perhaps, given his phlegmatic personality, George simply accepted Walt's surprising presence the same way he accepted his brother's inexplicable poetic effusions—with a shrug of his shoulders and large grain of salt.[5]

Walt, at any rate, showed enough emotion for both of them. When he finally located George on the afternoon of December 19, he told their mother, "O you may imagine how trifling all my little cares and difficulties seemed—they vanished into nothing." His overwhelming sense of relief may have been heightened by an unnerving sight he stumbled upon a short time after reaching the front. Outside the Lacy mansion, a local landmark pressed into service as a field hospital, he glimpsed "a heap of feet, legs, arms, and human fragments, cut, bloody, black and blue, swelled and sickening." The unwelcome thought that one of the lost limbs might be George's flashed through his mind. In the garden nearby he spied a row of dead bodies, "each covered with its brown woollen blanket. In the dooryard, toward the river, are fresh graves, mostly of officers, their names on pieces of barrel staves or broken board, stuck in the dirt."[6]

The mansion, built in 1771, stood on a barren hillside overlooking the Rappahannock River and the town of Fredericksburg. It was the former home of Moncure Conway, a Harvard Divinity School graduate who had visited Whitman in Brooklyn a few years earlier at the behest of Ralph Waldo Emerson. Its current owner, J. Horace Lacy, had watched the battle alongside Confederate commander Robert E. Lee and had patriotically asked Lee to direct the Rebel artillery to shell the house, which was then serving as Major General Edwin Sumner's field headquarters. Lee, ever the gentleman, declined to permit such an "unnecessary effusion of blood"—emphasis on the adjective—

and thus had probably saved the life of future American Red Cross founder Clara Barton, who was watching the battle from the mansion's second-floor balcony.[7]

Barton was still at the mansion when Whitman arrived, doing what she could for the hundreds of wounded and dying soldiers dumped unceremoniously on the carpeted floor. As Whitman had done before the war at the Broadway Hospital in New York, Barton had begun her one-woman ministry by distributing little gifts of food, tobacco, whiskey, and simple human kindness to the Union soldiers stationed in Washington, where she was working as a copyist for the U.S. Patent Office. Since then she had expanded her duties to the field of battle, following the army's fluctuating fortunes from Second Manassas to Antietam and on to Fredericksburg. She was, in her way, as remarkable a personality as Whitman himself. Barely five feet tall, with a round face, high cheekbones, wide mouth, and beautiful, expressive dark-brown eyes, the Massachusetts-born Barton had grown up "more boy than girl," ignored by her stern, unloving mother and taught to ride and shoot—she was a dead pistol shot—by her old, Indian-fighting father. Like Whitman, she was a bone-deep patriot who had prayed fervently that the war, once started, would reconfirm once and for all "not 'if' we have a Government, but *that* we have one." Unmarried by choice—a friend observed that "she was so much stronger a character than any of the men who made love to her that I do not think she was ever seriously tempted to marry any of them"—she nevertheless had many suitors, including one married Union colonel with whom she had a tempestuous love affair.[8]

In addition to her nursing career, Barton was also a pioneer in the area of women's rights, having withstood sexual harassment in the workplace to become the first woman to draw her own salary from the federal government (other women were filling in for disabled relatives and thus were paid under the men's names). Again like Whitman, she was proud of her physicality, eschewing all meats and stimulants, and she was capable of working long hours without sleep. Her favorite adjective to describe herself was "athletic." In many ways, she was Whitman's mirror image—stubborn, independent, sensitive, caring, affectionate, patriotic, robust, and kind. Of course, Whitman was also a literary genius, the one characteristic that Barton could not match him, strength for strength.[9]

Whitman did not enter the Lacy House that day. Instead, he continued searching for George amid the scattered tents and stacked arms of the 51st New York's winter encampment. After twenty-seven straight hours under fire, the regiment had finally been allowed to pull back across the river to its old camp. The men were disgusted, although not surprised, to find that while they were away their tents had been thoroughly rifled by the anonymous army of malingerers, malcontents, and camp followers known derisively as "dog robbers." Grateful to be still numbered among the living, the soldiers set to work rebuilding their winter "shebangs," which Whitman the former carpenter described admiringly as "half hut and half tent."[10]

Sometime late that afternoon Walt located George and immediately dispatched a message to their mother informing her of George's near-miraculous survival (a shell had burst directly at his feet). George had already written to her as well, but his letter had been delayed in the general pandemonium following the battle. In the meantime, a second notice had appeared in the newspapers, a cryptic reference in the *New York Times* on December 17: "Lieut. Whitman, Co. E., 51st New York—cheek." George, who had tried modestly to keep his name off the regimental honor roll, dashed off a second letter to his mother, telling her, "You cant imagine how sorry I was to hear how worried you have been about me, and all the while I was as well as ever, so you see how foolish it is to frett."[11]

Filial duties complete, the two brothers set about becoming reacquainted. Walt was particularly proud of the high regard the other soldiers had for George: "Everyone speaks so well of George—they say he is so brave, steady, is good natured, of few words—he is now Captain." Always at ease with working-class comrades, Whitman rapidly acclimated himself to army life. He left his kit in George's tent, which George was sharing with Captain Henry W. Francis, the company commander, while he finished constructing his own shebang. Walt, for some reason, did not take to Francis—"not a man I could like much; I had very little to say to him"—and he spent much of his time outside, strolling around camp and recording his impressions in his ever present notebook. Not surprisingly, he was fascinated by the soldiers' colorful lingo, jotting down a number of representative examples: new men were called "700 men" or "bounty regiments"; a shirker was either a "healthy beat" or a "dead beat," depending on whether he tried later to redeem himself; hard crackers and coffee were "army pies" and "wash"; coffee laced with whiskey was "western milk."[12]

He ate with the men — "the grub was good" — and took an avid artisan's interest in the way they had "improvised fireplaces in holes in the ground, with small subterranean passages and small mud chimneys, lengthened out by a barrel with both ends knocked out." In fifteen minutes' time, he observed, the soldiers "will have their camp fires burning in all directions, and the grub in process of cooking, coffee, pork, beef, potatoes boiling, chickens, or anything they stole or grabbed in any way." An inadvertent record of his meal taking may have been left by Northern artist Edwin Forbes, who was in Falmouth at the time recording the Battle of Fredericksburg and its aftermath for *Frank Leslie's Illustrated Newspaper*. In one sketch, Forbes depicted a line of Union soldiers drawing a meal of salt pork and hardtack from a couple of pots suspended on a pole over a campfire. The third man in line, wearing civilian clothes, a planter's hat, and high boots, bears a striking resemblance to Whitman. In the background are several rows of shebangs exactly like those described by the poet. If it is not Whitman, then it is his doppelganger.[13]

With his innate ability to draw out strangers and engage them in conversation, Whitman moved through camp unobtrusively, storing up impressions that would last a lifetime. He had always been a good listener, and around the campfires that December there was a lot to listen to. The main topic of conversation, naturally enough, was the recent misbegotten battle. From generals to privates, the men in the Army of the Potomac were angry, hurt, depressed, and disgusted. Most shared the opinion of an Ohio journalist who observed that "it can hardly be in human nature for men to show more valor, or generals to manifest less judgment, than were perceptible on our side that day."[14]

Leadership at the moment was in short supply. Commanding general Ambrose Burnside had suffered something of a nervous breakdown during the battle — he had to be forcibly restrained from personally leading a suicidal mounted attack — and now he was sulking in his tent, convinced that his subordinates had let him down by arguing against a renewal of fighting. He could take little consolation in a decidedly lukewarm message from Abraham Lincoln that offered the slight political comfort, "Although you were not successful, the attempt was not an error, nor the failure other than accident." In private, Lincoln was even less sanguine. "If there is a worse place than Hell," he told a visitor to the White House, "I am in it." George Whitman, in his own laconic way, cut to the heart of the matter. "The great battle of Fredericksburg," he noted, "was lost in my Opinion solely through incompetent Generalship for I am certain, never did men fight harder or better." Walt typically waxed more cosmic. The battle, he said, was "the most complete piece of mismanagement perhaps ever yet known in the earth's wars."[15]

Still, the Army of the Potomac was nothing if not resilient. The men might grumble around their fires, but they were committed to staying the course. Whitman listened sympathetically to their tales, noting that "to a stranger the men in the ranks appear great growlers: a large proportion of men in the world even the good fellows would burst if they couldn't grumble." He was struck again by how young they were: "The mass of our men in our army are young — it is an impressive sight to me to see the countless numbers of youths and boys. . . . On a parade at evening, there you see them,—poor lads, many of them already with the experiences of the oldest veterans." By the simple act of listening, he could share those experiences vicariously. At one campfire he heard the macabre tale of a soldier who had been sitting atop a split-rail fence when he was shot; the next morning was still sitting there, dead. "Then I heard of Charley Parker, a young man in Company E in the 51st; how he was shot on the advance at Fredericksburgh, died hard, suffered much, frothed at the mouth—his body on the return, found entirely stript by the Secesh."[16]

That in itself was not unusual; the ill-supplied Confederates frequently stripped the clothes from dead Yankees. At Fredericksburg they had numerous opportunities to do so—the wounded and dead lay unattended between the lines for two long days before Burnside formally requested a flag of truce. Walt himself talked to one Pennsylvania soldier who had spent fifty hours lying wounded on the battlefield, unable even to lift his head. In the meantime, Rebel marksmen enjoyed an uninterrupted turkey shoot, blazing away at anything—human or animal—that dared to move on the battlefield. By the time the first relief parties reached the scene, hundreds of wounded Union soldiers had joined the ranks of the frozen dead. They lay, said one witness, "in every conceivable position, some on their backs with gaping jaws, some with eyes as large as walnuts, protruding with glassy stare, some doubled up like a contortionist. Here lay one without a head, there one without legs, yonder a head and legs without a trunk, everywhere horrible expressions, fear, rage, agony, madness, torture, lying in pools of blood, lying with heads half buried in mud, with fragments of shell sticking in oozing brain, with bullet holes all over the puffed limbs."[17]

After nearly two years of war the men had grown inured to such sights, but Whitman, despite his strong stomach, was still new to the battlefield. The morning after he arrived, he came across a burial detail from the 51st New York and 11th New Hampshire regiments digging a long row of graves. He marveled at their matter-of-factness. "Death is nothing here," he wrote. "As you step out in the morning from your tent to wash your face you see before you on a stretcher a shapeless extended object, and over it is thrown a dark grey blanket—it is the corpse of some wounded or sick soldier of the reg't who died in the hospital tent during the night—perhaps there is a row of three of four of these corpses lying covered over. No one makes an ado. There is a detail of men made to bury them; all useless ceremony is omitted. (The stern realities of the marches and many battles of a long campaign make the old etiquets a cumber and a nuisance.)" In his notebook he hastily scrawled an outline for a new poem based on the scene: "Sight at daybreak—in camp in front of the hospital tent on a stetcher, (three dead men lying,) each with a blanket spread over him—I lift up one and look at the young man's face, calm and yellow,—'tis strange! (Young man: I think this face of yours the face of my dead Christ!)"[18]

He would turn that brief glimpse into an epiphany in the first artistically important poem he wrote about the war, "A Sight in Camp in the Daybreak Gray and Dim." Because of its centrality to Whitman's emerging sense of the war, as both a historic event and a dominant subject for his art, it is worth quoting in full:

A sight in camp in the daybreak gray and dim,
As from my tent I emerge so early sleepless,
As slow I walk in the cool fresh air the path near by the
   hospital tent,
Three forms I see on stretchers lying, brought out there
   untended lying,
Over each the blanket spread, ample brownish woolen
   blanket,
Gray and heavy blanket, folding, covering all.

Curious I halt and silent stand,
Then with light fingers I from the face of the nearest the
   first just lift the blanket;
Who are you elderly man so gaunt and grim, with well-
   gray'd hair, and flesh all sunken about the eyes?
Who are you my dear comrade?

Then to the second I step—and who are you my child and
   darling?
Who are you sweet boy with cheeks yet blooming?

Then to the third—a face nor child nor old, very calm, as
   of beautiful yellow-white ivory;
Young man I think I know you—I think this face is the
   face of the Christ himself,

Dead and divine and brother of all, and here again he
    lies.[19]

The poem, described by one critic as "gentle but lethal," de-
rives much of its power from its understated tone. Here for the
first time Whitman achieves a soft-spoken plainness entirely in
keeping with the hush of the moment. It is a brilliant marriage
of substance and style, anticipating by nearly half a century the
Imagist poetry of Amy Lowell and Ezra Pound and providing
more evidence — if any is needed — of Whitman's enduring mo-
dernity. One of the marks of any great writer is adaptability,
and Whitman, after a few short days in camp among the young
Northern soldiers, had already begun to grasp that his old enthusiastic style of writing was sadly unsuited for capturing the
grim realities of their war. A new approach was needed, one
that reflected more accurately the soldiers' homespun ways and
quiet courage. With his great gift for mimicry, Whitman would
begin to write poems that spoke in the drawling voices of the
men themselves, in accents he first heard around the campfires
at Fredericksburg. This was a new way of writing, not just for
Whitman but for American literature in general, and its importance can scarcely be overstated.[20]

    While George busied himself with the various responsibilities
attendant on his rank, Walt continued to enjoy the freedom of
camp. On Sunday morning, December 21, he took in a regimental inspection conducted by Colonel Robert S. Potter, the
51st New York's commanding officer. Potter, a Schenectady,
New York, lawyer, had entered the war as a militia private and
risen steadily to regimental command. He would continue

rising, all the way to major general, by virtue of his natural leadership ability and personal fearlessness—the latter a result, perhaps, of having lost his wife at a tragically young age. Potter had distinguished himself at Antietam, where he led his men across Burnside's Bridge, shouting and cursing at the top of his voice. A slight, balding man with muttonchop whiskers and a smooth-shaven chin, he was one of those instinctual civilian-soldiers who become transported in the heat of battle, and his men were a little in awe of his valor. Potter could see the same trait in others, and he cited George Whitman for bravery at Fredericksburg, saying that he had "particularly distinguished [him]self." Walt, in turn, praised Potter's "courage and coolness."[21]

Of the original one thousand soldiers who had enlisted in the regiment at the start of the war, only about two hundred still remained. "The men looked well to me," Whitman noted, "not in the sense of a march down Broadway, but with the look of men who had long known what real war was, and taken many a hand in—held their own in seven engagements, about a score of skirmishes &c—a regiment that had been sifted by death, disablement &c. from eleven hundred men, (including recruits,) down to about two hundred—any one of whom had now an experience, after eighteen months, worth more, and more wonderful, than all the romances ever written—whose story, if written out, would be first class." He toyed with the idea of writing such a history himself, but settled for a brief newspaper account of the regiment, "Our Brooklyn Boys in the War," which he published in the *Brooklyn Daily Eagle* shortly after leaving Falmouth.[22]

The same day as the regimental inspection, Whitman entered the charnel house at the Lacy mansion for the first time. Clara Barton was still there, but Whitman took no notice of her; his focus was on the wounded men. "The large mansion is quite crowded, upstairs and down, everything impromptu, no system, all bad enough, but I have no doubt the best that can be done; all the wounds pretty bad, some frightful, the men in their old clothes, unclean and bloody," he wrote. "I went through the rooms, downstairs and up. Some of the men were dying. I had nothing to give at that visit, but wrote a few letters to folks home, mothers, &c. Also talk'd to three or four, who seem'd most susceptible to it, and needing it."[23]

Whitman's observations, as usual, were sharp. A male nurse at Fredericksburg, William H. Reed, gave a similar account. "No available space was left unoccupied," he recalled. "The poor fellows just arrived had not had their clothes off since they were wounded, and were sleeping in blood and filth, and were swarming with vermin. They lay as close as they could be packed, the contaminated air growing worse every hour. . . . Here side by side they lay, through long days and longer nights of suffering, with no sound but the clock, the stifled moan, or the delirious muttering. The air was so close and nauseating that we often reeled with faintness at our work, while these poor fellows waited and bore all their burden in a brave endurance that was like a miracle."[24]

There was not room inside the Lacy House for more than a fraction of the wounded. Most were sheltered on the grounds in rude tent hospitals, one of which Whitman visited on December 22. There he found two members of the 51st New York, whose names and wounds he carefully catalogued in his notebook: "In the Hospital on the ground at Falmouth—John Lowerie—Co G. 51st N.Y.—arm amputated—plucky—(trade machinist)"; and "Amos H. Vliet—feet frozen—Hospital tent—51st N.Y." He also noted, but did not identify, a "man with his mouth blown out." Perhaps he was distracted by the timely appearance of a Union observation balloon, *Intrepid*, piloted by the grandly named Colonel Thaddeus Sobieski Constantine Lowe, a New Hampshire inventor and aeronaut who had dodged a blizzard of enemy fire at Fredericksburg to call down enemy troop dispositions and artillery coordinates. The poet, predictably, was much taken with the incongruously gay balloon, "a great huge, slow moving thing . . . [a] beautiful object to me."[25]

The scenes inside the hospital tents were not so diverting. "The results of the late battles are exhibited everywhere about here in thousands of cases, (hundreds die every day,) in the Camp, Brigade, and Division hospitals," Whitman noted. "These are merely tents, and sometimes very poor ones, the wounded lying on the ground, lucky if their blankets are spread on layers of pine or hemlock twigs or small leaves. No cots; seldom even a mattress. It is pretty cold. The ground is frozen hard, and there is occasional snow. I go around from one case to another. I do not see that I do much good, but I cannot leave them. Once in a while some youngster holds on to me convulsively, and I do what I can for him; at any rate, stop with him and sit near him for hours, if he wishes it."[26]

Bad as they were, the hospital tents represented a great advance in medical care over the previously inept handling of battlefield casualties. This was due largely to the work of one man,

Jonathan Letterman, the new medical director of the Army of the Potomac. Letterman, against the resistance of Secretary of War Edwin Stanton and other hidebound army regulars, had reorganized the ambulance service and field hospitals in the wake of the villainous performance of civilian teamsters at the Battle of Second Bull Run earlier that summer. Following the battle — another crushing Union defeat — hundreds of wounded soldiers had been left on the battlefield for up to a week, broiling in the sun without food or water, before being rescued. Meanwhile, the teamsters had broken into the surgeons' liquor supplies, stolen the wounded men's blankets and provisions, refused to load them into the ambulances, and rifled their pockets once they were inside.[27]

Apprised of the abuses, Letterman took the ambulances away from the Quartermaster Corps and set about training his own elite cadre of drivers and stretcher bearers. The new medical corpsmen, wearing specially designed uniforms, showed immediate improvement at the Battle of Antietam. There, the fledgling Ambulance Corps successfully transported every Union casualty to a field hospital by the end of the day's fighting. Three months later, at Fredericksburg, the army instituted Letterman's new system of field hospitals. Unlike the previous catch-as-catch-can method of wound dressing and surgery, Letterman's system was carefully organized. Each division was assigned a chief surgeon, who in turn was supported by regimental surgeons manning dressing stations at the front. After receiving their initial treatment, casualties were transported back to the tent hospitals by ambulance, where the chief surgeon examined their wounds and performed all necessary operations.

By modern standards it was still a barbarously crude system, but at least it was a system.[28]

When Whitman was not visiting the hospital tents, he took in the sights of an army at rest. On Tuesday, December 23, he watched from the hillside midway between the Lacy House and the railroad as George's regiment performed picket duty along the Rappahannock River. "The day is soft, brightly beautiful," he observed. "Down below is spread out a picturesque scene. The countless baggage wagons, with their white roofs, the numerous strings of mules, the railroad locomotive, the broad spread of slopes and hills winding their way over the railroad track, and making a huge S towards the river, which is only a few hundred yards distant, are the whole of the 51st N. Y. 51st Penn. and 100 men of the 11th N.H. on picket duty along the shore."[29]

The men were on patrol because Robert E. Lee was not going anywhere. Having seen the unmitigated hell his own men had inflicted on anyone rash enough to attempt to cross the river at Fredericksburg, Lee had no intention of reversing the attack. For the time being, he was content to wait and see whether Burnside was foolish enough to repeat his mistake. Not even Burnside was that obtuse, but the Union general did plan to resume the offensive the day after Christmas by crossing his army at Bank's Ford and U.S. Ford, a few miles west of Falmouth, and catching Lee's presumably unwary Confederates by surprise. It took an urgent, eleventh-hour message from Abraham Lincoln to prevent the general's latest ill-conceived adventure. Alerted to Burnside's intentions by his alarmed underlings, Lincoln summarily overruled him and directed that the army stay where it was and recuperate—as best it could—from Burnside's earlier brainstorm. A 2,500-man cavalry force already en route to spearhead the crossings was hastily recalled, and the army hunkered down over its cooking fires, blissfully unaware of how close it had come to another disaster.

Whitman may have witnessed the cavalry's misadventure. In a notebook entry dated "Christmas Afternoon, 1862," he mentioned that "a fine large troop of cavalry is just passing, the hoofs of the horses shake the ground, and I hear the clatter of sabres." In his poem "Cavalry Crossing a Ford," he describes a line of horsemen taking "a serpentine course" identical to that of the supply wagons mentioned in the note. The fact that it is a "large troop of cavalry" would seem to suggest that he had seen Burnside's vanguard, either setting out or returning. Whatever the case, it gave Whitman the opportunity to practice his new minimalist theory of poetry, and "Cavalry Crossing a Ford" has something of the timeless, sepia-tinged quality of a Mathew Brady photograph. By skillfully manipulating point of view, Whitman moves subtly from a long shot of the cavalry en masse to a close-up view of "splashing horses" and "brown-faced men . . . each person a picture." The men are individuals, but they are also part of a larger military family, and the near cinematic shift of perspective emphasizes both the democratic nature of the army and the way it has molded into a monolithic whole.[30]

With his trained newspaperman's eye, Whitman was a good observer. He watched the soldiers gather around their campfires, singing oddly merry songs and eating green corn "grated through tin pans with rough holes pierced in them." At dusk one afternoon he observed a horseman galloping through the camp "with something white thrown across the pommel of the saddle in front of him." It was a supply of newspapers, much treasured by the men for their connection to home. The cry, "Papers! papers!" brought the soldiers flying from their tents, and the vendor quickly sold his entire supply at the going rate of ten cents apiece for New York newspapers and five cents each for other dailies. Later, Whitman visited the camp of the 26th Pennsylvania, whose members had constructed a three-sided windbreak that did combination duty as a kitchen, public house, and reading room. There, he saw one soldier emerge from his tent "with a couple slices of beef, and some crackers, and commenced cooking the mess in a frying pan, for his breakfast. It looked very good." Inverately curious, Whitman peeked into the man's tent. Inside, "the ground [was] strewn with pine twigs, and protected on each side with a pine log for an entrance, the knapsacks piled at one end for pillows." In a fenced enclosure in the middle of the woods, he saw another group of men butchering cattle, their sleeves rolled up on their blood-stained arms.[31]

All these vivid images he put into an uncompleted poem titled "Sights—The Army Corps, Encamped on the War Field":

The cluster of tents—the brigades and divisions
The shelter tents—the peep through the open entrance flap—
    the debris around
The balloon up for reconnaisances
The sights of the hospital tent—the pale-faced wounded—
    the men lying flat on the ground, on the pine boughs,
The shebangs of branches,—the fires built
The men emerging from their tents in the gray of the
    morning

The great camp of army corps, the divisions, the brigades
   and camps of the regiments
The sound of the drums — the different calls, the assembly,
   the early reveille, the tatoo at night, & the dinner call,
   etc.
The rows of tents, the streets through them
The squads out on the open ground going through their
   evolutions
The long trains of baggage wagons — the huge clouds of
   smoke rising over the tents
The ambulances — [32]

The poem — or more accurately the lines — is less a finished
lyric than a collection of hasty travel notes. Whitman was more
concerned with getting down on paper the chaotic welter of
new impressions than he was with crafting a polished poem.
Despite his relationship to George and the ease with which he
moved through camp, he must have been uncomfortably aware
of his status as an outsider. The soldiers, he said beautifully, had
been "sifted by death" in a way that no civilian — not even a
great poet — could fully comprehend. On Christmas Day he pur-
posely removed himself from camp, spending an hour alone in
solemn contemplation on a deserted part of the battlefield. The
devastation caused by the war was plain to see; for miles around
the land had been stripped clear of all trees and vegetation, and
the black, bloated carcasses of dead horses and mules littered
the countryside. A seemingly endless line of supply wagons
passed nearby, adding to the heaping mounds of forage and hay
in the teamsters' camp beyond.[33]

Whitman being Whitman, he could not focus very long on the merely mundane. Instead, he "hear[d] plainly the music of a good band, at some Brigadier's headquarters, a mile and a half away; it is a beautiful, soft sunny Christmas day with thin haze in the air. Then the drum tap from one direction or other comes constantly breaking in. . . . I hear the sound of bugle calls, very martial, at this distance. . . . Amid all this pleasant scene, under the sweet sky and warm sun, I sit and think over the battle of last Saturday week."[34]

In nine days' time, Whitman had absorbed enough raw material for dozens of poems, letters, newspaper articles, and essays. Now it was time to leave. Probably with George's help, he obtained a pass from the army provost marshal to go by train to Aquia Landing, and a second pass signed by General Sumner himself to travel by government steamer back to Washington. He left Falmouth before sunrise on Sunday, December 28, riding alongside hundreds of wounded soldiers lying on beds of straw on an open platform car in the bitter weather. As they clattered past the sleeping camps ranged along the rail lines, "the soldiers guarding the road came out from their tents or shebangs of bushes with rumpled hair and half-awake look."[35]

At Aquia Landing a Sanitary Commission relief station had been set up, and civilian volunteers moved among the men handing out much needed blankets, shirts, and woolen underwear, along with hot meals and concentrated milk for those who were able to eat. During the three-hour wait for the steamer, Whitman went from man to man, collecting names and addresses to send word of their condition to the folks back home. He had his hands full, he said, on the ensuing boat ride to

Washington, and one of the men he was caring for died before they docked at the Sixth Street wharf.[36]

Leaving the wounded to make their own way to the hospital, Whitman went to retrieve his belongings from William O'Connor's home at 394 L Street. O'Connor's wife, Ellen, had heard a lot about the poet from her novelist husband, but she had missed Whitman's earlier visit. That afternoon the couple was just sitting down to lunch when they were interrupted by a knock at the door of their third-floor apartment. "There stood the man whom Mr. O'Connor afterwards christened 'The Good Gray Poet,' " she recalled. "He was immediately made known to me by name, but I could not have had a moment's doubt, for he looked as his pictures at that time represented him."[37]

The outdoor sojourn had invigorated Whitman; he was now as healthy—mentally and physically—as he was ever again to be. His only ailment, he told Nelly O'Connor, was the occasional intense headache that he attributed to a severe sunstroke he had suffered a few years earlier while strolling about hatless after getting a haircut. The summer sun made his daily walks a little perilous, and not even his Keatsian ability "to make his brain 'negative' " insured Whitman against future attacks. To lessen the danger, he carried an umbrella with him wherever he went.[38]

Whitman intended to stay in Washington for a week or ten days, he told the O'Connors, to visit some of the Brooklyn boys confined to the hospitals. He had a list, probably obtained from Charles Eldridge, of likely boarding houses to look into, and O'Connor volunteered to help him search for new living quarters. None of the recommended places proved suitable, but there was "a werry little bedroom" on the second floor of the

O'Connors' own lodgings, and Whitman moved into the spartan quarters and gratefully accepted an invitation from the couple to take his meals with them until he could find permanent accommodations.[39]

It was the beginning of a deep friendship between Whitman and the O'Connors, whose rather problematical marriage had been strained even further by the recent death from smallpox of their two-year-old son, Philip. Except for a shared commitment to abolitionism, women's rights, and prohibition, the couple seemed a poor match. Boston-born William was the stereotypical hot-blooded Irishman, one who fought his frequent word battles the way earlier courtiers had fought with swords. His childhood nickname was D'Artagnan. Extending the comparison, O'Connor's friend Wendell Phillips once told him, "You ought to have lived in Sidney's day when knightly service was in fashion."[40]

From the time of their first meeting in the spring of 1860 at Eldridge's office in Boston, O'Connor and Whitman shared a passionate intellectual and emotional bond. Walt could not help but notice the slender, blue-eyed, vivacious novelist, who was twelve years younger and was "personally and intellectually the most attractive man I had ever met." O'Connor, he said, "was a gallant, handsome, fine-voiced, glowing-eyed man; lithe-moving on his feet, of healthy magnetic atmosphere and presence, and the most welcome company in the world." The attraction was mutual. "The great Walt is very grand and it is health and happiness to be near him," O'Connor wrote to his longtime mentor, Sarah Helen Whitman (no relation to the poet); "he is so large and strong—so pure, proud and tender, with such an ineffable bon-hommie and wholesome sweetness of presence; all the young men and women are in love with him."[41]

It was, for all its ardor, a purely platonic relationship; O'Connor was entirely—and extremely—heterosexual, and therein lay the heart of the problem between him and his wife. While Nelly stayed home tending to their five-year-old daughter, Jeannie, O'Connor roamed freely about the city, often staying out until well past midnight. He said he was working late at the office (he was a clerk at the Light-House Board), but soon he was telling Whitman about the beautiful young women he encountered on his rounds and implying that he had gotten to know some of them quite well in the process.[42]

Thin, sharp-featured, and plain, Nelly O'Connor was no match for the capital beauties her husband described. Even Walt, who quickly became her lifelong friend, found Nelly "rather intellectual than physical." Her straitened childhood— she had grown up a factory girl in Lowell, Massachusetts, before escaping the mills to become a governess and schoolteacher in Washington—had ill equipped her for marriage to a moody, high-strung, occasionally brilliant writer. Her own niece, Grace Ellery Channing, said flatly that Nelly was "the very last [woman] a man of imagination or genius should have married. . . . She was expressly and particularly framed to see life from the opposite standpoint of O'Connor and to quietly and unviolently frustrate every attempt of his native talent. She was the best stifler of self-expression in others I have ever known. Against the calm rock of her opposition, the great waves of his aspirations beat in vain. They ought to have separated as quickly as possible."[43]

After the failure of his well-received but little-purchased novel, *Harrington*, Nelly had persuaded William to take the Light-House Board job. It was steady work, and besides, as she confessed to Whitman, "I have a great love of good housekeeping, care too much, I fear, for the trifles." Meanwhile, her artist-husband chafed incessantly at his confinement. "I am like a caged tiger walking around and around endlessly," he told a friend, "mad as I can be that I am wasting my life in this infamous office." Unwittingly, Whitman had entered a household on the verge of imploding.[44]

That implosion would not occur for several more years, and in the meantime Walt and the O'Connors formed a sort of surrogate family to replace the even more dysfunctional family he had left behind in Brooklyn. "The O'Connor home was my home," Whitman recalled many years later. "They were beyond all others—William, Nelly—my understanders, my lovers; they more than any others. I was nearer to them than any others—oh! much nearer. A man's family is the people who love him—the people who comprehend him." Whether they truly comprehended Whitman—who really did, for that matter?—unquestionably they loved him, perhaps too much. It was lucky for Walt that they did—he was about to embark on the most difficult, soul-testing, and spirit-sapping interlude of his life. The man who had once written, "Agonies are one of my changes of garments," would soon be changing his costume yet again. The open road, with its lithe young men and their sunburnished limbs, now led inexorably to the hospital door, and the war-ruined bodies that lay bleeding beyond it.[45]

CHAPTER THREE

The Great Army
of the Sick

Safely settled in his new quarters, Whitman spent the next few days catching up on his letter writing. As always, his first allegiance was to his mother, and he wrote to her on December 29, describing in detail his trip to Fredericksburg, his struggles to locate George, his joy and relief at finding him safe, and his life-altering stay among the young soldiers. "Now that I have lived for eight or nine days amid such scenes as the camps furnish," he told her, "and realize the way that hundreds of thousands of good men are now living, and have had to live for a year or more, not only without any of the comforts, but with death and sickness and hard marching and hard fighting, (and no success at that,) for their continual experience — really nothing we call trouble seems worth talking about." Everything was unsettled at the moment, he said, but "I will stay here for the present, at any rate long enough to see if I can get any employment at any thing, and shall write what luck I have." He listed his return address as "care of Major Hapgood, paymaster, U.S. Army, corner 15th and F streets, 5th floor, Washington D.C."[1]

His second letter, written the same day, was to Ralph Waldo Emerson. With his "New York stagnation" broken up for good, Whitman reported that he had arrived in Washington "in harsh and superb plight—wretchedly poor, excellent well, (my only torment, family matters)—realizing at last that it is necessary for me to fall for the time in the wise old way, to push my fortune, to be brazen, and get employment, and have an income—determined to do it, (at any rate until I get out of the horrible sloughs)." Whether these sloughs applied to family matters, money concerns, or his old depression was left unclear. For the time being, he wanted Emerson to write letters of introduction for him to present to Secretary of State William Seward, Secretary of the Treasury Salmon P. Chase, and Massachusetts senator Charles Sumner, three of the most powerful men in Washington.[2]

Emerson was dubious about the enterprise, particularly given Whitman's quirky insistence on applying for government work "on literary grounds, not political"—as though anything got done in Washington for any other reason. Nevertheless, he set his hand to crafting a letter of recommendation that was remarkable chiefly for its reservations. "Permit me to say that he is known to me as a man of strong original genius," Emerson wrote to the three politicians, "combining, with marked eccentricities, great powers & valuable traits of character: a self-relying, large-hearted man, much beloved by his friends; entirely patriotic & benevolent in his theory, tastes, & practice. If his writings are in certain points open to criticism, they yet show extraordinary power, & are more deeply American, democratic & in the interest of political liberty, than those of any other poet. He is indeed a child of the people, & their champion. . . . [I]f the Government has work that he can do, I think it may easily find, that it has called to its side more valuable aid than it bargained for."[3]

It would take Emerson the better part of two weeks to produce the letter. In the meantime, Whitman freely explored his adopted city. On December 31 he looked in on Brooklyn druggist George J. Holman at the hospital camp across the Potomac in Alexandria, where Holman was serving as a hospital steward for the 87th New York. The next day he and O'Connor ran into Ohio poet John James Piatt and his wife in front of Willard's Hotel. The Piatts were en route to the president's annual New Year's Day reception at the White House, and O'Connor introduced them to Whitman. Piatt remembered shaking hands with a "large, gray-haired, gray bearded man, dressed rather shabbily, in what might be called 'country clothes.' " Since there is no mention in Whitman's notes or letters of attending the presidential open house, it is likely that he and O'Connor were merely out for a morning stroll. They could not have known, at any rate, that this was to be one of the most significant days in Lincoln's presidency.[4]

The summer before the president had begun thinking seriously about issuing a special proclamation freeing all the slaves held within the rebellious southern states. He urged congressional leaders in the contested border states to take the lead by endorsing a plan of federally compensated emancipation. "As you would perpetuate popular government for the best people in the world," Lincoln told them, "I beseech you that you do in no wise omit this." The congressmen, predictably, declined to take such a drastic and politically risky step, and Lincoln delayed acting on his own until he could do so from a position of strength, after a decisive Union victory in the field. The Battle of Antietam, although militarily a draw, gave Lincoln the opening he needed, and on September 22, 1862, he issued the Emancipation Proclamation. If, by January 1, 1863, the South had not ended its state of rebellion, Lincoln warned, he would sign a final draft of the order.[5]

On the afternoon of New Year's Day, 1863, he followed through on his threat. All slaves in the still-rebellious states, the document read, "are, and henceforward shall be free." The war had entered a new phase. George Whitman, with his customary succinctness, pointed out the inherent flaw in Lincoln's plan: by freeing only those slaves living within areas not yet under Union control, he had done nothing concrete for the millions of black Americans still held in chains, while unalterably stiffening the resolve of those who kept them there. "I don't know what effect it is going to have on the war," George wrote to Walt after the Emancipation Proclamation, "but one thing is certain, he has got to lick the south before he can free the niggers."[6]

It was just as well that Whitman and O'Connor had not gone to the White House that morning to shake Lincoln's hand: such a visit might have fatally strained their growing friendship. The basic incompatibility of their racial views was a constant source of friction between the two. Like everyone, they were products of their upbringing and environment. O'Connor had the sort of mind that tended to divide all issues—no pun intended—into black and white. Driven from his own home at the age of eight by a violent father who once threw a flat iron at his head, he had grown up alone on the mean streets of Boston, a congenital underdog who identified personally with the struggles of blacks, women, and other oppressed minorities.

In *Harrington* O'Connor had written eloquently of the lack of opportunity that blacks faced, even in the North, in the decade before the Civil War. "They had a narrow range of humble employments and avocations, such as window-cleaning, white-washing, boot-blacking, cab-driving, porterage, domestic service, and the like," he wrote. "They were shut out of the mechanic occupations; shut out of commerce; shut out of the professions. They were excluded from the first-class car; excluded from the theatres unless the manager could make a place for them . . . excluded from some of the churches by express provision, and from most, if not all, of the others, by tacit understanding; excluded from the common schools, and allotted caste-schools where to learn anything was against nature; excluded from the colleges; excluded from the decent dwellings; excluded from the decent graveyards; excluded from almost everything. They were, however, freely admitted to the gallows and the jail."[7]

Whitman, unlike O'Connor, had grown up in a part of the North that was almost Southern in its racial attitudes. His great-grandfather had owned slaves (the practice was legal in Long

Island until 1828, when Whitman was nine), and one of his closest companions as a youth was a freed slave named Old Mose who was the living embodiment of Harriet Beecher Stowe's Uncle Tom. "He was very genial, correct, manly, and acute," Whitman recalled, "and a great friend of my childhood." When the family moved to Brooklyn, Whitman mingled freely with the blacks who made up 10 percent of the borough's population and were even poorer—if that was possible—than the Whitmans and their working-class neighbors. Although Whitman would later salute the "dim-descended, black, divine-soul'd African, large, fine-headed, nobly-form'd, superbly destin'd, on equal terms with me," he was rather less welcoming to the African Americans of his own country. "Who believes that Whites and Blacks can ever amalgamate in America?" he asked in an editorial written for the *Brooklyn Daily Times* in May 1858. "Or who wishes it to happen? Nature has set an impassable seal against it. Besides, is not America for the Whites? And is it not better so?"[8]

He would put the matter even more crudely in an aside to Horace Traubel thirty years later. "That is one reason why I never went full on the nigger question," he said. "The nigger would not turn—would not do anything for himself—he would only act when prompted to act. No! no! I should not like to see the nigger in the saddle—it seems unnatural." Given such views, it is not surprising that Whitman's erstwhile publisher, Charles Eldridge, would later observe: "I never knew him to have a friend among the negroes while he was in Washington. Of the negro race he had a poor opinion. He said that there was in the constitution of the negro's mind an irredeemable trifling or volatile element, and he would never amount to much in the scale of civilization."[9]

From the first day they met, Whitman worried that O'Connor's "ardent abolitionism" would drive them apart. Certainly, his own opinion of Northern abolitionists was negative in the extreme. Going back as far as 1846, when he was editor of the *Brooklyn Daily Eagle*, Whitman had castigated the antislavery activists as "a few . . . foolish red-hot fanatics," and warned that "the dangerous and fanatical insanity of 'Abolitionism' [is] as impracticable as it is wild." He despised equally the abolitionists and the proslavery hotheads of the South whom he blamed—not without cause—for the fracture of the Union. In his poetry he had tried to find a balance between the two:

> I am the poet of slaves and of the masters of slaves,
> I go with the slaves of the earth equally with the masters
> And I will stand between the masters and the slaves,
> Entering into both so that both shall understand me
>   alike.[10]

The difficulty in finding such a balance—and it was certainly not limited to Whitman alone—was that although he fervently supported the maintenance of the Union, he could never bring himself to hate all Southerners—far from it. As he later confided to Traubel, "I must admit that my instinct of friendship towards the South is almost more than I like to confess." On another occasion, he went even further, telling Traubel, "I know enough of Southern affairs, have associated with Southern people to feel convinced that if I lived South I should side with the Southern whites." A three-month sojourn as editor of the *New Orleans Crescent* in 1848 had deepened his affection for the "glistening perfumed South, my South," a place where even the peculiar institution of slavery could be seen—at a comfortable remove—in its idealized state:

> There are the negroes at work in good health, the ground
>   in all directions cover'd with pine straw;
> In Tennessee and Kentucky slaves busy in the coalings, at
>   the forge, by the furnace-blaze, or at the corn-shucking,
> In Virginia, the planter's son returning after a long
>   absence, joyfully welcom'd and kiss'd by the aged mu-
>   latto nurse.[11]

One wonders what O'Connor made of such bucolic lines, or how he reconciled them with his almost religious devotion to the man he would later christen the Good Gray Poet. To be sure, the two argued fiercely over slavery and black suffrage throughout the war and beyond. Eventually, it would become the catalyst, if not perhaps the final straw, in the ultimate breakdown of their friendship. But for now, Whitman and O'Connor were inseparable. After chatting with the Piatts, they stopped by to visit Eldridge at the paymaster's office on the top floor of the Corcoran Building at 15th and L streets. Major Hapgood's office provided a splendid view of the capital, all the way to Arlington, but Whitman's enjoyment of the vista was tempered somewhat by the sight of dozens of "poor sick, pale, tattered soldiers" who had made their way painfully up five flights of stairs in search of their pay. "They climb up here, quite exhausted, and then they find it is no good, for there is no money to pay them," Whitman wrote. "[T]he scenes of disappointment are quite affecting. Here they wait in Washington, perhaps week after week, wretched and heart sick—this is the greatest place of delays and puttings off, and no finding the clue to anything . . . many of them day after day, disappointed and tired out." Many of the men had been invalided out of the army, but without money to get home they were stuck in the hospitals and convalescent camps, surrounded by sick and dying comrades— the only places where they could find shelter. Others, even less lucky, were reduced to living on the streets and begging for bread.[12]

Whitman made himself at home in Hapgood's office, writing letters and holding court, and within a few days he was put on the payroll as a part-time copyist, spending two or three hours a day duplicating government vouchers, orders, memoranda, and reports. It was easy if unexciting work, and it left the afternoons free for more important things: he had begun to visit the hospitals. As with most of the turning points in Whitman's life, the visits started casually, with no particular plan or purpose. The day after New Year's he called at Campbell Hospital to look in on the two Brooklyn soldiers, John Lowery and Amos Vliet, whom he had met at Fredericksburg. They had somehow gotten a note to him asking him to visit, and as always Whitman was happy to oblige. The men were recuperating nicely, Lowery from an amputated forearm and Vliet (who also knew Jeff Whitman) from frozen feet. Considerably worse off was a young Bridgewater, Massachusetts, soldier, Private John A. Holmes, whom Whitman happened upon one afternoon in Ward 6 of the hospital. Holmes, a twenty-one-year-old shoemaker by trade, had enlisted in Company C of the 29th Massachusetts Regiment in May 1861. The regiment, one of the first three-year units raised in the state, had seen action in the Peninsula campaign and at Antietam, where, as part of the celebrated Irish Brigade, it had helped turn the tide of battle at the infamous Bloody Lane.[13]

Holmes had managed to avoid being wounded during any of the bitter fighting, but he could not escape the war's greatest, if most basic, peril—diarrhea. The disease, which affected some 54 percent of all Union soldiers and a staggering 99 percent of all Confederates, would eventually claim nearly one hundred thousand lives in the course of the war. Thousands of others, including the fearsome Southern cavalry leader Nathan Bedford Forrest, would suffer from chronic diarrhea for the rest of their prematurely shortened lives. Holmes had fallen prey to the illness sometime prior to the Battle of Fredericksburg. His subsequent treatment—or mistreatment—was a textbook example of the way that sick and wounded soldiers were still being handled as late as the second winter of the war.

Unable to eat and vomiting repeatedly, Holmes had been left to lie on the ground for several days in camp until he was evacuated by open rail car to Aquia Creek. There, too weak to sit up by himself, he was again left to suffer alone, without anything to eat or drink, until he was placed aboard a hospital steamer bound for Washington. That night he found himself too weak to undo the blankets in his knapsack; he asked a passing deckhand to untie them for him. The man brusquely demanded to know why he could not do it for himself, and Holmes replied that he had been trying for half an hour to do just that. Unmoved, the man left Holmes to his own devices, and the exhausted young soldier spent the rest of the frigid December night uncovered, alternately wracked by fever and chills.[14]

Arriving in Washington, Holmes was deposited unceremoniously on the Sixth Street wharf, still without food or water. Eventually he managed to get a ride to Campbell Hospital. Falling facedown onto a bed, he was immediately ordered to get up by the ward-master, who said that it was against hospital rules for anyone to lie down in bed with his clothes on. Holmes was then made to go to the common bathroom, where callous attendants scrubbed him down roughly with cold water until he suddenly collapsed in their arms.[15]

Taking up Holmes's story in an article he wrote for the *New York Times*, Whitman angrily detailed the result of the young man's suffering: "Poor boy! the long train of exhaustion, deprivation, rudeness, no food, no friendly word or deed, but all kinds of upstart airs and impudent, unfeeling speeches and deeds, from all kinds of small officials (and some big ones), cutting like razors into that sensitive heart, had at last done the job. He now lay at times out of his head but quite silent, asking nothing of anyone, for some days, with death getting a closer and a surer grip upon him; he cared not, or rather he welcomed death. His heart was broken."[16]

Whitman happened to pass Holmes's bed on his way out of the ward and noticed "his glassy eyes, with a look of despair and hopelessness, sunk low in his thin, pallid-brown young face." Immediately recognizing the look of a dying man, Whitman stopped and made some encouraging remark; Holmes did not reply. "I saw as I looked that it was a case for ministering to the affection first, and other nourishment and medicines afterward," Whitman wrote. "I sat down by him without any fuss; talked a little; soon saw that it did him good; led him to talk a little himself; got him somewhat interested; wrote a letter for him to his folks in Massachusetts . . . soothed him down as I saw he was getting a little too much agitated, and tears in his eyes; gave him some small gifts and told him I should come again soon." Holmes said he would like to buy a glass of milk from the woman who peddled it in the wards, and Whitman gave him a little change. The young man immediately burst into tears. Whitman continued to check on Holmes, who remained quite sick for several weeks before eventually recovering his health and rejoining his unit. He rose to the rank of corporal, was wounded at the Battle of Bethesda Church in June 1864, and served out the remainder of the war with honor, if not distinction. Before leaving the hospital, Holmes told Whitman that his bedside visit that first day had saved his life.[17]

Visiting the hospitals quickly became the focal point of Whitman's day. His life took on an unwonted regularity. Never an early riser, he would eat a leisurely breakfast with the O'Connors at eight-thirty, having first fetched a pitcher of fresh cold water from the pump at the corner. Morning discussions centered on Emerson, Wordsworth, Tennyson, and other leading poets of the day—Whitman was particularly intrigued with guessing how the "calm and sweet" Emerson would have reacted to the battle scenes at Fredericksburg. The trio laughed derisively at the more punctual government clerks hurrying to their desks along the street below, and Whitman once suggested, tongue in cheek, that O'Connor write a short story entitled, "The Faithful Clerk, a Tale of the Treasury—Dedicated to the Nine O'Clockers, by a Half-past Tener."[18]

The rest of the morning Whitman spent at his desk in the paymaster's office, copying documents or writing letters, before going to visit one of the hospitals in the afternoon. He generally spent the hours between noon and 4 P.M. with the soldiers, then returned to his room for a long, restorative bath before sharing dinner with the O'Connors. From six to nine, he went again to the hospitals, sometimes spending the night beside a particularly difficult patient. Then he walked home alone, enjoying the myriad sights of the capital by starlight, although he readily confessed that some areas of Washington, filled as they were with army deserters, runaway slaves, drunken soldiers, hard-faced prostitutes—male as well as female—and other assorted denizens of the night, made such ventures decidedly "pokerish."[19]

More often than not, the evening would conclude with a lively discussion at the O'Connors' involving Whitman, O'Connor, and a regular cast of visitors drawn from the city's governmental and journalistic communities. Among those stopping by to exchange views and voice opinions were Charles Eldridge, John Piatt, Assistant Attorney General J. Hubley Ashton, *New York Times* correspondent William Swinton (brother of Walt's good friend John Swinton, the *Times*'s managing editor), Dr. Frank Baker, medical historian for the Smithsonian

Institution, and Polish count Adam Gurowski, an old standby from the bohemian days at Pfaff's who was working as a translator for the State Department. "The discussion upon all topics was always open and ready, and the fun and good-natured banter always free," recalled Nelly O'Connor. "No subject under the sun was neglected." Topics ranged widely, from free trade to free love, the latter evoking for some reason "the fiercest denunciations that were ever heard from Whitman."[20]

The discussions may not always have been as pacific as Mrs. O'Connor remembered. On at least one occasion a policeman came to the door to see what all the yelling was about—"neighbors were convinced that a furious quarrel was going on." Years later Whitman would tell Traubel that "we had the hardest discussions in the old days—brutal ones, I should say. [O'Connor] would go for me in the fiercest way, denounce me—appear to regard me as being negligent, as shirking a duty." Nor did Whitman necessarily step back from an argument. "Walt, with his strong lungs and loud voice, did his full share of the roaring," said Nelly, "and by no means as gently as the sucking dove." She sometimes worried—with good reason, as events would prove—that such habitual arguing would one day ruin their friendship.[21]

For the time being, however, the late-night wrangles were a welcome respite for Whitman, whose daily trips to the hospitals were already beginning to tax him physically, mentally, and emotionally. Nothing in his far from sheltered life had prepared him for the sights, the sounds, and the smells of the army hospitals—they were literally a world unto themselves. At the end of 1862 there were approximately thirty-five hospitals in and around Washington, accommodating some thirteen thousand suffering soldiers. Despite the recent influx of wounded from Fredericksburg, the winter of 1862–63 actually represented something of a downtime for the hospitals after the extended bloodletting that followed Major General George McClellan's Peninsula campaign, the Seven Days battles, Second Manassas, South Mountain, and Antietam, when a grand total of 56,050 cases had been treated in Washington during the last four months of the year.[22]

As always, raw numbers could be misleading; there may have been fewer soldiers confined to the hospitals at the time of Whitman's arrival in the capital, but those who languished in the whitewashed wooden sheds, converted government buildings, and outlying tent hospitals were, practically speaking, the sickest and most gravely wounded of all. By the time they had made their way to Washington, the soldiers had already endured the disease-ridden squalor of camp life, the exhaustions of marching, the terrors of combat, the chills of fever, the hammering of bullets, the slicing of canister, and the dull grinding rasp of the field surgeon's saw. In many ways their greatest trials still lay ahead. Before they could return to their regiments or, better yet, walk through the gates of their peacetime homes, honorably discharged from the army with an empty sleeve or a brace of crutches, they first had to survive the hospitals.

Like the soldiers who filled them, the hospitals in Washington were a variable lot. They ranged in size and richness of appointment from the private mansions of Douglas Hospital to the filthy, mud-encrusted tents of the contraband camp on the outskirts of town. At the start of the war, patients had been housed indiscriminately in churches, taverns, jails, schoolrooms, stables, hotels, warehouses, and homes; many had been left out in the open in vacant lots. The ensuing two years had witnessed a boom in hospital building, although the new facilities were far from standardized. The three-thousand-bed Harewood Hospital, constructed on a rolling farm northwest of the city, was modeled after an English estate, with landscaped grounds, terraced flower gardens, and a well-tended vegetable plot. By contrast, the hastily built Lincoln Hospital consisted of rough canvas tents stretched across wooden frames on the marshy flood plain east of the Capitol. State-of-the-art hospitals included Armory Square and Judiciary Square, which had been constructed on the modern "pavilion plan" that featured separate wards, or pavilions, radiating from a central corridor. The new pavilion hospitals, based on the British design first used in the Crimean War, emphasized open air and ample ventilation: "noxious effluvia"—bad smells—were still believed to be the chief cause of the rampant infections that raced unchecked through the hospital wards and carried off postoperative patients by the thousands.

Whatever their design, the hospitals in Washington were places to be feared and despised by any soldier. Medical care in the early 1860s was not much advanced from the Middle Ages. The great discoveries in bacteriology and antisepsis by such European medical pioneers as Louis Pasteur, Robert Koch, and Joseph Lister were still a few years in the future. American doctors, by and large, were poorly trained and woefully underequipped. (Harvard Medical School, for example, did not even own a microscope until 1869.) The cause and prevention of disease were unknown. Typhoid fever, malaria, and diarrhea, the three most prevalent and deadly killers of the Civil War, tore through every hospital and camp, spread by infected drinking water, fecally contaminated food, and disease-transmitting mosquitoes. Meanwhile, attending physicians ascribed the ills to such imaginative and fantastical causes as "malarial miasms," "mephitic effluvia," "crowd poisoning," "sewer emanations," "depressing mental agencies," "lack of nerve force," "exhalations," "night air," "sleeping in damp blankets," "choleric temperament," "decay of wood," "odor of horse manure," "effluvia of putrefying corpses," and "poisonous fungi in the atmosphere."[23]

Given such thinking, together with the endemic overcrowding and poor sanitary practices common to both armies, it is no wonder that Civil War soldiers were four times as likely to fall ill as civilians—and five times as likely to die if they did. It was not that the hometown doctors were dramatically better at their work—most of the eleven thousand physicians who served the Union Army in camp, field, or hospital were volunteers drawn from the same pool of peacetime practitioners—the problem lay in the system itself. In 1860, one year before the start of the Civil War, there were forty existing medical schools in the United States, three-fourths of them in the North, with a total enrollment of approximately five thousand students. The demand for doctors far outstripped the number of schools, and students characteristically rushed through their classes in a year or less and then were free to hang out their shingles without (as was still common in Europe) serving a professional apprenticeship. Low standards of education, combined with a dismaying ignorance of European medical advances, meant that all Americans — soldiers and civilians — received less than satisfactory medical treatment during the war. And the sheer volume of cases — more than four hundred thousand wounded and six million sick in the Union Army alone during the four years of war — insured that even the most competent doctors were swamped with more cases than they could effectively handle.[24]

Once ill, the soldiers could expect little in the way of practical help from their doctors. Indeed, many of the physicians' favorite remedies made matters worse by violating the most basic of all medical tenets: first, do no harm. Civil War–era doctors were apt to prescribe a bewildering and generally ineffective array of drugs at the first sign of illness. Diarrhea was treated with laxatives, opium, epsom salts, castor oil, ipecac, quinine, strychnine, turpentine, camphor oil, laudanum, blue mass, belladonna, lead acetate, silver nitrate, red pepper, and whiskey. Malarial symptoms called for large doses of quinine — one unfortunate patient received 120 grains in seventeen hours — whiskey, opium, epsom salts, iodide of potassium, sulphuric acid, wild cherry syrup, morphine, ammonia, cod liver oil, spirits of nitre, cream of tartar, barley water, and cinnamon. Typhoid sufferers were dosed with quinine, blue mass, carbonate of ammonia, turpentine, opium, and brandy. When all else failed, as it frequently did, doctors harkened back to more primitive methods of treatment: bleeding, cupping, blistering, leeching, binding, and chafing. Flannel belly bands were also widely if ineffectively used.[25]

By far the most widely prescribed and damaging drug was

calomel, or mercurous chloride. Dissolved in a chalky, bitter-tasting liquid, calomel was administered in massive doses for virtually every disease that Civil War physicians encountered. This was the era of "heroic dosing," when patients were virtually drenched in medicines, on the seemingly unassailable theory that any drug worth taking in moderation was doubly worth taking in excess. Unfortunately, it did not require much calomel to induce chronic mercury poisoning, with horrific short-term and insidious long-term aftereffects. Some patients were given a dram of calomel every hour, causing their faces to swell, their tongues to jut out of their mouths, and their saliva to gush forth at the rate of anywhere from a pint to a quart every twenty-four hours. Heavy doses caused victims' teeth and hair to fall out, and in extreme cases they developed mercurial gangrene, a particularly loathsome disease that rotted the soft tissue in the inside of the mouth and caused it to slough off in a putrid mass.[26]

Abuses were so widespread that in May 1863 Union Surgeon General William A. Hammond felt compelled to issue a directive banning the use of calomel and a related mercury-based compound, tartar emetic, in all army hospitals. "No doubt can exist," said Hammond, "that more harm has resulted from the misuse of both these agents . . . than benefit from their administration." Hammond's farsighted order was widely ignored, and its unpopularity among other physicians contributed greatly to his removal from office a few months later. At any rate, the directive came too late to help Northern author Louisa May Alcott, who had come to Washington not long before Whitman to serve as a nurse in the hospitals. Contracting typhoid fever after only three weeks at Union Hotel Hospital, Alcott was heroically dosed with calomel, lost most of her hair and teeth, and suffered from shooting pains in her arms and back for the rest of her life.[27]

Sharing hospital space with the ill were soldiers who had been wounded in combat. Frequently, this meant that they were recuperating from amputations of their arms or legs and, more often than not, were also battling some sort of postoperative fever caused by the incredibly filthy conditions of Civil War surgery. Antisepsis was almost entirely unknown during the war, and the rough nature of field hospitals precluded even minimal standards of cleanliness, much less sterility. The common image of the Civil War "butcher" at work in a charnel house of severed limbs and screaming victims has some basis of truth, but with important qualifications. The popular notion of a wounded soldier biting down on a bullet while a drunken surgeon sawed away clumsily at his ruined arm is a romantic—or antiromantic—figment of the screenwriter's imagination. To begin with, most wounded soldiers were effectively anesthetized before surgery, chloroform being the overwhelming agent of choice. Soldiers were often given a drink of whiskey upon their arrival at field hospitals, but this was done erroneously to combat symptoms of shock, not for anesthetic reasons.

Amputations were performed at a staggering rate after a major battle, not out of callousness or stupidity but as accepted medical practice stemming from the experience of British surgeons during the Crimean War. The number of amputated limbs was high because the number of wounds to soldiers' extremities was also high—71 percent of all Civil War wounds were to the arms, legs, hands, or feet. The wounding agent was almost always a bullet—surprisingly, only 6 percent of wounds were caused by artillery fire—and three-forths of all bullet wounds were inflicted by .58-caliber Minie bullets, wrongly called balls. The damage done to the human body by such a lethal projectile, fired from a rifled musket with great accuracy at a range of upwards of one thousand yards, is difficult to exaggerate. The relatively slow muzzle speed of Civil War muskets, coupled with the heavy weight of the cone-shaped lead bullet, resulted in large, jagged wounds, copious bleeding, and catastrophically shattered bones. (By comparison, the modern steel-jacketed, .30-caliber bullet, traveling at a much faster speed, is effectively sterilized by the sheer heat of its velocity and typically makes a smaller, neater, utterly aseptic hole while passing completely through the victim's body.)[28]

More often than not, it was this shattering of bones that compelled immediate amputation during the Civil War. As one wartime surgeon described it, "The shattering, splintering, and splitting of a long bone by the impact of the minie or Enfield ball were, in many instances, both remarkable and frightful, and early experience taught surgeons that amputation was the only means of saving life." Furthermore, it was accepted practice that operations should take place within twenty-four hours of the patient's wounding, before the "irritative," or infected, stage of the injury had set in, meaning that the amputations of necessity took place in rough field hospitals, not in better-equipped surgeries farther to the rear.[29]

It was not so much the amputations themselves that caused such traumatic medical aftereffects in Civil War soldiers but the frightful and literally ignorant way in which they were carried out. No modern description of the procedure can equal the eyewitness account of Union surgeon W. W. Keen, a young Philadelphia physician who went through the war with the Army of the Potomac and later became one of the country's most respected neurologists. Writing in 1918, half a century removed from the horrors he had witnessed at Bull Run, Gettysburg, and Spotsylvania, Keen could not suppress an almost perceptible shudder. "We operated in old blood-stained and often pus-stained coats," he wrote. "We used undisinfected instruments from undisinfected plush-lined cases, and still worse, used marine sponges which had been used in prior pus cases and had been only washed in tap water. If a sponge or an instrument fell on the floor it was washed and squeezed in a basin of tap water and used as if it were clean. . . . The silk with which we sewed up all wounds was undisinfected. If there was any difficulty in threading the needle we moistened it with . . . bacteria-laden saliva, and rolled it between bacteria-infected fingers. We dressed the wounds with clean but undisinfected sheets, shirts, tablecloths, or other old soft linen rescued from the family ragbag. We had no sterilized gauze dressing, no gauze sponges. . . . We knew nothing about antiseptics and therefore used none."[30]

The predictable result of such hurried and horrific operations was postoperative infections, of which there was no shortage of dreadful candidates. Pyemia, septicemia, erysipelas, osteomyelitis, tetanus, gangrene—the very names of the so-called "surgical fevers" are terrifying, and with good reason. Caused by the ever teeming streptococcus or staphylococcus bacteria, the fevers routinely followed invasive surgery (erysipelas was the exception, often occurring idiopathically, or spontaneously, without the necessity of an open wound). Pyemia, or "pus in the blood," was the most dreaded of all, with a mortality rate of 97.4 percent. Sufferers experienced profuse sweating, high fevers, chills, jaundice, and the affliction's mordant trademark, multiple abcesses, before being carried off within a few days of its onset.[31]

One Union surgeon graphically charted the fever's course: "Many a time have I had the following experience: A poor fellow whose leg or arm I had amputated a few days before would be getting on as well as we then expected—that is to say, he had pain, high fever, was thirsty and restless, but was gradually improving. . . . Suddenly, over night, I would find that his fever had become markedly greater; his tongue dry, his pain and restlessness increased; sleep had deserted his eyelids, his cheeks were flushed; and on removing the dressings I would find the secretions from the wound dried up, and what there were were watery, thin, and foul smelling, and what union of the flaps had taken place had melted away. Pyemia was the verdict, and death the usual result within a few days."[32]

Less deadly than pyemia, but perhaps more distressing to both victims and onlookers because of their hideous outward manifestations, were tetanus and hospital gangrene. Tetanus, or lockjaw, is caused by the bacillus tetani, found frequently in the very soil the soldiers fought over. It was easily spread by horse manure (horses being a popular host of the germ), and the largest single outbreak of the disease during the war came after the Battle of Antietam, when many of the Union wounded were treated at a field hospital located in a stable that was ankle deep in manure. Once securing a foothold in a deep puncture wound — the bacillus cannot survive in the open air — tetanus releases a variety of toxins that grotesquely affect the central nervous system, causing the familiar fixed smile and frozen jaws of the terminal victim. There was no effective treatment at the time, and the mortality rate was a fearsome 89 percent. Doctors tried large doses of brandy and opium, administered through stomach tubes or enemas, but without noticeable effect. "To enumerate the means used for the relief of tetanus would require a volume," a surgical manual explained, "but to record those entitled to confidence does not demand a line." Few who saw a tetanus victim thrashing his life away on a hospital cot, held down by half a dozen straining attendants, ever forgot the hideous sight.[33]

Hospital gangrene, now mercifully extinct, was even more terrible to behold. The infection typically began with a small black spot the size of a dime appearing on the surface of the wound. Within a few days' time, the spot would grow into a rotten-smelling mass of decayed tissue, gray, blue, green, or black in color. Because its characteristic odor and repulsive appearance were upsetting to fellow patients, doctors, and staff, gangrene cases were sometimes kept in isolated wards or separate hospitals, such as the Confederates' Empire Hospital in Macon, Georgia. Treatment included surgically removing the dead tissue or burning it off with corrosive chemicals such as nitric acid, chlorine, or bromine. Charcoal, yeast, turpentine, and carrot poultices were also frequently applied to the wounds, with predictably low rates of success.[34]

Understandably, if wrongly, confusing the cause of the disease with its most noticeable symptom, doctors attributed hospital gangrene to the catchall culprit "sewer effluvia." Pails of bromine were scattered about the wards to combat the smell, although one Confederate surgeon actually opposed the practice on the grounds that it was "like removing the beacon that warns the watchful mariner of the certain death that lurks beneath the surface." Patients trapped in nearby beds no doubt disputed that nautical reasoning.[35]

This, then, was the universe that Walt Whitman entered in January 1863, when it sometimes seemed as though America herself had been "brought to Hospital in her fair youth— brought and deposited here in this great, whited sepulchre of Washington." Whitman was not unaccustomed to hospitals— he had been going to see his injured stage driver friends in New York's Broadway Hospital for several years—but this was different: there were so many patients, and they were so young. Two weeks after he began his visits, he described to Emerson their effect on him: "The first shudder has long passed over," he wrote, "and I must say I find deep things, unreckoned by current print or speech. The Hospital, I do not find it, the repulsive place of sores and fevers, nor the place of querulousness, nor the bad results of morbid years which one avoids like bad s[mells]."[36]

Instead, and perhaps to a degree that he could not admit even to himself, he found the hospitals—and the handsome young men within them—surprisingly fertile ground for his art. Very early in his career as a hospital volunteer, he began planning to write a book about his experiences, one that would commemorate "this other freight of helpless worn and wounded youth, genuine of the soil, of darlings and true heirs to me the first unquestioned and convincing western crop, prophetic of the future, proofs undeniable to all men's ken of perfect beauty, tenderness and pluck that never race yet rivalled . . . the imperial blood and rarest marrow of the North." Without imputing too cynical a motive to Whitman's actions, it nevertheless is fair to say that he found the soldiers—and himself— exceptionally good copy. Dozens of new poems, newspaper articles, essays, and books came out of his work in the hospitals. And while no one should deny Whitman proper credit for his good deeds, he was himself honest enough to admit that his virtue, in a way, was its own reward. "People used to say to me, Walt you are doing miracles for those fellows in the hospitals," he told Horace Traubel. "I wasn't. I was doing miracles for myself."[37]

His hospital visits were good therapy—for him as much as the soldiers. The brave young men who were fighting and dying so uncomplainingly for the Union restored his belief in the inherent goodness of the American people and his idealized concept of comradely love. Coming as they did on the heels of a half decade of drift and depression, his experiences in Washington were nothing short of life changing. As he told Traubel, "There were years in my life—years there in New York—when I wondered if all was not going to the bad with America—the tendency downwards—but the war saved me: what I saw in the war set me up for all time—the days in the hospitals." Within a few weeks the visits went from being a temporary diversion to a way of life. "I cannot give up my Hospitals yet," Walt told his brother Jeff. "I never before had my feelings so thoroughly and (so far) permanently absorbed, to the very roots, as by these huge swarms of dear, wounded, sick, dying boys—I get very much attached to some of them, and many of them have come to depend on seeing me, and having me sit by them a few minutes, as if for their lives."[38]

It seems clear, in retrospect, that Whitman's love for the young soldiers had a sexual, if largely sublimated, component to it. Modern gay writers have seized on the poet as an early role model of unembarrassed male love, some going so far as to read into every casually expressed, written endearment a hidden level of sexual activity that, given the tenor of the times and the sheer physical overcrowding of the hospitals, seems highly unlikely if not ridiculous. Whitman, at any rate, did not go to the hospitals to make romantic conquests—he went to help. And although he did on occasion grow more than casually attached to some few of the soldiers he met there, his feelings were most often those of a fond, avuncular uncle or brother. Three decades later, describing his relationships with the soldiers to Traubel, Whitman mentioned particularly "the revelation of an exquisite courtesy—man to man—rubbing up there together. I could say in the highest sense, *propriety—propriety*, as in the doing of necessary unnameable things, always done with exquisite delicacy." In other words, even when making intimate physical contact with the patients, changing a bedpan or washing a limb, Whitman was careful to maintain a proper professional distance—or at least give the appearance of doing so, which in itself was half the fight.[39]

With the peculiar predictive power of genius, Whitman had already foreseen his labors in *Leaves of Grass*:

Behold, I do not give lectures or a little charity,
When I give I give myself.

　．．．

To any one dying, thither I speed and twist the knob of
　　the door,
Turn the bed-clothes toward the foot of the bed,
Let the physician and the priest go home.

I seize the descending man and raise him with resistless
　　will,
O despairer, here is my neck,
By God, you shall not go down! hang your whole weight
　　upon me.

I dilate you with tremendous breath, I buoy you up,
Every room of the house do I fill with an arm'd force,
Lovers of me, bafflers of graves.

Sleep—I and they keep guard all night,
Not doubt, not decease shall dare to lay finger upon you,
I have embraced you, and henceforth possess you to
　　myself,
And when you rise in the morning you will find what I tell
　　you is so.[40]

Sometimes, of course, there was nothing anyone could do to
prevent death from "tapping lightly . . . some poor young
man," and Whitman would pray by his bedside:

Come sweet death! be persuaded O beautiful death!
In mercy come quickly.[41]

Again, he had already anticipated the experience, and he could
console and be consoled in turn by the thought that the dead

> . . . are alive and well somewhere,
> The smallest sprout shows there is really no death,
> And if ever there was it led forward life, and does not wait
>   at the end to arrest it,
> And ceas'd the moment life appear'd.
> All goes onward and outward, nothing collapses,
> And to die is different from what any one supposed, and
>   luckier.[42]

It was not the dead who most required Whitman's attention
but those still clinging precariously to life. He prepared for his
daily visits—one might almost say his ministry—as carefully as
a general prepares for a battle. He soon discovered that outward
appearance counted greatly with the men, and he always made
it a point to bathe, dress, and eat a good meal before starting
his rounds. "In my visits to the Hospitals I found it was in the
simple matter of Personal Presence, and emanating ordinary
cheer and magneticism, that I succeeded and help'd more than
by medical nursing, or delicacies, or gifts of money, or anything
else," he recalled. "My habit, when practicable, was to prepare
for starting out on one of those daily or nightly tours, of from
a couple to four or five hours, by fortifying myself with previous

THE GREAT ARMY OF THE SICK

rest, the bath, clean clothes, a good meal, and as cheerful an appearance as possible."[43]

He bought himself a good, sober, wine-colored suit, a pair of black Morocco boots, and a widebrimmed hat with a gold and black drawstring and gold acorns at the bottom. His arthritic mother chipped in from Brooklyn, painfully knitting him a number of new white shirts that he wore beneath an invariable necktie. "I am as well and hearty, and I suppose . . . as much of a beauty as ever," he told her, "not only as much but more so—I believe I weigh about 200, and as to my face, (so scarlet,) and my beard and neck, they are terrible to behold. I fancy the reason I am able to do some good in the hospitals among the poor languishing and wounded boys, is, that I am so large and well— indeed like a great wild buffalo, with much hair. Many of the soldiers are from the West, and far North, and they take to a man that has not the bleached shiny and shaved cut of the cities and the East."[44]

He realized, of course, that the soldiers needed more than his mere presence to comfort and inspire them. With the luminous example of Ellen Eyre freshly before him, Whitman began assembling a grab bag of little treats that he carried slung over his shoulder in a canvas haversack wheedled from his new friend Elijah Allen, who ran an army-navy store on Pennsylvania Avenue. Into the sack went anything Whitman could beg, borrow, or buy to make the soldiers' lot easier. He regularly brought them fruit, tobacco, candy, jelly, pickles, preserves, cookies, wine, brandy, shirts, socks, handkerchiefs, and underwear. In hot weather he sometimes brought ice cream for the men as a special treat. All these gifts he distributed informally and unostentatiously, knowing full well that the proud young soldiers would resist instinctively any suggestion of charity. He kept track of his dispersals in small pocket notebooks he made by stitching together sheets of folded paper with bits of string. Each day he jotted down whatever he could learn from the patients he visited—name, rank, company, regiment, bed number, ward, hospital, nature of wound or illness, and the names and addresses of parents and wives. He soon saw that the best thing he could give the men was writing supplies; those who were unable to write for themselves he cheerfully assisted at dictation. An inveterate letter writer himself, he knew how important it was to keep in touch with the folks back home.

As the soldiers became more familiar with Whitman, they began telling him things they would like him to bring. A sample entry from his notebooks reveals how pitifully little the soldiers really wanted and how assiduously he sought to meet their requests: "Bed 53 wants some licorice; Bed 6 (erisypelas), bring some raspberry vinegar to make a cooling drink with water; Bed 18 wants a good book—a romance; Bed 25 (a manly, friendly young fellow, independent young soul) refuses money and eatables, so I will bring him a pipe and tobacco, for I see how much he enjoys a smoke; Bed 45 (sore throat and cough) wants horehound candy; Bed 11, when I come again, don't forget to write a letter for him. . . . One poor German, dying—in the last stages of consumption—wished me to find him in Washington a German Lutheran clergyman and send him to him. . . . One patient will want nothing but a toothpick, another a comb, and so on." When twenty-one-year-old Henry Boardman of the 27th Connecticut told Whitman that he craved some rice pudding as a break from the unpalatable hospital food, the poet had Nelly O'Connor make some especially for him. Boardman, in turn, proudly insisted a few days later that Whitman share a box of food with him that had just arrived from his parents in North-ford, Connecticut.[45]

All these little kindnesses—they were not so little to the sol-diers who received them—cost money, and Whitman was con-stantly on the lookout for additional sources of income. During his first two weeks at work in the paymaster's office, he received twenty-seven dollars in pay, and he immediately spent ten dol-lars of it on gifts for the soldiers. On February 6 he wrote to his brother Jeff, asking him to start a fund-raising drive among Jeff's coworkers at the Brooklyn Water Works. This netted an-other six dollars, but Walt admonished Jeff for sending five dol-lars of his own money and a dollar of their impecunious mother's. "What ought to be done by our family, I feel that *I* am doing, and have done myself," he told Jeff, adding, "I wouldn't take a thousand dollars for the satisfaction it has been to me." He hit up old friends and casual acquaintances—four dollars came from a man named Wood who lived near the army-navy store on Pennsylvania Avenue—and he fell back on his training as a journalist to produce two well-paying articles on the hospitals in Washington for the *New York Times* and the *Brooklyn Daily Eagle*.[46]

The first article, "The Great Army of the Sick," featuring the sad story of Massachusetts Private John Holmes, appeared in the *Times* on February 26. In it, Whitman gave a good picture of the new pavilion design of hospitals: "The Government . . . is gradually settling down to adopt the plan of placing the hos-

pitals in clusters of one-story wooden barracks, with their ac-
companying tents and sheds for cooking and all needed purposes. . . . These sheds now adopted are long, one-story edifices,
sometimes ranged along in a row, with their heads to the street,
and numbered either alphabetically, Wards A or B, C, D, and
so on; or Wards 1, 2, 3, etc. The middle one will be marked by
a flagstaff, and is the office of the establishment, with rooms for
the ward surgeons, etc. One of these sheds, or wards, will contain sixty cots; sometimes, on an emergency, they move them
close together and crowd in more. . . . Each ward has a ward-
master, and generally a nurse for every ten or twelve men. A
ward surgeon has, generally, two wards—although this varies.
Some of the wards have a woman nurse; the Armory-square
wards have some very good ones."[47]

Whitman's account stressed his missionary work among the
soldiers and openly solicited other volunteers. "A benevolent
person, with the right qualities and tact, cannot, perhaps make
a better investment of himself, at present, anywhere upon the
varied surface of the whole of this big world, than in these
military hospitals, among such thousands of most interesting
young men," he wrote. "Reader, how can I describe to you the
mute appealing look that rolls and moves from many a manly
eye, from many a sick cot, following you as you walk slowly
down one of these wards? To see these, and to be incapable of
responding to them, except in a few cases (so very few com-
pared to the whole of the suffering men), is enough to make
one's heart crack."[48]

Whitman was far from the only visitor in the hospitals. Indeed, one signal characteristic of Civil War–era hospitals was

the easy access that the general public had to the men. This access was not always an unalloyed blessing, as one disgusted Indiana soldier recalled later, remembering the "broken-down, short-winded, long-faced, seedy preachers of all denominations" who prayed regularly over the men "without having smiled on a single soldier or dropped a word of comfort or cheer," and the "batch of sightseers, do-nothings, idlers, time-killers, fops, and butterflies [who] skip through the hospital, and like summer shadows, leave no trace behind." Doubtless there were some patients who considered Whitman a similar nuisance—in the words of one modern editor, "a funny-looking, intrusive old fruit." There is no suggestion in any of his writings that he was ever less than universally accepted, but then every man is the hero of his own autobiography. At any rate, he had more than enough to do keeping up with the vast majority of men who welcomed his company.[49]

For a brief time Whitman served under the auspices of the Christian Commission, a wartime adjunct of the YMCA. How he came to be connected with the agency is unclear, but it seems likely that he approached them for help in supplying items requested by the soldiers, including in one instance a bottle of "first-rate brandy" that he secured for two patients at Armory Square Hospital "imperatively requiring stimulus." His formal commission, dated January 20, 1863, enjoined him to carry on the work of "distributing stores where needed, in hospitals and camps, circulating good reading matter amongst soldiers and sailors; visiting the sick and wounded to instruct, comfort and cheer them, and aid them in correspondence with their friends at home; aiding surgeons on the battle-field and elsewhere in the care and conveyance of the wounded to hospitals; helping chaplains in the ministrations and influence for the good of the men under their care; and addressing soldiers and sailors, individually and collectively, in explaining the work of the Christian Commission and its delegates, and for their personal instruction and benefit, temporal and eternal."[50]

This last, evangelical instruction may have been a sticking point; Whitman was no proselytizer. Union Colonel Richard Hinton, a former associate of John Brown's in Kansas, was recuperating from wounds suffered at Antietam when he first met Whitman at Armory Square Hospital. His postwar account in the *Cincinnati Commercial* favorably contrasted Whitman's methods with those of other visitors at the time. Noting that Whitman "seemed to have ready what everybody wanted," Hinton added, "When this old heathen came and gave me a pipe and tobacco, it was about the most joyous moment of my life. . . . I don't mean to say he was the only one who visited the hospital. There were plenty of others I assure you. The little bay at the head of my cot was full of tracts and testaments, and every Sunday there were half a dozen old roosters who would come into my ward and preach and pray and sing to us, while we were swearing to ourselves all the time, and wishing the blamed old fools would go away. Walt Whitman's funny stories, and his pipes and tobacco were worth more than all the preachers and tracts in Christendom. A wounded soldier don't like to be reminded of his God more than twenty times a day. Walt Whitman didn't bring any tracts or Bibles; he didn't ask if you loved the Lord, and didn't seem to care whether you did or not."[51]

THE GREAT ARMY OF THE SICK

In light of such unorthodox views, it was inevitable that Whitman would soon part ways with the Christian Commission, although he continued to hold its members in high regard for their selfless (and unpaid) devotion to duty. He had considerably less use for the salaried members of the United States Sanitary Commission, a quasi-military organization whose cool, clinical approach to aiding the soldiers was summed up by one female volunteer who recommended that hospital nurses "put away all feelings. Do all you can and be a machine—that's the way to act; the only way." It was not Whitman's way, and he broadcast his dislike in a letter to his mother, calling the members of the Sanitary Commission "hirelings" who "get well paid, & are always incompetent & disagreeable."[52]

One Sanitary Commission member, Harriet Hawley of Connecticut, returned Whitman's antipathy in spades. "There comes that odious Walt Whitman to talk evil and unbelief to my boys," she wrote in a letter to her husband, Union Colonel Joseph Hawley. "I think I would rather see the Evil One himself—at least if he had horns and hooves. . . . I shall get him out as soon as possible." Mrs. Hawley, of course, was not lying wounded at the time. At any rate, Whitman soon withdrew from any formal connection with any agency, public or private. "I am not connected with any society," he advised readers of the *Brooklyn Daily Eagle*, "but go on my own individual account, and to the work that appears to be called for." Like a latter-day Johnny Appleseed he made his solitary rounds, "distributing myself and the contents of my pockets and haversack in infinitesimal quantities, with faith that nearly all of it will, somehow or other, fall on good ground."[53]

Preoccupied as he was with his work in the hospitals, Whitman suspended indefinitely his sporadic attempts to find better-paying government work. He had already undergone three fruitless interviews with Massachusetts senator Charles Sumner, complaining afterwards that Sumner had told him oracularly that "every thing here moves as part of a great machine, and that I must consign myself to the fate of the rest." Eventually, Sumner passed him off to New York senator Preston King, who, after first dismissing Whitman as looking "for all the world like an old Southern planter," came up with a generalized letter of endorsement for Secretary of the Treasury Salmon P. Chase and Quartermaster General Montgomery C. Meigs. By then, Whitman had grown bored with supplicating "some big bug," and he shelved King's letter for several months, reasoning that "I cannot give up my Hospitals yet." His only outside source of income remained his occasional newspaper work.[54]

"The Great Army of the Sick" was well received by readers and earned Whitman a congratulatory letter from *Times* managing editor John Swinton praising the article and adding perceptively, "I am glad to see you are engaged in such good work in Washington. It must be even more refreshing than to sit by Pfaff's privy and eat sweet-breads and drink coffee, and listen to the intolerable wit of the crack-brains. I happened in there the other night, and the place smelt as atrociously as ever." By then, Pfaff's must have seemed like a distant memory. *Times* publisher Henry Raymond liked the article so well that he sent Whitman an extra fifty-dollar check.[55]

Three weeks later, Whitman wrote a second article, "Life Among Fifty Thousand Soldiers," for the *Brooklyn Daily Eagle*.

The article was geared specifically to its hometown readers, and Whitman took pains to mention by name as many of the local soldiers as he could. "At a rough guess, I should say I have met from one hundred and fifty to two hundred young and middle-aged men whom I specifically found to be Brooklyn persons," he wrote. "Many of them I recognized as having seen their faces before, and very many of them knew me. Some said they had known me from boyhood. Some would call to me as I passed down a ward, and tell me they had seen me in Brooklyn. I have had this happen at night, and have been entreated to step and sit down and take the hand of a sick and restless boy, and talk to him and comfort him awhile, for old Brooklyn's sake."[56]

Whitman concluded the article with an angry dig at a particularly annoying ward master he had encountered recently on his rounds. "Some pompous and every way improper persons, of course, get power in hospitals, have full spring over the helpless soldiers," he wrote. "There is great state kept at Judiciary-square hospital, for instance. An individual who probably has been waiter somewhere for years past has got into the high and mighty position of sergeant-of-arms at this hospital; he is called 'Red Stripe' (for his artillery trimmings) by the patients, of whom he is at the same time the tyrant and the laughing-stock. Going in to call on some sick New York soldiers here the other afternoon, I was stopped and treated to a specimen of the airs of this powerful officer. Surely the Government would do better to send such able-bodied loafers down into service in front, where they could earn their rations, than keep them here in the idle and shallow sinecures of military guard over a collection of sick soldiers to give insolence to their visitors and friends."[57]

The problem with Red Stripe was not an isolated one; the system was as much to blame as the individual. Few rational men—sick or well—wanted to be in the hospitals. Nevertheless, military doctrine mandated that a certain number of soldiers be detailed to the hospitals as attendants. Some were drawn from nearby garrisons—generally the most expendable soldiers. These shiftless, surly, and often simple-minded individuals were joined by convalescent soldiers and invalids who proved physically and emotionally unable to meet the challenges confronting them in the wards. The male attendants, who outnumbered female nurses by a margin of five or six to one, were noticeably ill suited for the job. They balked at doing "women's work," shirked their cleaning duties, mishandled patients (or ignored them altogether), and were fumble-fingered when assisting at surgery. Civilians hired to augment their numbers were even worse. They were universally regarded as "a filthy, saucy lot," and they frequently augmented their salaries of $20.50 a month by stealing from patients or selling them extra doses of morphine.[58]

In April 1863 the Army came up with a new organization, the Invalid Corps, to help hard-pressed hospital administrators. In theory the Invalid Corps was to be a "Corps of Honor" comprised of "meritorious and deserving" individuals whose physical handicaps precluded them from returning to the battlefield. In practice, however, its ranks were filled with a volatile combination of unwilling soldiers who wanted to get back to the front, unhealthy soldiers who wanted to get home, and unvalorous soldiers who wanted to get out of active duty. To a man, the members of the Invalid Corps loathed their new,

eye-catching sky-blue uniforms and Corps insignia—"I.C."—
which unfortunately duplicated the governmental stamp on
broken-down horses and inferior materiel: "Inspected and Con-
demned." In time the name was changed to the more dignified
Veteran Reserve Corps, but the quality of care it provided to
those confined to the hospitals remained conspicuously poor
and grudging.[59]

Given such undertrained and unmotivated attendants, it is
not surprising that mistakes were made—sometimes fatally—in
the treatment of patients. Whitman was on hand for the tragi-
comic denouement of one such incident. On January 4, 1863,
at Campbell Hospital, a middle-aged private named Joshua
Ford, of Company E, 1st Delaware Regiment, was orally given
a fatal dose of ammonia nitrate that had been intended for use
as a foot wash. He lingered for nine days before dying and
seemed to take the mishap with amazing aplomb, helped no
doubt by the liberal libation of rum and water that the attending
physician permitted him. "Now give me another plug of tobacco—I'm going to die soon," he would say, or, "Now give
me some more toddy." A childless widower, Ford "did not seem
to mind death at all—took it very phlegmatically—spoke of it
with perfect coolness," Whitman observed. He died early on
the morning of January 13 after taking a last lingering drink of
rum and water. Another soldier, Private Frederick Huse of the
35th Massachusetts, was accidentally given an overdose of opium
and laudanum by the same "ignorant ward master" and died a
short time later as well.[60]

Not all deaths were as easy as Ford's or as swift as Huse's.
At Armory Square Whitman came across Thomas Haley, a

young cavalryman in the 4th New York. Haley had emigrated
from Ireland to enlist in the Union cause; his zealotry earned
him a bullet in the lung. "I saw Tom when first brought here,
three days since, and didn't suppose he could live twelve hours,"
Whitman wrote. "He lies there with his frame exposed above
the waist, all naked, for coolness, a fine built man, the tan not
yet bleach'd from his cheeks and neck. It is useless to talk to
him, as with his sad hurt, and the stimulants they give him, and
the utter strangeness of every object, face, furniture, &c., the
poor fellow, even when awake, is like a frighten'd, shy animal.
. . . Poor youth, so handsome, athletic, with profuse beautiful
shining hair. One time as I sat looking at him while he lay
asleep, he suddenly, without the least start, awaken'd, open'd
his eyes, gave me a long, long steady look, turning his face
slightly to gaze easier—one long, clear silent look—a slight
sigh—then turn'd back and went into his doze again. Little he
knew, poor death-stricken boy, the heart of the stranger that
hover'd near."[61]

Haley's death, at least, was quick. Another Union soldier,
Private John Mahay, Company A, 101st New York, languished
for fifteen months at Armory Square before succumbing in the
autumn of 1863. Mahay, called Johnny by his friends, had been
shot through the bladder at Second Bull Run. "He had suffer'd
much," Whitman noted, "the water came out of the wound by
slow but steady quantities, for many weeks—so that he lay almost constantly in a sort of puddle—and there were other disagreeable circumstances." Walt gave Mahay a piece of horehound candy for his sore throat and later sat with him during
his death throes: "The water ran out of his eyes from the intense

pain, and the muscles of his face were distorted, but he utter'd nothing except a low groan now and then. Hot moist clothes were applied, and reliev'd him somewhat. Poor Mahay, a mere boy in age, but old in misfortune. He never knew the love of parents, was placed in his infancy in one of the New York charitable institutions, and subsequently bound out to a tyrannical master in Sullivan County, (the scars of whose cowhide and club remain'd yet on his back.) His wound here was a most disagreeable one, for he was a gentle, cleanly and affectionate boy." When he died, Mahay was given "quite a funeral ceremony."[62]

Following the failed Union offensive at Chancellorsville, Virginia, in May 1863, the hospitals began filling up again with wounded—Northern losses alone were over seventeen thousand. Among the casualties was twenty-one-year-old Oscar Wilber, a private in Company G, 154th New York Infantry. Wilber, the eldest son in a family of eight children, was his widowed mother's chief support (the family worked a small farm in the town of Humphrey, in Cattaraugus County, New York). Wilber was wounded on the first day of the Battle of Chancellorsville when a Confederate shell fragment struck him with such force that it broke his thighbone completely in two. He lay unattended for ten days on the field before being taken by his Rebel captors to a field hospital at Aquia Creek. He arrived at Armory Square Hospital on June 16.[63]

By the time Whitman encountered him, five weeks later, Wilber had been further reduced by chronic diarrhea. Yet somehow he hung on, buoyed by an intense religious faith that Walt witnessed at first hand. "He ask'd me to read to him a chapter in the New Testament," said Whitman. "I complied, and ask'd him what I should read. He said: 'Make your own choice.' I open'd at the close of one of the first books of the Evangelists, and read the chapters describing the latter hours of Christ, and the scenes at the crucifixion. The poor, wasted young man ask'd me to read the following chapter also, how Christ rose again. I read very slowly, for Oscar was feeble. It pleas'd him very much, yet the tears were in his eyes. He ask'd me if I enjoy'd religion. I said, 'Perhaps not, my dear, in the way you mean, and yet, maybe, it is the same thing.' He said: 'It is my chief reliance.' He talked of death, and said he did not fear it. I said: 'Why, Oscar, don't you think you will get well?' He said: 'I may, but it is not probable.'" Nine days later Wilber died.[64]

In the aftermath of Chancellorsville, Whitman suffered a temporary crisis of faith. One evening he went down to the Sixth Street Wharf to see the arriving flood of wounded, and was profoundly disheartened by what he saw. "The men in charge of them told me the bad cases were yet to come," he wrote. "If that is so I pity them, for these are bad enough. You ought to see the scene of the wounded arriving at the landing here. . . . Two boat loads came up about half-past seven last night. A little after eight it rain'd a long and violent shower. The poor, pale, helpless soldiers had been debark'd, and lay around on the wharf and neighborhood anywhere. The rain was, probably, grateful to them; at any rate they were exposed to it. . . . All around — on the wharf, on the ground, out on side places — the men are lying on blankets, old quilts, &c., with bloody rags bound round heads, arms, and legs. . . . The men generally make little or no ado, whatever their sufferings. A few groans that cannot be suppress'd, and occasionally a scream of pain as they lift a man into the ambulance." The wounded were arriving at the rate of nearly one thousand per day.[65]

The steady influx of casualties and the seeming inability of Union commanders to defeat Robert E. Lee induced in Whitman an uncharacteristic pessimism. "The condition of things here in the hospital is pretty bad," he told his mother on May 5, "the wounded from the battles around Fredericksburg are coming up in large numbers. It is very sad to see them." Even the arrival of Confederate prisoners in the capital depressed, rather than elated, him: "Mother, while I have been writing this a very large number of Southern prisoners, I should think 1,000 at least, has passed up Pennsylvania avenue, under a strong guard. I went out in the street, close to them. Poor fellows, many of them mere lads — it brought the tears; they seemed our flesh and blood too, some wounded, all miserable in clothing, all in dirt and tatters — many of them fine young men. Mother, I cannot tell you how I feel to see those prisoners marched."[66]

Equally distressing was the death of Private John Elliott of the 2nd Pennsylvania Cavalry, which Whitman also witnessed at the time. Elliott, who had been wounded severely in the leg, had died on the operating table under anesthesia. "The surgeons put off amputating the leg, he was so exhausted, but at last it was imperatively necessary to amputate," wrote Whitman. "Mother, I am shocked to tell you, that he never came alive off the amputating table — he died under the operation . . . poor young man, he suffered much, very very much, for many days & bore it so patiently — so it was a release to him — Mother, such things are awful — not a soul here he knew or cared about, except me . . . how contemptible all the usual little worldly prides & vanities & striving after appearances seems in the midst of such scenes as these. . . . To see such things & not be able to help them is awful—I feel almost ashamed of being so well & whole."⁶⁷

He betrayed the strain on his emotions in a heated conversation with Unitarian minister William Henry Channing, a friend of the O'Connors who happened to drop by one evening. Pacing the floor and wringing his hands, Whitman suddenly exclaimed: "I say stop this war, this horrible massacre of men." Channing pacified him: "You are sick; the daily contact with these poor maimed and suffering men has made you sick; don't you see that the war cannot be stopped now? Some issue must be made and met." And when O'Connor added that "the issues are not settled yet; slavery is not abolished," Whitman replied sharply, "I don't care for the niggers in comparison with all this suffering and the dismemberment of the Union." Whitman may have been recalling this conversation when he told Horace Traubel years later: "The people who like the wars should be compelled to fight the wars."⁶⁸

Contributing to Whitman's low mood was the deteriorating state of his own health. After five months of going to the hospitals on a daily basis, he now was complaining of "quite an attack of sore throat & distress in my head. . . . I am told that I hover too much over the beds of the hospitals, with fever & putrid wounds, &c." In retrospect his scarlet face, coupled with a persistent humming and deafness in his ears, seems to have been a harbinger of an even more serious breakdown still to come. Nor was his situation helped when he suffered a bad cut to his hand while assisting at an operation. The hand became infected and he had to keep it carefully wrapped to avoid the ever present threat of gangrene. For several weeks he also suffered a recurrence of headaches. He began skipping a day or two of visits to the men, "as I have several cautions from the doctors, who tell me that one must beware of continuing too steady and long in the air and influence of the hospitals." He revealed, perhaps, more than he intended of his current state of mind when he wrote to his mother on May 26: "O the sad, sad things I see—the noble young men with legs and arms taken off—the deaths—the sick weakness, sicker than death, that some endure, after amputations . . . just flickering alive, and O so deathly weak and sick."[69]

Still, despite his physical and emotional setbacks, Whitman could not give up his hospital visits. The young men he saw there each day represented to him a pure distillation of the American spirit. He tried to explain it in a letter to his old New York friends Nat Bloom and Fred Gray. "These thousands, and tens and twenties of thousands of American young men, badly wounded, all sorts of wounds, operated on, pallid with diarrhea, languishing, dying with fever, pneumonia, &c. open a new world somehow to me," he wrote, "giving closer insights, new things, exploring deeper mines than any yet, showing our humanity, (I sometimes put myself in fancy in the cot, with typhoid, or under the knife,) tried by terrible, fearfulest tests, probed deepest, the living soul's, the body's tragedies, bursting the petty bonds of art. To these, what are your dramas and poems, even the oldest and the tearfulest? . . . For here I see, not at intervals, but quite always, how certain, man, our American man — how he holds himself cool and unquestioned master above all pains and bloody mutilations. It is immense, the best thing of all, nourishes me of all men."[70]

His own ongoing role in the war received its fullest treatment in a new poem, "The Wound-Dresser," which he completed about this time. Whitman did not ordinarily dress patients' wounds — he was not, after all, a nurse but a visitor — but in the poem he imagines himself in the caregiver's role in order to make, perhaps, a more visceral connection to the wounded men:

Bearing the bandages, water and sponge,
Straight and swift to my wounded I go,
Where they lie on the ground after the battle brought in,
Where the priceless blood reddens the grass the ground,
Or to the rows of the hospital tent, or under the roof'd
    hospital,
To the long rows of cots up and down each side I return,
To each and all one after another I draw near, not one do
    I miss,
An attendant follows holding a tray, he carries a refuse pail,
Soon to be fill'd with clotted rags and blood, emptied, and
    fill'd again.

I onward go, I stop,
With hinged knees and steady hand to dress wounds,
I am firm with each, the pangs are sharp yet unavoidable,
One turns to me his appealing eyes — poor boy! I never
    knew you,

Yet I think I could not refuse this moment to die for you,
    if that would save you.

On, on I go, (open doors of time! open hospital doors!)
The crush'd head I dress, (poor crazed hand tear not the
    bandage away,)
The neck of the cavalry-man with the bullet through and
    through I examine,
Hard the breathing rattles, quite glazed already the eye, yet
    life struggles hard,
(Come sweet death! be persuaded O beautiful death! In
    mercy come quickly.)

From the stump of the arm, the amputated hand,
I undo the clotted lint, remove the slough, wash off the
    matter and blood,
Back on his pillow the soldier bends with curv'd neck and
    side-falling head,
His eyes are closed, his face is pale, he dares not look on
    the bloody stump,
And has not yet look'd on it.

I dress a wound in the side, deep, deep,
But a day or two more, for see the frame all wasted and
    sinking,
And the yellow-blue countenance see.

I dress the perforated shoulder, the foot with the bullet-
    wound,

Cleanse the one with a gnawing and putrid gangrene, so
  sickening, so offensive,
While the attendant stands behind aside me holding the
  tray and pail.

I am faithful, I do not give out,
The fractur'd thigh, the knee, the wound in the abdomen,
These and more I dress with impassive hand, (yet deep in
  my breast a fire, a burning flame.)[71]

In the weeks between the dispiriting Union defeat at Chancellorsville and the landmark triumph at Gettysburg, Whitman, like the nation as a whole, would regain his equilibrium. Never again, in the remaining twenty-three months of the war, would he question so deeply either himself or his cause. He was faithful, he would not give out. The fire that he nursed within his heart for the gallant young men in the great army of the sick would prove to be, in the face of harsher trials to come, a steadfast and abiding flame.

CHAPTER FOUR

The Real Precious
& Royal Ones of This Land

Toward the end of June 1863, William and Ellen O'Connor moved out of the house at 394 L Street, leaving Whitman to fend for himself. Their erstwhile Irish landlord, motivated perhaps by the combative late-night talkfests in the O'Connors' third-floor apartment, had decided to sell the house. It would take him three months to do so, and in the meantime Whitman retained his little room on the second floor, but his daily association with the O'Connors was over.

The practical effect of the change was to induce him to spend even more time than usual at the hospitals. The spring and summer campaigns had brought a fresh influx of patients to Washington, and Walt was irresistibly swept along by the deluge. Still nursing his infected hand, he stepped up his efforts to aid the wounded. On a single day, June 18, at Armory Square, he recorded a dizzying array of cases. He sat with one dying cavalryman, gave "good, strong green tea" to a middle-aged patient recovering from pneumonia, pressed gifts of tobacco and money on a reticent Pennsylvania soldier, and found some tobacco (perhaps to mask the smell) for a New Hampshireman suffering from gangrene of the feet. After consulting with a doctor, he scrounged a small bottle of horseradish for another patient who was craving something spicy to eat. And to critically ill Marcus Small of the 7th Maine, who had grown discouraged by his long bout with dysentery and typhoid fever, Whitman spoke "in a cheering, but slow, low and measured manner." Pennsylvania cavalryman Thomas Lindly, suffering from an agonizingly painful bullet wound to the foot, received a "large handsome apple" to roast for his breakfast; Whitman also wrote two letters for him. In the bed directly opposite Lindly was Amer Moore of the 2nd U.S. Artillery, who was dying slowly from a gunshot wound to the head that had paralyzed him from the hips down. His mother, an elderly Quaker, sat by his bed, and Whitman made a point of speaking to them both when he passed.[1]

The weather in Washington was hot and dry; the unpaved streets raised heavy clouds of dust from marching soldiers and passing wagons. Whitman complained to Nelly O'Connor that every time he took a bath and changed into clean clothes "the dust hunted him out, and pursued him." He carried an umbrella and a fan with him—he was "quite a Japanee," he told his mother. It was not an idle affectation; one day Whitman saw two people keel over from sunstroke, along with several street-car horses.[2]

The hot weather brought with it a new outbreak of typhoid fever, and Whitman spent the better part of two weeks nursing one such victim of the disease, Private Livingston Brooks of the 17th Pennsylvania Cavalry. The Missouri-born Brooks, like John Holmes five months earlier, first attracted the poet's attention through the sheer abjectness of his suffering. "I found him in what appeared to be a dying condition, from negligence, & a horrible journey of about forty miles, bad roads & fast driving," Whitman wrote to his mother. "[T]hen after he got here, as he is a simple country boy, very shy & silent, & made no complaint, they neglected him—I found him something like I found John Holmes last winter—I called the doctor's attention to him, shook up the nurses, had him bathed in spirits, gave him lumps of ice, & ice to his head, he had a painful bursting pain in his head, & his body was like fire—he was very quiet, a very sensible boy, old fashioned—he did not want to die, & I had to lie to him without stint, for he thought I knew everything, & I always put in of course that what I told was exactly the truth & that if he got really dangerous I would tell him & not conceal it." When doctors attempted to move Brooks to a special fever ward, "the poor boy got it immediately in his head that he was marked with death, & was to be removed on that account."[3]

Whitman persuaded the physicians to let Brooks stay in the main ward a little longer and dropped by his bed for a week to feed him quartered orange slices until the fever broke and he began to recover. "I will say, whether any one calls it pride or not, that if he does get up & around again, it's me that saved his life," Whitman boasted with pardonable satisfaction. Eventually, Brooks recovered and returned to his regiment in Virginia, afterward sending Whitman several fond letters addressed to his "dear uncle."[4]

Another typhoid case did not turn out so happily. Erastus Haskell, a young musician with the 141st New York, had been sick for several weeks before coming to Armory Square. Whitman sketched the boy's suffering — he was only nineteen — in a letter he wrote to Mrs. Whitman while sitting beside Haskell's bed. "He is a shy, and seems to me a very sensible boy — has fine manners — never complains," Whitman observed. "The first week this July was brought up here — journey very bad, no accommodations, no nourishment, nothing but hard jolting, and exposure enough to make a well man sick . . . a silent dark-skinn'd Spanish-looking youth, with large very dark blue eyes, peculiar looking." Alarmed by Haskell's limp appearance, Whitman called over one of the ward physicians, "but he laugh'd, and would not listen to me." Whitman came back with the head surgeon of Armory Square, Willard Bliss, and the first doctor quickly changed his tune — "he said the boy would probably die, but they would make a hard fight for him."[5]

Whitman sat with Haskell as much as possible during his final days. "Mother, I wish you could see the whole scene," he wrote. "This young man lies within reach of me, flat on his back, his hands clasp'd across his breast, his thick hair cut close; he is dozing, breathing hard, every breath a spasm — it looks so cruel. He is a noble youngster, — I consider him past all hope." He wrote a brief note to Haskell's parents, Mr. and Mrs. Samuel Haskell, in Breesport, New York, warning them that "Erastus seems to me very sick" and enclosing an envelope for them to send to their son, who, he admonished gently, "had some one write to you two weeks ago, but has received no answer. . . . [P]ut a stamp on it, & write soon."[6]

Whether the Haskells had time to write is doubtful; Erastus died two weeks later. The death of the quiet, modest young fifer—"I am not much of a player yet," he confessed to Whitman—affected the poet deeply and occasioned the most poignant, and in some ways the most revealing, letter that Whitman wrote during the war. Once again, it was addressed to Mr. and Mrs. Haskell. "Dear friends," Whitman began, "I thought it would be soothing to you to have a few lines about the last days of your son Erastus Haskell of Company K, 141st New York Volunteers. I write in haste, & nothing of importance— only I thought any thing about Erastus would be welcome. From the time he came to Armory Square Hospital till he died, there was hardly a day but I was with him a portion of the time—if not during the day, then at night. I had no opportunity to do much, or any thing for him, as nothing was needed, only to wait the progress of his malady. I am only a friend, visiting the wounded & sick solders." He told them about the doctor's initial downplaying of Haskell's condition and his own angry remonstrance, adding, "Maybe it would not have made any difference any how—I think Erastus was broken down, poor boy, before he came to the hospital here."[7]

The bulk of the letter was given over to a frank description of Haskell's death. It must have been painful for his parents to read; certainly, it was painful for Whitman to write. The Haskells, of course, did not know Whitman, and they must have wondered why a self-confessed stranger should have had such a strong reaction to their son's death. Clearly, it moved him beyond the bland impersonality of most bedside letters, almost into the realm of a lover's sense of loss. If Whitman sensed such feelings within him, it did not inhibit him from writing the boy's parents with a naked, unselfconscious candor. For once his mask of impassivity slipped. "Somehow I took to him," Whitman wrote, "he was a quiet young man, behaved always correct & decent, said little—I used to sit on the side of his bed—I said once, You don't talk any, Erastus, you leave me to do all the talking—he only answered quietly, I was never much of a talker. . . . [O]nce I tried to tell him some amusing narratives, but after a few moments I stopt, I saw that the effect was not good, & after that I never tried again—I used to sit by the side of his bed, pretty silent, as that seemed most agreeable to him, & I felt so too—he was generally opprest for breath, & with the heat, & I would fan him . . . sometimes when I would come in, he woke up, & I would lean down & kiss him, he would reach out his hand & pat my hair & beard a little, very friendly, as I sat on the bed & leaned over him. . . .

"I was very anxious he should be saved, & so were they all— he was well used by the attendants—poor boy, I can see him as I write—he was tanned & had a fine head of hair, & looked good in the face when he first came, & was in pretty good flesh too. . . . He never complained—but it looked pitiful to see him lying there, with such a look out of his eyes. He had large clear eyes, they seemed to talk better than words—I assure you I was attracted to him much—Many nights I sat by in the hospital till far in the night—The lights would be put out—yet I would sit there silently, hours, late, perhaps fanning him—he always liked to have me sit there, but never cared to talk—I shall never forget those nights, it was a curious & solemn scene, the sick & wounded lying around in their cots, just visible in the darkness, & this dear young man close at hand lying on what proved to be his death bed — I do not know his past life, but what I do know, & what I saw of him, he was a noble boy — I felt he was one I should get very much attached to. I think you have reason to be proud of such a son, & all his relatives have cause to treasure his memory.

"I write you this letter, because I would do something at least in his memory — his fate was a hard one, to die so — He is one of the thousands of our unknown American men in the ranks about whom there is no record or fame, no fuss made about their dying so unknown, but I find in them the real precious & royal ones of this land, giving themselves up, aye even their young & precious lives, in their country's cause — Poor dear son, though you were not my son, I felt to love you as a son, what short time I saw you sick & dying here — it is as well as it is, perhaps better — for who knows whether he is not better off, that patient & sweet young soul, to go, than we are to stay? So farewell, dear boy — it was my opportunity to be with you in your last rapid days of death — no chance as I have said to do any thing particular, for nothing could be done — only you did not lay here & die among strangers without having one at hand who loved you dearly, & to whom you gave your dying kiss."[8]

Here in one extraordinary letter is the unmediated essence of Whitman's Civil War experience, a snapshot almost of his inner and outer selves. Sitting in the dark in the hospital ward, holding the hand of a dying young man, he is at once doctor and nurse, mother and father, friend and lover, angel and Death. The "stranger that hover'd near," leaning over the ebbing youth, is in the end no stranger at all, but the summoner from the other realm, calling to him in "whispers of heavenly death":

> From all the rest I single out you, having a message for
>   you,
> You are to die—let others tell you what they please, I can-
>   not prevaricate,
> I am exact and merciless, but I love you—there is no
>   escape for you.
>
> Softly I lay my right hand upon you, you just feel it,
> I do not argue, I bend my head close and half envelop it,
> I sit quietly by, I remain faithful,
> I am more than nurse, more than parent or neighbor,
> I absolve you from all except your spiritual body, that is
>   eternal, you yourself will surely escape,
> The corpse you will leave will be but excrementitious.
>
> The sun bursts through in unlooked-for directions,
> Strong thoughts fill you and confidence, you smile,
> You forget you are sick, as I forget you are sick,
> You do not see the medicines, you do not mind the weep-
>   ing friends, I am with you,
> I exclude others from you, there is nothing to be
>   commiserated,
> I do not commiserate, I congratulate you.[9]

One can only guess what those congratulations, multiplied hundreds or thousands of times, cost Whitman mentally and emotionally. He was, after all, a man who hated goodbyes; in one of his last poems, "After the Supper and Talk," he pictures himself "shunning, postponing severance — seeking to ward off the last word ever so little . . . loth, O so loth to depart." And yet his work in the hospitals inevitably required him to say goodbye. Sooner or later the soldiers he comforted either got well and went back to their regiments, or partially recovered and went back to their homes, or else they died. Whatever the case, Whitman was forever bidding farewell to someone, even as a relentless stream of new patients took over the beds of the lately departed. It is not surprising, then, to find him growing especially attached to certain individual soldiers, young men who somehow had differentiated themselves from the crowd. *Eros* and *Thanatos*, as the Greeks remind us, are often conjoined; and the hothouse atmosphere of the army hospitals, with their endless supply of fresh-faced, suffering boys, weakened Whitman's usual reserve.[10]

Two soldiers, in particular, laid claim to his heart: Lewis Brown and Thomas Sawyer. "Lewy" Brown of Elkton, Maryland, had enlisted in Purnell's Legion in March 1862, when he was eighteen. He was wounded on August 19, 1862, at Rappahannock Station, where a Confederate shell shattered his left leg. Suffering from a compound fracture, he lay semiconscious for four days among other wounded prisoners before being exchanged and transferred to Armory Square Hospital. Sawyer, a twenty-one-year-old soapmaker from Cambridgeport, Massachusetts, enlisted in the 11th Massachusetts Infantry in June 1861 and was wounded ten days after Brown at the Second Battle of Bull Run.[11]

Brown and Sawyer apparently became friends in the hospital, but it is not clear when Whitman first made their acquaintance. A diary note for April 20, 1863, says simply that he had "spent the evening in Armory Sq. with Lew Brown." By then, Sawyer had returned to his regiment, and Whitman sent him a letter the next day. "Tom, I thought I would write you a few words, and take chances of its getting to you," he began. He told him of sitting for a long time with Brown, who was "planning to go home to Maryland, go to school, and learn to write better, and learn a little bookkeeping . . . so that he can be fit for some light employment. Lewis is so good, so affectionate—when I came away, he reached up his face, I put my arm around him, and we gave each other a long kiss, half a minute long."[12]

At the far end of another century, it is possible to read too much into that kiss. Same-sex affection had not yet become eroticized, and overt demonstrations of affection between men—kissing, hugging, stroking, and petting—were commonplace. Behavior that would instantly attract attention today went virtually unnoticed in the mid-nineteenth century. Nevertheless, the fervency of Whitman's affection, particularly for Sawyer, seems to have exceeded mere wartime camaraderie. And Sawyer, for his part, may have sensed as much. Whitman had set aside for his young friend "a good strong blue shirt, a pair of drawers & socks," and he invited Sawyer to come by his room and pick them up before returning to the front. Sawyer failed to show. "I am sorry you did not come up to my room to get the shirt & other things you promised to accept from me and take when you went away," Whitman complained. "I got them all ready . . . and it would have been a satisfaction to me if you had accepted them. I should have often thought now Tom may be wearing around his body something from me, that it might contribute to your comfort, down there in camp on picket, or sleeping in your tent."[13]

Sawyer responded—to Brown, significantly, not to Whitman—saying that he had simply forgotten his "prommice" to the older man. "I came away so soon that it sliped my mind and I am very sorry for it, tell him that I shall write to him my self in a few days, give him my love and best wishes forever." For all his good intentions, it would be nearly a year before Sawyer wrote to Whitman in his own hand, although he did dictate a painfully formal reply that unintentionally must have hurt its recipient with the sheer impersonality of its prose: "I fully reciprocate your friendship as expressed in your letter and it will afford me great pleasure to meet you after the war will have terminated or sooner if circumstances will permit."[14]

Whitman sent a flurry of unanswered letters to Sawyer, alternately hectoring and imploring him. "You must not forget me, for I never shall you," he wrote in one characteristic note. "My love you have in life or death forever. I don't know how you feel about it, but it is the wish of my heart to have your friendship, and also that if you should come safe out of this war, we should come together again in someplace where we could make our living, and be true comrades and never be separated while life lasts—and take Lew Brown too, and never separate from him. Or if things are not so to be—if you get these lines, my dear, darling comrade, and any thing should go wrong, so that we do not meet again, here on earth, it seems to me, (the way I feel now,) that my soul could never be entirely happy, even in the world to come without you, dear comrade."[15]

As Sawyer's silence continued, the letters became even more insistent. "I have not heard from you for some time, Lewy Brown has received two letters from, you, & Walter in Ward E has received one," Whitman wrote. Another letter fretted: "I do not know what is the reason I have been favored with nary a word from you, to let me know whether you are alive & well." By now, Whitman seemed to sense a deeper reason for Sawyer's reticence. "My dearest comrade," he told him, "I cannot though I attempt it, put in a letter the feelings of my heart—I suppose my letters sound strange & unusual to you as it is, but as I am only expressing the truth in them, I do not trouble myself on that account. As I intimated before, I do not expect you to return for me the same degree of love I have for you." Despite that disavowal, Whitman continued to pursue the absent soldier. "You did not write any answer to my last two letters, now quite a while ago, still I will write again," he told him. "Dear brother, how I should like to see you. . . . I cant understand why you have ceased to correspond with me. Any how I hope we shall meet again, & have some good times."[16]

A little desperately, perhaps, Whitman sought to use Lewy Brown as an intermediary, advising him: "Lew, when you write to Tom Sawyer you know what to say from me—he is the one I love in my heart, & always shall till death & afterwards too." Nothing availed, and Whitman ultimately was driven to demand of Sawyer: "I do not know why you do not write to me. Do you wish to shake me off? That I cannot believe." Or perhaps, given his much greater experience in such matters, Whitman could believe it only too well. He was accustomed to losing his boys — to death, to marriage, or to distance — and now he could sense that he was losing another. He still had Lewy Brown, as well as an inexhaustible supply of new soldiers to pet, but it would not be until nearly the end of the war that he would rekindle his personal, as opposed to his altruistic, interest in another young man, this time a former Confederate soldier turned streetcar conductor named Peter Doyle.[17]

Whitman, at any rate, needed to conserve his emotional energy for the trying months to come. Washington, with its bulging hospitals, bristling forts, and crowded streets, had become even more a "harrowing city." The Confederate Army, although decisively bested at Gettysburg, still rested on its arms uncomfortably near. All male residents of the capital between the ages of eighteen and forty-five were mustered into the militia and told to be ready at a moment's notice to resist an invasion that many thought was imminent. Whitman, being a legal resident of Brooklyn, was exempt from such duty, but, as he told his mother, "I am getting so callous that it hardly arouses me at all. I fancy I should take it very quietly if I found myself in the midst of a desperate conflict here in Washington." He watched the long wagon loads of wounded pass up Fourteenth Street at sundown and thought, "This is the way the men come in now, seldom in small numbers, but always in these long, sad processions." And when a large cavalry force rode by, spearheaded by a band of buglers and drummers, he had conflicting emotions. "A man feels so proud on a good horse," he mused, but immediately added: "Alas! how many of these healthy, handsome, rollicking young men will lie cold in death before the apples ripen in the orchard."[18]

Preoccupied as he was by such gloomy thoughts, Whitman could still spare a moment of empathy for the man who was sending the young soldiers off to their deaths. Just before the Battle of Gettysburg, the poet happened to see Abraham Lincoln ride past in his shabby barouche, bound for the Soldiers' Home on the outskirts of town. "He looks more careworn even than usual," Whitman observed, "his face with deep cut lines, seams, and his complexion gray through very dark skin — a curious looking man, very sad. I said to a lady who was looking with me, 'Who can see that man without losing all wish to be sharp upon him personally?' "[19]

As it happened, there were many who entertained such wishes, and they were not all fire-breathing Southerners. In New York City, Lincoln's institution of the new draft law, which allowed anyone able to scrape together three hundred dollars to buy his way out of the service, touched off some of the worst rioting in American history. For five days and nights, from July 11 to July 16, 1863, hundreds of rioters drawn from the ranks of the urban poor terrorized the city, setting fire to draft headquarters, battering policemen who sought to quell them, and lynching any blacks who fell into their hands. Many of the rioters were recent Irish immigrants who felt, with some justice, that the burden of the draft had fallen unfairly upon them. The focus of their resentment centered inevitably on the city's large black population, whom the immigrants blamed for causing the war in the first place by carelessly allowing themselves to be brought to America in chains.

Incited and condoned by Democratic officials who winked at their selective destruction of Republican-owned homes and businesses, the rioters disported themselves with little outside interference until the federal government rushed in troops from the Gettysburg front. These battle-hardened veterans mowed down their fellow Northerners with as little compunction as they had shown the Rebel legions of Longstreet and Lee. In the end, peace returned to the troubled city at the cost of 105 lives and five million dollars' worth of property damage, including the Colored Orphan Asylum, which was burned to the ground. Eventually, the city council appropriated funds to buy its residents out of the draft, some of them no doubt the same men who had taken to the streets in the first place.[20]

As a native New Yorker, Whitman was caught in the middle. In *Leaves of Grass* he had advised Americans as a general rule to "resist much, obey little," and now he told his mother, "I do not feel it in my heart to abuse the poor people, or call for a rope or bullets for them, but that is all the talk here, even in the hospitals." When the wounded soldiers, naturally enough, denounced the rioters as cowardly shirkers and blazed out as "savage and hot as fire against New York," Whitman diplomatically held his tongue, "partly amused, partly scornful" at the talk. But as he learned more about the horrific cruelty of the rioters, he applauded the government's decision to send in troops. "I thought when I first heard of the riot in N.Y. I had some feeling for them," he wrote, "but soon as I found what it really was, I felt it was the devil's own work all through. I guess the strong arm will be exhibited this time up to the shoulder."[21]

That was fine with Jeff Whitman, who told Walt that he only regretted "that they did not kill enough of 'em. . . . I am perfectly rabid on an irishman. I hate them worse than I thought I could hate anything." George Whitman, in camp with the Union Army in Kentucky, was equally blunt in his denunciations. "Its almost enough to make a fellow ashamed of being a Yorker," he wrote. "I could hardly believe, that a thing of that kind would be alowed to get such headway in the City of New York. . . . I would have went into that fight with just as good a heart, as if they had belonged to the rebel army." Fellow New Yorker Herman Melville was untypically succinct. "The town," he said, "is taken by its rats."[22]

Ironically, the same day the racially motivated rioting began in New York, Whitman was on an island in the middle of the Potomac River watching a regiment of African American soldiers receive their pay. His superior, Major Lyman Hapgood, had invited him along to witness the event, together with William and Nelly O'Connor and their daughter, Jeannie. Whitman, mildly diverted, watched for a time as Hapgood and his assistant, Charles Eldridge, handed out pay packets from a table in front of an old stucco house that had been the birthplace of U.S. senator James Mason, author of the much hated Fugitive Slave Act and now a Confederate diplomat in Europe. The men of the 1st Regiment, U.S. Colored Troops, were "manly enough, bright enough, look as if they had the soldier-stuff in them," Whitman allowed, adding that despite their "thoroughly African physiognomies . . . I have to say that I do not see one utterly revolting face." Some of the men, having been soldiers for only a few weeks, received only a few cents in pay, which they angrily refused. Others stepped aside and counted their money "with a pleas'd, half-puzzled look."[23]

Whitman quickly lost interest in the financial transactions and wandered off to a solitary part of the island to listen to bird songs at the river's edge. If the paymaster's actions had been designed to improve the poet's overall opinion of blacks, they did not succeed. The next spring, when five regiments of black troops paraded past Abraham Lincoln on their way to the front, Whitman was still complaining that "it looked funny to see the President standing with his hat off to them just the same as the rest."[24]

Back in the city, the summer sweltered on. Whitman returned to the hospitals, fanning the heat-wracked soldiers hour after hour and worrying that the hot, moist weather was having a harmful effect on their wounds. Lewy Brown had gone home to Elkton on medical furlough, and he and Walt exchanged a series of fond letters. The untutored Brown, in his dispatches to "Dear Freind Walter," worried that his letters were "verry porely wrote," but Whitman assured him that such was not the case. "My darling boy," he said, "when you write me, you must write without ceremony, I like to hear every little thing about yourself & your affairs—you need never care how you write to me, Lewy, if you will only—I never think about literary perfection in letters either, it is the *man* & the *feeling*." As for his own feelings, Whitman suddenly burst forth: "O Lewy how glad I should be to see you, to have you with me—I have thought if it could be so that you & one other person & myself could be where we could work & live together, & have each other's society, we three, I should like it so much—but it is probably a dream." He did not have to tell Brown who the third person in the fantasy was.[25]

With his favorite soldiers gone and the O'Connors moved to another apartment, Whitman fell prey to an unfamiliar malady: homesickness. His letters to his mother reflected a new weariness with the war and his own small but increasingly stressful role in it. "Mother, I want to see you and all very much," he wrote on August 18. "[D]on't you miss Walt loafing around, and carting himself off to New York toward the latter part of every afternoon? . . . How I should like to take a walk on Old Fort Greene — tell Mannahatta her Uncle Walt will be home yet, from the sick soldiers, and have a good walk all around, if she behaves to her grandmother and don't cut up." Two weeks later he wrote again. "O how I want to see Jeff and you, mother," he exclaimed. "I sometimes feel as if I should just get in the cars and come home." He mentioned that he had been in touch with Samuel Haskell, Erastus's father, and that he had asked for Walt's address in Brooklyn. "Mother," he added, "when I come home I will show some of the letters I get from mothers, sisters, fathers, etc. — they will make you cry." He had just visited two Brooklyn soldiers, George Monk and Stephen Redgate, both of whom were only eighteen. "O mother," he said, "it seems to me as I go through these rows of cots as if it was too bad to accept these *children*, to subject them to such premature experiences."[26]

Part of Whitman's homesickness was the result of worry over the declining health of his brother Andrew. Jeff had told him that Andrew's throat was giving him a great deal of trouble, and Walt replied, "I hope it will go over, and that a little time will make him recover—I think about it every day." Walt suggested that Mrs. Whitman take some money from George's next paycheck (which George sent home to her to save) and give it to Andrew to buy some simple comforts. But even this act of thoughtfulness created friction. The easily alarmed Jeff wrote to say that Mrs. Whitman was economizing so severely that her health, and that of her other dependent sons, Jesse and Edward, was worsening. "Jeff thinks you show your age more, and failing like," Walt wrote. "O my dear mother, you must not think of failing yet. I hope we shall have some comfortable years yet. Mother, don't allow things, troubles, to take hold of you; write a few lines whenever you can; tell me exactly how things are. Mother, I am first rate and well—only a little of that deafness again."[27]

Physically, Whitman may have been fine, but emotionally he was becoming more and more fragile. Death and suffering were all around him. On September 16 he witnessed the death of Lorenzo Strong of the 9th U.S. Cavalry, who had been brought into Armory Square Hospital two days earlier after being wounded by a shell and having his right leg amputated on the field. Strong, true to his name, was a "perfect specimen of physique, one of the most magnificent I ever saw." He had seemed to be holding his own until he suddenly took a turn for the worse and "a strangely rapid and fatal termination ensued."[28]

Whitman, although busy himself with other patients, stayed to watch the young man die. "It was a death-picture characteristic of these soldier's hospitals," he wrote, "the convulsive spasms and working of muscles, mouth, and throat. There are two good women nurses, one on each side. The doctor comes in and gives him a little chloroform. One of the nurses constantly fans him, for it is fearfully hot. He askes to be rais'd up, and they put him a half-sitting posture. He call'd for 'Mark' repeatedly, half-deliriously, all day. Life ebbs, runs now with the speed of a mill race; his splendid neck, as it lays all open, works still, slightly; his eyes turn back . . . a crowd, including two or three doctors, several students, and many soldiers, has silently gather'd. It is very still and warm, as the struggle goes on, and dwindles, a little more, and a little more—and then welcome oblivion, painlessness, death. A pause, the crowd drops away, a white bandage is bound around and under the jaw, the propping pillows are removed, the limpsy head falls down, the arms are softly placed by the side . . . and the broad white sheet is thrown over everything."[29]

Such scenes, although commonplace, had the effect of wearing down the watcher. That same month Whitman told his mother: "One's heart grows sick of war, after all, when you see what it really is; every once in a while I feel so horrified and disgusted—it seems to me like a great slaughter-house and the men mutually butchering each other." And in early October he wrote again, describing the physical attractions of Washington and reflecting: "It is lucky I like Washington in many respects, and that things are upon the whole pleasant personally, for every day of my life I see enough to make one's heart ache with sympathy and anguish here in the hospitals, and I do not know as I could stand it if it was not counterbalanced outside. It is curious, when I am present at the most appalling things—deaths, operations, sickening wounds (perhaps full of maggots)—I do not fail, although my sympathies are very much excited, but keep singularly cool; but often hours afterward, perhaps when I am home or out walking alone, I feel sick and actually tremble when I recall the thing and have it in my mind again before me." Post-traumatic stress disorder had not yet been identified, but Whitman clearly was a candidate for it. Sometimes, he told his mother, he had to bustle about mindlessly to keep from crying.[30]

One way for a writer to deal with stress is by writing, and Whitman kept up a busy pace. Between August and October he wrote three articles for the *New York Times*: "Washington in the Hot Season," "Our National City," and "Letter from Washington." The newly established *Brooklyn Union* also published his short letter describing the capital's anxiety about the inconclusive late-summer campaigning. In addition, Whitman was working sporadically on a series of poems bearing the doubly evocative title, *Drum-Taps*. These poems ranged from the early recruiting poem "Beat! Beat! Drums!" to the battlefield poems "Cavalry Crossing a Ford," "By the Bivouac's Fitful Flame," and "A Sight in Camp in the Daybreak Gray and Dim," and the hospital poem "The Wound-Dresser." It is not known definitively when Whitman wrote each poem; he may not have remembered himself. Years later he told Horace Traubel that *Drum-Taps* had been "put together by fits and starts, on the field, in the hospitals, as I worked with the soldier boys."[31]

By now Whitman felt close enough to the boys to speak in their behalf. On September 7 he wrote a brief note to a fellow hospital worker, a Miss Gregg, who was leaving Washington the next day for a much needed rest. The note, which must have meant a lot to the young woman, was a prime example of Whitman's inherent kindness and tact. "Dear friend," he began. "You spoke the other day, partly in fun, about the men being so undemonstrative. I thought I would write you a line as I hear you leave the hospital tomorrow for a few weeks. Your labor of love and disinterestedness here in Hospital is appreciated. I have heard the ward A patients speak of you with gratitude, sometimes with enthusiasm. They have their own invariable ways (not outside eclat, but in many American hearts however rude however undemonstrative to you). I thought it would be sweet to your tender and womanly heart to know that I have so often heard from the soldiers about you as I sat by their sick cots. I too have learnt to love you, seeing your tender heart, and your goodness to these wounded and dying young men— for they have grown to seem to me as my sons or dear young brothers. As I am poor I cannot make you a present, but I write you this note dear girl, knowing you will receive it in the same candor and good faith it is written."[32]

Besides his poems and journalism, Whitman had resumed contemplating a book based on his experiences in the hospitals. He had first mentioned the idea in a letter to Ralph Waldo Emerson the previous January, not long after his arrival in Washington. "I desire and intend to write a little book out of this phase of America, her masculine young manhood, its conduct under most trying of and highest of all exigency, which she, as by lifting a corner in a curtain, has vouchsafed me to see," he told Emerson. "A new world here I find as I would show—a world full of its separate action, play, suggestiveness— surely a medium world, advanced between our well-known

practised one of body and of mind, and one there may be somewhere on beyond, we dream of, of the soul."[33]

In October he returned to the idea of the book, motivated
in part by the publication of Louisa May Alcott's *Hospital
Sketches* earlier that summer. Alcott's publisher was James Redpath, abolitionist author of a well-received biography of John
Brown for Whitman's own former publishers, Thayer and Eldridge. Whitman had been in touch with Redpath recently during the poet's endless quest for money to fund his hospital
work. Now he suggested bringing out "a book of the time,
worthy the time—something considerably beyond mere hospital sketches—a book for sale perhaps in a larger American market—the premises or skeleton memoranda of incidents, persons,
places, sights, the past year (mostly jotted down either on the
spot or in the spirit of seeing or hearing what is narrated) . . .
full of interest I think—in some respects somewhat a combination in handling of the Old French Memoires, & my own
personality (things seen through my eyes, & what my vision
brings)."[34]

One particular aspect of the book, Whitman continued,
would be "to push forward the very big & needed truth, that
our national military system needs shifting, revolutionizing &
made to tally with democracy, the people—The officers should
almost invariably rise from the ranks—there is an absolute want
of democratic spirit in the present system & officers—it is the
feudal spirit exclusively—nearly the entire capacity, keenness &
courage of our army are in the ranks." (How this tallied with
the fact that George Whitman, with no more social or political
connections than the lowliest serf, had risen in two years' time

from private to captain, he neglected to explain.) The book would "have much to say of the hospitals. . . . I have many hospital incidents, will take with the general reader—I ventilate my general democracy with details very largely & with reference to the future—bringing in persons, the President, Seward, Congress, the Capitol, Washington City, many of the actors of the drama—have something to say of the great trunk America, the West &c&c—do not hesitate to diffuse *myself*—the book is very rapid—is a book that can be read by the five or ten minutes. . . . I should think two or three thousand sales ought to be certainly depended on here in hospitals in Washington."[35]

Despite his florid sales pitch, Whitman set aside *Memoranda of a Year*—the book's proposed title—and returned his attention to the wounded and dying. It would be another dozen years and many changes later before he would publish the book privately, under its revised title, *Memoranda During the War*. By then the target audience, like the hospitals themselves, would belong to the past, dispersed across the very Union that they had helped to save. In the meantime, life went on inside—and unlikely as it sometimes seemed—even outside the hospitals. One night Whitman walked down Pennsylvania Avenue to Seventh Street, then circled back around the U.S. Patent Office. "Somehow," he wrote, "it look'd rebukefully strong, majestic, there in the delicate moonlight. The sky, the planets, the constellations all so bright, so calm, so expressively silent, so soothing after those hospital scenes. I wander'd to and fro till the moist moon set, long after midnight." Two days later, standing on the corner of Louisiana Avenue and Sixth Street, he watched the sunset, "the most languidly gorgeous I have ever seen, the crimson golden light flooding the west, flooding all with the same peculiar hue, slightly veiled with haze."[36]

The ugliness of war had a way of intruding on any scene, however poetic, and Whitman's attention was caught by a parade of three hundred Union deserters being marched along Pennsylvania Avenue under heavy guard. They were a motley collection, he noted, wearing "all sorts of rig, all sorts of hats and caps, many fine-looking young fellows, some of them shame-faced, some sickly, most of them dirty, shirts very dirty, and long worn." Some spectators laughed at the men as they were passing, but Whitman for his part "felt like anything else but laughing."[37]

On October 16, 1863, Whitman moved into new living quarters at 456 6th Street, between E and D streets. The three-story house was owned by Mrs. E. S. Baker, an elderly widow who lived there with her five-year-old granddaughter. The little girl's calls, "Grandma, Grandma," reminded Whitman of his niece Mannahatta. He gave Mrs. Baker five dollars — half a month's rent — and settled in, telling his mother contentedly that the room would "prove a very good winter room, as it is right under the roof and looks south; has low windows, is plenty big enough, I have gas." He was particularly pleased with the fact that the room was off by itself and overlooked "a great old yard with grass and some trees back, and the sun shines in all day, etc., and it smells sweet, and good air — good big bed; I sleep first rate." He told his friend Nat Bloom that he was living "a sort of German or Parisian life," an observation that was seconded by Boston novelist John Townsend Trowbridge, who stopped by to visit one morning while he was in town to prepare a campaign biography for would-be presidential candidate Salmon P. Chase.[38]

Trowbridge had spent the night in Chase's sumptuous mansion, which was located across Pennsylvania Avenue from Whitman's humble new quarters. For all the good Whitman's proximity to the elegant, ambitious secretary of the treasury did him, he might just as well have lived on the moon. A year earlier Whitman had heard that Chase, finding a copy of *Leaves of Grass* on a friend's table, had complained, "How is it possible you can have this nasty book here?". Remembering Chase's attitude, the poet had hesitated to use his letter of introduction from Emerson. Trowbridge offered to act as go-between. He took the letter across the street to Chase and gave it to him the next morning after breakfast. Chase, whose highly developed sense of morality did not prevent him from scheming tirelessly to undercut Abraham Lincoln and take the White House from him in 1864, still could not countenance Whitman's "very bad book." He considered the poet, he told Trowbridge, "a decidedly disreputable person." Nevertheless, as an amateur autograph collector, Chase was glad to have a letter with Emerson's signature on it. He rejected the application but pocketed the letter.[39]

Whitman did not blame Trowbridge for Chase's lack of support. "It's about what I expected," he said — Chase was "just the meanest & biggest kind of shyster." Whitman did manage to put one highly placed connection to good use. Through the intercession of William O'Connor, he was able to obtain from Lincoln's private secretary, John Hay, a free railroad pass to New York, on the somewhat spurious grounds that Whitman was going home to Brooklyn to campaign for the Republican party in the off-year election. Calling at the White House for his ticket, Whitman caught sight of Abraham Lincoln standing nearby, "talking to a gentleman, apparently a dear friend. . . . His face & manner have an expression & are inexpressibly sweet—one hand on his friend's shoulder, the other holds his hand. I love the President personally." As always, Whitman declined the opportunity to speak to Lincoln, preferring to admire him from a polite distance. For all his later identification with the martyred president, he and Lincoln never spoke.[40]

Shortly before leaving for New York, Whitman met a man who would prove to be one of his most devoted followers. At Elijah Allen's army-navy store he was introduced to a twenty-six-year-old former schoolteacher from upstate New York, John Burroughs. The meeting was no accident: Burroughs had been following Whitman's career for years and had even gone to New York City in April 1862 to seek out the poet at Pfaff's beer cellar. He had missed Whitman that day, but he did meet Henry Clapp, Ada Clare, and Adah Isaacs Menken, the last of whom had tried unsuccessfully to take Burroughs home to bed. Now Burroughs had been in Washington for several days, seeking employment with the government and sleeping on a cot in the back of Allen's store. The two were friends of long standing, having met when Burroughs was teaching school in Allen's hometown of Orange, New Jersey.[41]

Whitman took one look at the slender, wide-eyed young man and said approvingly, "His face is like a field of wheat." Burroughs, for his part, was even more approving. "If that is not the face of a poet," he said, "then it is the face of a god." In

Whitman he beheld "a well-dressed, large, benevolent-looking man, cleanly and neat, with a grizzly, shaggy appearance about the face and open throat. Without rising he reached out to me a large, warm, soft hand, and regarded me with a look of infinite good nature and contentment. I was struck with the strange new beauty of him as he sat there in the gas light—the brightness of his eyes, the glow of his countenance, and the curious blending of youth and age in his expression." Not just Whitman's appearance impressed the younger man: "I was struck likewise with his rich mellow voice—a voice that was at once an index to the man, implying not only deep human sympathies and affinities, but the finest blood and breeding, a gentle, strong, cultivated soul."[42]

One Sunday afternoon a few days later, Burroughs, a budding naturalist, ran into Whitman in the woods outside the city. The poet was on his way to one of the outlying hospitals, his haversack bulging with gifts for the men. Whitman invited Burroughs to come along. At the hospital Burroughs marveled at Whitman's magnetic effect on the soldiers: "The lusterless eye brightened up at his approach; his commonplace words invigorated; a bracing air seemed to fill the ward, and neutralize the bad smells." Later, walking with Whitman near the Capitol, Burroughs witnessed another instance of the older man's habitual charity. "We met a soldier—dirty, travel-stained, and ragged, with a friendless care-worn expression, whom Walt kindly accosted," Burroughs remembered. "I shall never forget how the soldier alter[ed] the tone in which he was about answering him, as he looked Walt in the face. . . . The sympathy and deep, yearning love that spoke in this man's voice and beamed in his face completely disarmed him; and in a blushing, bashful way he answered Walt's questions."[43]

The young soldier was probably a deserter or a former Rebel, Whitman told Burroughs afterwards; as usual, the poet made no distinction. Instead, "Walt, in his tender, curious way, asked him if he should not help him a little; not enough to hurt him, but enough to get him a bit of food, for he looked hungry. The soldier did not know how to meet this charge, and came near breaking down outright; and as Walt placed some small notes in his hand and turned away, he found his tongue to say, in that awkward, constrained way, that he hoped he would have good health and keep well. . . . That youth will not forget as long as he lives, the great kind man who accosted him under the walls of the Capitol, and spoke the first words of human sympathy and tenderness, perhaps, he had heard since his mother bid him farewell."[44]

Burroughs, who bore a passing resemblance to William O'Connor, soon replaced O'Connor as Whitman's closest companion. The two regularly visited the hospitals, took long walks in the woods outside of town, ate picnic lunches beside a brook, and communed easily with nature. Burroughs was already an expert ornithologist; he could identify dozens of separate bird calls by ear. Whitman listened sympathetically to Burroughs's plans to "liberate the birds from the scientists" and become an "Audubon of prose." He encouraged the younger man to write a book of nature essays based on strict firsthand observation but taking off on "a kind of winged, ecstatic reasoning, quite above and beyond the real facts." Eventually, Burroughs would follow

Whitman's advice and bring out the book that started his long, successful career as a naturalist, *Wake-Robin*. With its lyrical intermingling of the pure, natural world and the author's personal reaction to it, the book owed an obvious debt to *Leaves of Grass*. Even its title was selected by Whitman.[45]

Burroughs's book was still several years in the future. For now he was content to share Whitman's company, basking in the glow of an established artist whom he clearly worshipped as a hero. Soon after meeting Whitman, he boasted to a friend: "I have been much with Walt. Have even slept with him. I love him very much. The more I see and talk with him, the greater he becomes to me. He is as vast as the earth, and as loving and noble. He is much handsomer than his picture represents him. . . . I am convinced that Walt is as great as Emerson, though after a different type. Walt has all types of men in him, there is not one left out." Later, to the same correspondent, New York poet Myron Benton, Burroughs enthused: "The more I see of Walt, the more I like him. . . . He is by far the wisest man I have ever met. There is nothing more to be said after he gives his views. It is as if Nature herself had spoken. And so kind, sympathetic, charitable, humane, tolerant a man I did not suppose was possible. He loves everything and everybody. I saw a soldier the other day stop on the street and kiss him. He kisses me as if I were a girl."[46]

Despite such kisses, Whitman's relations with Burroughs were entirely chaste. The younger man was obviously heterosexual, and his slight build and intellectual inclination were totally at odds anyway with Whitman's usual taste in roughhewn, lower-class lads. Nevertheless, there may have been an unsettling undercurrent in their relationship, at least at first. The rather sheltered Burroughs could not put his finger on the problem, but "nothwithstanding the beauty and expressiveness of his eyes, I occasionally see something in them as he bends upon me, that almost makes me draw back. I cannot explain it—whether it is more, or less, than human. It is as if the earth looked at me—dumb, yearning, relentless, immodest, inhuman. . . . It is not piercing, but absorbing and devouring—the pupil expanded, the lid slightly drooping, and the eye set and fixed." Whether or not Whitman intended anything overtly sexual with those looks, he soon settled into a more mutually congenial role as Burroughs's fatherly confidant.[47]

On November 2, 1863, Whitman took leave of Burroughs and the rest of Washington and caught a train for New York. The daylong journey took him through Baltimore, Philadelphia, and other eastern cities, and Whitman marvelled at the prosperous appearance and apparent peacefulness of the Northern homefront. "It looks anything else but war," he observed, "everybody well drest, plenty of money, markets boundless & of the best, factories all busy." The farther he got from Washington, the more the capital seemed like a fever dream, its squalid hospitals and pale, suffering soldiers receding like phantoms in the smoky evening air. He arrived in Brooklyn at eight o'clock that night, having been gone from home for ten and one-half months. He was delighted to find his mother "very well indeed for her age, which is 67." She was "cheerful and hearty" and ever ready to hear his stories about the soldiers he had met. He held Jeff's new baby daughter, California, whom he was seeing for the first time since her birth four months earlier, and pronounced her "a most splendid child." "I am not sure but the Whitman breed gives better women than men," he observed.[48]

The rest of the family was about the same. Walt sincerely regretted Andrew's condition—he was doing "very poorly indeed, & I fear will never be much better"—but he did not spend much time with his brother, possibly because of Andrew's wife, Nancy, a once and future prostitute who was then four months pregnant with the luckless couple's third child. None of the family could abide Nancy, who cursed and drank like a sailor, neglected her children, allowed her home to sink to the level of a Bowery flophouse, and complained lachrymosely that Andrew wanted to spend more time with his mother than he did with her. Even Walt, who was notably accepting where prostitutes were concerned, seems to have avoided Nancy whenever possible. His other sister-in-law, Jeff's wife, Mattie, was a different matter. Judging from her photographs, Mattie Whitman was not much to look at, but she was an affectionate, good-natured girl, and Walt gave her the highest praise possible when he mentioned her in the same breath as his mother as being one of "the two best and sweetest women I have ever seen or known or ever expect to see." He kept his promise to take her to the opera, where they saw Josephine Medori sing the title role of *Lucrezia Borgia* at the New York Academy of Music.[49]

Besides squiring his sister-in-law around town, Whitman permitted himself to be carried off by his old New York friends on a dizzying round of eating, drinking, and late-night carousing. "My New York boys are good, too good," he told Eldridge, "if

I staid here a month longer I should be killed with kindness." Beneath the patina of goodwill and hale fellowship, however, something was missing—or perhaps something had been added: the gray, speechless ghosts of the soldiers back in Washington. In a long, rambling letter to Lewy Brown and the other patients at Armory Square, he wrote: "I have now been home about a week in the midst of relations, & many friends, many young men, some I have known from childhood, many I love very much. I am out a great deal, as we are glad to be with each other. . . . But truly, my dear comrades, I never sit down, not a single time, to the bountiful dinners & suppers to which I am taken in this land of wealth & plenty without feeling it would be such a comfort to all, if you too, my dear & loving boys, could have each your share of the good things to eat & drink, & of the pleasure & amusement. . . . [O]ften in the midst of the profusion, the palatable dishes to eat, & the laughing & talking, & liquors &c, my thoughts silently turn to Washington, to all who lie there sick & wounded, with bread & molasses for supper."[50]

Whitman told another soldier he had befriended, Elijah Douglass Fox, that after three full weeks of steady partying, "[I] have had enough of going around New York—enough of amusements, suppers, drinking, & what is called *pleasure*. . . . I do not think one night has passed in New York or Brooklyn when I have been at the theatre or opera or afterward to some supper party or carouse made by the young fellows for me, but what amid the play or the singing, I would perhaps suddenly think of you—& the same at the gayest supper party, of men, where all was fun & noise & laughing & drinking. . . . I would see your face before me in my thought as I have seen it so often there in Ward G, & my amusement or drink would be all turned to nothing."[51]

He did not wish to disparage his New York friends, Whitman assured Fox, "there are so many of them & all so good, many so educated, traveled, &c., some so handsome & witty, some rich &c., some among the literary class . . . all good— many of them educated & polished, & brilliant in conversation, &c—& I thought I valued their society & friendship. . . . But, Douglass, I will tell you the truth, you are so much closer to me than any of them that there is no comparison—there has never passed so much between them & me as we have."[52]

Fox, an orphan, had just been invalided out of the army and returned to his wife in Kalamazoo, Michigan. His letters to Whitman are eloquent examples of the depth of affection the poet engendered in many of the young soldiers he had helped. "Dear Father," Fox began one letter. "You will allow me to call you Father wont you. I do not know that I told you that both of my parents are dead but it is true and now Walt you will be a second Father to me wont you, for my love for you is hardly less than my love for my natural parent. I have never before met with a man that I could love as I do you still there is nothing strange about it for 'to know you is to love you' and how any person could know you and not love you is a wonder to me." And in another letter, Fox wrote: "I am afraid I shall never be able to recompense you for your kind care . . . while I was sick in the hospital unless you are already paid by knowing you have helped the sick and suffering soldiers many of them will never cease to remember you and to ask God's blessing to rest upon you while you and they live."[53]

The fact of the matter was that the previous eleven months Walt had spent with Fox and the other young Union soldiers in the hospitals around Washington had "veteranized" him to such an extent that he was now unfit for civilian life. His real family, as opposed to the troublesome covey of blood relatives who nested unhappily on Portland Avenue in Brooklyn, consisted of the war-damaged young men he had come to know and love at their bedsides. "I am only a friend, visiting the sick & wounded soldiers," he had modestly told Erastus Haskell's parents earlier in the year. Now he was more. He was their father, their mother, their brother, and their friend. Above all he was—his favorite word—their comrade.

Whitman returned to Washington on December 1; two days later he received a telegram from Jeff informing him that Andrew had died. Suffering from tuberculosis of the throat, Andrew had wanted to go to his mother's house to die, but "nancy made a great adue and said you shant have him he belongs to me," Mrs. Whitman told Walt a few days later. Instead, everyone trooped to Andrew's house and instituted a daylong death watch. "Andrew was very desirous of having us all around him when he died," said Jeff. "The poor boy seemed to think that that would take nearly all the horror of it away."[54]

At length Andrew turned his head to the wall, gave a last long look at Walt's and George's photographs, and died "like any one going to sleep." Jesse, raging with syphilis, "took on very much and looked a little strange." At home he screamed at three-year-old Mannahatta, threatened Mattie, and "looked just like a madman." Mrs. Whitman jumped into the fray, attempting to calm him down, but Mattie "told him he better try it if he dare to when he flew at me again and said he did not mean to hurt me but now he Be D— —if he wouldn't knock my brains out such a D— —fool as I was hadn't right to live." Jeff, who usually managed to miss all conflicts, national or personal, raged in an after-the-fact letter to Walt: "Had I been home, so help me God i would have shot him dead on the spot. . . . I wish to God he was ready to put alongside of Andrew. There would be but few tears shed on my part I can tell you." Walt, for his part, professed to being "very very sorry now that I did not stay while I was at home," but he was no doubt also relieved that he had missed the ensuing uproar.[55]

Back in Washington, Whitman resumed his visits to the men, renewing his vow to "continue as a Missionary among them as surely as I live." He interrupted his duties on New Year's Eve to usher in the new year with the O'Connors and their friends on L Street. It had been snowing when he arrived, Nelly recalled, and "after entering, and shaking and stamping off the soft snow from his garments, he began to unload his pockets. . . . Out of those capacious receptacles he brought forth a small bottle of Scotch whiskey, a lemon, and some lump sugar, and he said we would welcome in the New Year."[56]

Painstakingly, Whitman measured out the makings for hot toddies, "and then came the gay and merry discussion of any and every thing under the sun and stars, while the punch so carefully concocted was slowly sipped till the midnight bells pealed out the hour of twelve, and the guests departed, wishing each other all sorts of piquant and jolly good wishes." On that fleetingly festive note the terrible year of 1863 ended, and the still more terrible year of 1864 began. By the time the next New Year's bells had tolled, thousands fewer would be around to hear them ring, having answered by then the valedictory summons of an altogether different sort of bell.[57]

Walt Whitman in 1863, when he began his hospital visits. (LIBRARY OF
CONGRESS)

George
Washington
Whitman, 51st
New York
Volunteers.
(LIBRARY OF
CONGRESS)

Louisa Whitman, the
poet's beloved mother.
(LIBRARY OF
CONGRESS)

Walt Whitman
taken from life 1863
war time Washington
to Horace L. Traubel   DC
from his friend WW
June 1888—

After only a few months, the strain is etched on Whitman's face.

Ellen O'Connor, one of
Whitman's "understanders."

Two recent amputees among the wounded in the Wilderness.

A sight in camp. The dead await burial at Fredericksburg. (USAMHI)

A hard-pressed surgeon, foreground, examines a soldier's leg wound, Virginia 1862. (LIBRARY OF CONGRESS)

Armory Square Hospital, where Whitman spent most of his time.
(USAMHI)

Interior of Armory Square, with 4th of July holiday decorations.
(USAMHI)

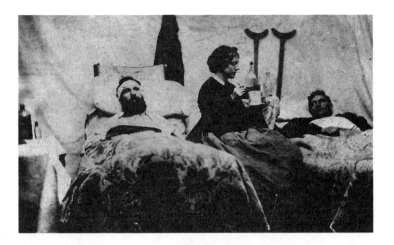

Rare photo of a female nurse with the men. Her name was Anne Bell. (USAMHI)

Army ambulances parading down Pennsylvania Avenue in the Grand Review. (LIBRARY OF CONGRESS)

Whitman with Peter Doyle—"Pete the Great"—in 1865. (LIBRARY OF CON-
GRESS)

CHAPTER FIVE

The Melancholy Tide

The first week of the new year brought with it new worries: Lewy Brown's broken leg, having stubbornly failed to mend properly, would have to be amputated. On January 5, at Brown's request, Whitman attended the operation. "Today after dinner Lew Brown had his left leg amputated six inches below the knee," he recorded in his notebook. "I was present at operation most of the time in the Army hosp. It was under ether. The surgeon in charge amputated but did not finish the operation being called away—as they were stitching it up Lew came out of the influence of the ether. It bled & they thought an artery had opened. They were about to cut the stitches again and make a search, but after some time concluded it was only surface bleeding. They then stitched it up again & Lew felt every one of those stitches . . . I could hear his cries & sometimes quite loud, & half-coherent talk & caught glimpses of him through the open door."[1]

Following the traumatic operation, Brown was understandably exhausted. Whitman stayed by his bedside throughout the night, anxiously monitoring Brown's condition. Brown, he said, "talked quite a good deal. His face was very pale, & his eyes dull. He asked often about me. He remained very sick, opprest for breath, with deathly feeling . . . in the stomach, head, &tc., & great pain in the leg. As usual in such cases he could feel the lost foot & leg very plainly. The toes would get twisted & not possible to disentangle them." Whitman spent the next night as well at Brown's side and continued checking on him religiously every day. By the beginning of February, Brown had recovered sufficiently to get around on crutches, although it would be another six months before he was released for good from the hospital.[2]

Whitman's personal attention to Brown did not deter him from his usual rounds. He brought apples, oranges, and crab apple jelly to William Widner of the 2nd New York Cavalry, who was suffering from heart disease, and peppermint candy to James Taylor of the 33rd New York Artillery, who was hospitalized with scurvy. On January 31 and February 1 he visited with Charles Davis of the 1st Michigan Cavalry and Walter Sibbett of the 126th New York, both of whom were "pretty low with Diarrhea." The next day he wrote to his mother: "There has been several hundred sick soldiers brought in here yesterday. I have been around among them to-day all day—it is enough to make me heart-sick, the old times over again; they are many of them mere wrecks, though young men (sickness is worse in some respects than wounds) . . . I have been feeding some their dinners. It makes me feel quite proud, I find so frequently I can do with the men what no one else at all can, getting them to eat (some that will not touch their food otherwise, nor for any-body else) — it is sometimes quite affecting, I can tell you. I found such a case to-day, a soldier with throat disease, very bad. I fed him quite a dinner; the men, his comrades around, just stared in wonder, and one of them told me afterwards that he (the sick man) had not eat so much at a meal in three months."[3]

Congress had reconvened in early December, and Whitman and Burroughs occasionally walked over to the Capitol to hear the debates. Among Whitman's new acquaintances was Ohio congressman James A. Garfield, who had taken his seat in the House of Representatives after serving for two years in the Army of the Cumberland. Always more politician than soldier, Garfield was busily laying the groundwork for his own success-ful presidential bid in 1880, a presidency that would be cut short after only four months in office by a deranged assassin's bullet. Whitman's close friend Willard Bliss, chief of staff at Armory Square Hospital, would oversee the team of physicians attend-ing the stricken president. Given his vast experience with gun-shot wounds and infections during the war — to say nothing of the great medical advances in the intervening two decades — Bliss ought to have been of some practical use. Instead, he prob-ably contributed more than anyone to Garfield's death by stick-ing an unwashed finger into the president's wound, thus doom-ing Garfield to two and a half months of feverish, pain-wracked suffering from a fatal case of blood poisoning. After Garfield's demise on September 19, 1881, Whitman published a brief poem lamenting his passing, "The Sobbing of the Bells," in the *Boston Daily Globe*. The gentle poem drew an angry rebuke from William O'Connor, who in typical iconoclastic fashion lambasted the martyred president as "personally and politically base."[4]

By early January Burroughs had managed to secure employment as a clerk in the Treasury Department, the same department whose high-flown secretary had denied Whitman a similar post a few weeks earlier. Typically, Whitman did not hold that against his young friend. Instead, as he had done with the O'Connors, he became a frequent breakfast guest at Burroughs's newly rented home near the Capitol. By then Burroughs had brought his wife, Ursula, to Washington to live with him, and the couple set up housekeeping in a small red-brick house, complete with a plot of potatoes, some succulent plum trees, a brood of chickens, and a milk cow named Chloe. The formidable Ursula did not much care for Whitman's poetry, nor that of any other "scribblers," for that matter, but she soon warmed to Whitman himself. She even managed to turn an indulgent, if not blind, eye on his habitual tardiness. "Walt was usually late for breakfast," Burroughs recalled, "and Ursula, who was as punctual as the clock, would get in a pucker. The coffee would boil, the griddle would smoke, and car after car would go jingling by, but no Walt. The situation at times verged on the tragic. But at last a car would stop, and Walt would roll off it and saunter up to the door — so cheery, and so unaware of the annoyance he had caused, that we soon forgot our ill-humor."[5]

Ursula Burroughs was rather less forgiving of some other visitors that winter: William and Nelly O'Connor and their daughter, Jeannie. Homeless again after yet another house had been sold from under them, the O'Connors moved into the Burroughs's attic until they could find more permanent quarters. From the start their bohemian lifestyle rankled the proper Mrs. Burroughs. O'Connor, fueled by great quantities of coffee and cigarettes, habitually shut himself up in the attic every Sunday and wrote all day and night, leaving Burroughs to toss fresh plums through his open window "to remind the poor man that there was a good green world waiting outside for him." Other nights, the couple would host loud, raucous parties—some attended by Whitman—and leave empty whiskey bottles on the stairs leading up to the attic. Worst of all, from Ursula's point of view, was O'Connor's habit of sneaking girlfriends into the apartment whenever his wife was out of the house. In this, she may have objected more forcefully than Nelly O'Connor herself, who by this time had managed to convince herself that she was in love with Walt Whitman.[6]

When Whitman was away the previous November, Nelly had sent him a number of lovelorn letters. "To tell you that we miss you *awfully* would not be news would it?" she wrote. "I do have a most uncomfortable sense of 'goneness' all the time, & I shall welcome you home here *very heartily*." In another letter she sighed: "I feel as if a large part of myself were out of the city,—I shall give you a good kiss when you come, so depend upon it. My love to your good, noble mother, whom I shall some day know. Kiss her for me & tell her that I love her boy Walt."

As he was always to do when confronted by the unsought ardor of the opposite sex, Whitman declined to respond to Nelly O'Connor's obvious overtures. Nor did he respond a few months later when she became even more bold, telling him that

"I have missed you terribly every minute of the time. I think I never in my life felt so wholly blue and unhappy about anyone's going away as I did, and have since, about your going. . . . Ah! Walt, I don't believe other people need you as much as we do. I am *sure* they don't need you as much as I do. . . . [I]n the evening when I hear a car coming, I find myself watching for you, listening for you." Coquettishly, she enclosed a new photograph of herself, asking Whitman how he liked it. "I got my pictures last week," she wrote, "& they are rather bad, the front face, or rather three quarter face is hideous. . . . The side face is—well what do you say of it. I think it is *very* sharp, & I should not like anybody that looked like it, do *you?*" Walt liked Nelly well enough, but as with Ellen Eyre and other women who occasionally put themselves forward on his account, he was not sufficiently interested to rise to the bait.[7]

The war, at any rate, still dominated his life. He hardly had time for the one good meal a day he allowed himself to eat in the cheap restaurants near Armory Square—much less time to carry on an affair with the emotionally needy wife of a friend. Despite the new influx of patients, most of whom were sick rather than wounded (the spring campaign having not yet begun), Whitman began to weary of his daily routine. He talked to an unidentified but "pretty high officer" about his "great desire to be present at a first-class battle." The officer told Whitman to stick around for three or four more weeks and "my wish would probably be gratified."[8]

As it happened, the officer's prediction was three months premature; the Union Army's advance into northern Virginia would not occur until the beginning of May. Whitman could not wait that long. On February 6 he joined Major Hapgood and Charlie Eldridge on a paymaster's mission to the Culpeper, Virginia, winter camp of the Army of the Potomac, to deliver cash bounties of four hundred dollars each to those soldiers who had reenlisted for the duration of the war. In all a total of 136,000 veterans reenlisted, including about half the Army of the Potomac, leaving the other half to be filled by "the most thorough-paced villains that the stews of New York and Baltimore could furnish—bounty-jumpers, thieves, and cutthroats," as one disgruntled Connecticut artilleryman complained. A recruitment officer in Illinois was even more scathing. In his eyes the new enlistees, many of them hired substitutes, were "branded felons . . . blotched and bloated libertines and pimps . . . thieves, burglars and vagabonds . . . the riff-raff of corruption and scoundrelism of every shade and degree of infamy which can be swept into the insatiable clutches of the vampires who fatten upon the profits of the execrable business." To differentiate the veterans from the incoming rabble, the old-timers were given bright new chevrons to wear on their sleeves.[9]

At Culpeper, Whitman took a room in the home of a Mrs. Ashby, whose late husband had been a kinsman of Confederate General Turner Ashby (the same Ashby who had fatally wounded Fitz-James O'Brien, Whitman's old drinking companion from Pfaff's, in the Shenandoah Valley in 1862). He found Mrs. Ashby well mannered and handsome, but also "quite melancholy," which was understandable, given the fact that she was being forced to provide room and board to a large number of freeloading Union officers and their guests. "She & her sister paid me the compliment of talking friendlily & nearly exclusively with me," Whitman reported. "[S]he was dressed in very faded clothes but her manners were fine, seems to be a travelled well educated woman . . . said she had remained through fearful troubles & changes here on acct of her children . . . poor lady, how I pitied her, compelled to live as one may say on chance & charity, with her high spirit."[10]

Whitman did not spend much time in his new quarters. Instead, he went out among the men, renewing acquaintances with many of the same soldiers he had met when visiting George's camp outside Fredericksburg fourteen months earlier. His intent, he explained in a letter to John Townsend Trowbridge on February 8, was "to see more of camp life and war scenes, & the state of the army this winter." Trowbridge, for his part, sent along a large box of books, which the poet donated to a field hospital for army teamsters. Whitman soon got his wish, witnessing a large-scale demonstration that the Army of the Potomac undertook on February 6 to distract Robert E. Lee from an assault on Richmond by Major General Benjamin Butler.[11]

Whitman was asleep when the soldiers came trooping back into camp at 3 A.M. after making a halfhearted feint across the Rapidan River at Raccoon Ford. Awakened by their "tremendous cries," the poet "got up & went out, & found it was some of the men returning from the extreme front . . . it was a curious sight to see the shadowy columns coming in two or three o'clock at night." Despite the failure of their assault, Whitman found the soldiers surprisingly chipper. "The men had their usual burdens, overcoats, knapsacks, guns and blankets," Whitman wrote. "Along and along they filed by me, with often a laugh, a song, a cheerful word, but never once a murmur. It may have been odd, but I never before so realized the majesty and reality of the American people *en masse*. It fell upon me like a great awe."[12]

The predawn return of the troops may have inspired Whitman to write the evocative, dreamlike poem, "By the Bivouac's Fitful Flame":

> By the bivouac's fitful flame,
> A procession winding around me, solemn and sweet and
>   slow—but first I note,
> The tents of the sleeping army, the fields' and woods' dim
>   outline,
> The darkness lit by spots of kindled fire, the silence,
> Like a phantom far or near an occasional figure moving,
> The shrubs and trees, (as I lift my eyes they seem to be
>   stealthily watching me,)
> While wind in procession thoughts, O tender and won-
>   drous thoughts,
> Of life and death, of home and the past and loved, and of
>   those that are far away;
> A solemn and slow procession there as I sit on the ground,
> By the bivouac's fitful flame.[13]

Four days later Whitman went down to the front to visit New York captain Henry Lowd Cranford's battery of horse artillery, which was camped within a half mile of the outer picket line. "I asked him if he did not think it dangerous," Whitman told his mother, "he said no, he could have a large force of infantry to help in there, in very short metre, if there was any sudden emergency." Still, the nearness to the front made Whitman a little nervous. In his poem "The Artilleryman's Vision" he imagines a cannoneer much like Cranford lying in bed beside his wife long after the war has ended. Jolted awake in "the vacant midnight," the artilleryman experiences something akin to what Vietnam War veterans call a "flashback," a vivid sensory memory of combat:

> There in the room as I wake from sleep this vision presses
> upon me;
> The engagement opens there and then in fantasy unreal,
> The skirmishers begin, they crawl cautiously ahead, I hear
> the irregular snap! snap!
> I hear the sounds of the different missiles, the short *t-h-t!*
> *t-h-t!* of the rifle-balls,
> I see the shells exploding leaving small white clouds, I hear
> the great shells shrieking as they pass,
> The grape like the hum and whirr of wind through the
> trees, (tumultuous now the contest rages,)
> All the scenes at the batteries rise in detail before me
> again.[14]

In his letter to his mother, Whitman added a lengthy description of the army encampment. "The troops here are scattered all around," he wrote, "much more apart than they seemed to me to be opposite Fredericksburg last winter. They mostly have good huts and fireplaces, etc. I have been to a great many of the camps, and I must say I am astonished how good the houses are almost everywhere. I have not seen one regiment, nor any part of one, in the poor uncomfortable little shelter tents that I saw so common last winter after Fredericksburg. . . . A good many of them would be comfortable enough to live in under any circumstances." He was proud of the cheerful welcome he had received from the men, adding that he was surprised at the number who still remembered him from the year before.[15]

Whitman looked in on the various field hospitals dotting the hills above Culpeper. "I suppose you know that what we call hospital here in the field is nothing but a collection of tents on the bare ground for a floor," he explained to his mother. In the tents he found "some poor creatures crawling about pretty weak with diarrhoea; there is a great deal of that; they keep them until they get very bad indeed, and then send them to Washington. This aggravates the complaint, and they come into Washington in a terrible condition. O mother, how often and how many I have seen come into Washington from this awful complaint after such an experience as I have described—with the look of death on their poor young faces; they keep them so long in the field hospitals with poor accommodations the disease gets too deeply seated." Long after the war Whitman told Horace Traubel—without exaggeration—that the conflict had been "about nine hundred and ninety-nine parts diarrhea to one part glory."[16]

While Walt was in Culpeper, George was back home in Brooklyn on furlough. After briefly considering leaving the army, George renlisted in his old unit, the 51st New York, and returned to the front on February 25. In true military fashion, the regiment was shipped west from New York to Indianapolis, then east to Louisville, then south to Nashville and Chattanooga, then north to Knoxville, then east to Mossy Creek, then west to Knoxville, and finally back north to Annapolis, Maryland. In the meantime Walt had returned to Washington, where he saw ominous portents of a huge new military buildup. Not only were large squads of fresh recruits and veteran troops passing through the capital daily, but the hospitals were filling up with previously sick and wounded soldiers unable to stand the rigors of a new campaign.

Some six hundred of the army rejects arrived by train one rainy afternoon, and Whitman rushed to Armory Square to help prepare a place for them. "I could not keep the tears out of my eyes," he told his mother. "Many of the poor young men had to be moved on stretchers, with blankets over them, which soon soaked as wet as water in the rain. . . . Mother, it was a dreadful night . . . pretty dark, the wind gust, and the rain fell in torrents." One emaciated young soldier, barely eighteen, died before he could be carried through the hospital gate. The worst thing about it, said Whitman, was "that he is entirely unknown — there was nothing on his clothes, or any one with him to identify him, and he is altogether unknown. Mother, it is enough to rack one's heart. . . . Very likely his folks will never know in the world what has become of him. Poor, poor child."[17]

Like other experienced observers, Whitman could see what was coming, and he was not at all certain that he was equal to the task. "Mother, to think that we are to have here soon what I have seen so many times, the awful loads and trains and boat loads of poor bloody and pale and wounded young men—for that is what we certainly will, and before very long," he worried. "I see all the little signs, getting ready in the hospitals, etc.; it is dreadful when one thinks about it. I sometimes think over the sights I myself have seen, the arrival of the wounded after a battle, and the scenes on the field too, and I can hardly believe my own recollections. What an awful thing war is! Mother, it seems not men but a lot of devils and butchers butchering each other."[18]

A week later he was still uncommonly anxious. "I feel lately as though I must have some intermission," he wrote. "I feel well and hearty enough . . . but my feelings are kept in a painful condition a great part of the time. Things get worse and worse, as to the amount and suffering of the sick . . . and those who have to do with them are getting more and more callous and indifferent. Mother, when I see the common soldiers, what they go through, and how everybody seems to try to pick upon them, and . . . how even the dying soldier's money stolen from his body by some scoundrel attendant, or from some sick one, even from under his head . . . I get almost frightened at the world."[19]

He had good reason to be apprehensive. Newly promoted Lieutenant General Ulysses S. Grant, Whitman noted on March 31, "has just come in town from the front. The country here is all mad again." Grant, he said, "is determined to bend everything to take Richmond and break up the banditti of scoundrels that have stuck themselves up there as a 'government.' He is in earnest about it; his whole soul and all his thoughts night and day are upon it. He is probably the most in earnest of any man in command or in the government either." Diffident and physically unprepossessing, Grant was a new kind of warrior for a new kind of war, one based less on grand heroics and noble gestures than on the simple ciphering of sums that he had learned in his brother's Galena, Illinois, dry-goods store. With the war now entering its fourth spring, the North had roughly twice as many soldiers as the South, and the new Union general in chief, with Abraham Lincoln's enthusiastic backing, intended to improve those odds by forcibly subtracting, one by one, the enemy's dwindling stock of defenders. When enough Rebels had been subtracted, the North would win. It was as simple — and brutal — as that.[20]

To bolster his chances, Grant planned to keep the Confederates off balance by having the various Union armies attack simultaneously on all fronts. He had already discussed his grand scheme with his close friend and confidant, William Tecumseh Sherman, who now commanded the main Union army in the western theater of the war. While Grant's Army of the Potomac led the way across the Rapidan River into Virginia, Sherman would send his forces south from Chattanooga, Tennessee, into northern Georgia, with the vital city of Atlanta as his ultimate goal. Meanwhile, smaller Union armies on the Virginia peninsula, in the Shenandoah Valley, and in Louisiana would also take the offensive, more as a nuisance than a real threat. Describing their subsidiary role, Lincoln employed a favorite backwoods metaphor. "Those not skinning," he said, "can hold a leg."[21]

Grant was waiting for the spring rains to stop and the roads to dry before launching his ambitious campaign. In the meantime he continued augmenting his numbers. On April 25, ten days before the offensive began, Major General Ambrose Burnside led his old 9th Corps into Washington en route to the front. Whitman was standing with John Burroughs on the curbside at 14th Street and Pennsylvania Avenue, just opposite Willard's Hotel, hoping to catch a glimpse of his brother George amid the thirty thousand soldiers marching past. Amazingly enough, he succeeded. After three hours of patient watching, during which time a number of men whom Whitman had nursed broke ranks to give him a quick kiss or an affectionate hug, the poet caught sight of George in the company of the 51st New York. Delighted, he fell in step alongside his brother, startling him so badly with his sudden materialization that George momentarily forgot military protocol and neglected to salute the president as he passed. "He was a little annoyed at forgetting it," Walt reported to their mother the next day. He and George had "had quite a talk" before the column marched out of Washington and across Long Bridge into enemy-held Virginia.[22]

George's regiment scarcely had time to take its place in line before the long-anticipated Union onslaught began at dawn on May 4, 1864. Walt had heard from someone, perhaps George, that the 51st New York would be kept in reserve, guarding the Orange & Alexandria Railroad back to Washington. Plans soon changed. Grant had hoped rather optimistically to steal a march on Lee by bypassing the Confederate defensive line below Culpeper and moving swiftly through the seventy-mile-wide, thirty-mile-long stretch of second-growth timber, thorny underbrush, brackish water, and barren soil aptly named the Wilderness. Once through the Wilderness, he would head due south toward

Richmond, forcing Lee to confront him in the open countryside outside the Rebel capital. Lee, however, had no intention of fighting the war on Grant's terms, and the day after the Union advance he struck first, sending two corps of hard-eyed veterans crashing into the Northern lines as they inched apprehensively through the gloom.

For two endless days and nights the opposing armies fought savagely, if blindly, in the tree-shrouded woods around a ramshackle tavern marking the intersection of the two best roads to Richmond. The fighting was unparalleled in its awfulness: gun smoke hung so heavily among the trees that no one could see more than a few feet in front of him; bullets whizzed from every side. Brushfires ignited by red-hot projectiles filled the air with the loathsome stench of burning flesh. Cartridge belts exploded around soldiers' waists, sending jagged shards of metal slicing through their bowels. Many of the wounded, unable to move, committed suicide to escape the flames that snaked implacably toward them. One North Carolinian remembered the battle as "a butchery pure and simple . . . unrelieved by any of the arts of war." To another Confederate, it was not even a formal battle but simply "bushwhacking on a grand scale." Grant's own aide de camp, Colonel Horace Porter, searched for a suitable biblical analogy. "It seemed as though Christian men had turned to fiends," he wrote, "and hell itself had usurped the place of earth."[23]

Back in Washington, Whitman waited along with the rest of the nation for news from the front. Grant had forbidden newspaper correspondents to use the telegraph lines, and for several days there were no reports, however limited, of the fighting.

Lincoln was reduced to haunting the halls of the War Department, waiting for word from his new commander. When word finally came, it was frustratingly brief and incomplete. "Everything pushing along favorably," Grant reported tersely. Meanwhile, Whitman passed along what news he could glean to his fretful mother in Brooklyn. Given his limited access, it was remarkably accurate. "Grant has advanced his army or portion of it to the region of Chancellorsville battle of just a year ago & has either flanked Lee as they call it (got in on his army between him & Richmond) — or else that Lee has hurried back or is hurrying back to Richmond," he reported on May 6. Three days later he reassured her: "The fighting has been hard enough, but the papers make lots of additional items, and a good deal that they just entirely make up." The 9th Corps, he learned, had been thrown into the battle, "but from the wounded I have seen I don't think that Corps was deeply in."[24]

On May 12 a new batch of wounded men arrived in Washington from the Wilderness, and Whitman eagerly questioned them about George's regiment. Corporal Fred Saunders, from George's own company, told Walt that as of Tuesday, May 10, his brother remained safe and unhurt. Others in the 51st New York were not as fortunate — regimental losses amounted to twenty killed and another forty or fifty wounded. On May 18 Whitman wrote again to his mother: "I will only write you a hasty note this time, as I am pretty tired, and my head feels disagreeable from being in too much. I was up yesterday to Carver hospital and again saw the man of the 51st, Thos. McCowell, who told me of George, up to the latter part of Thursday, 12th inst. I questioned him, and his story was very clear, so I felt perfectly satisfied. . . . Mother, I see such awful things, I expect one of these days, if I live, I shall have awful thoughts and dreams." His poem, "Old War-Dreams," dramatizes just such a war-troubled sleep:

> In midnight sleep of many a face of anguish,
> Of the look at first of the mortally wounded, (of that inde-
>   scribable look,)
> Of the dead on their backs with arms extended wide,
> I dream, I dream, I dream.
>
> . . .
>
> Long have they pass'd, faces and trenches and fields,
> Where through the carnage I moved with a callous compo-
>   sure, or away from the fallen,
> Onward I sped at the time — but now of their forms at
>   night,
> I dream, I dream, I dream.[25]

Following the two-day Battle of the Wilderness, which cost the Army of the Potomac a staggering 17,500 casualties — 985 in the 9th Corps alone — the Northern troops fully expected to retreat to Washington. That had been the pattern in previous campaigns — a bloody battle followed by a panicky withdrawal — but Grant was not like previous commanders. Instead of turning north, the army continued south, this time toward Spotsylvania Courthouse, a key crossroads village twelve miles southeast of the Wilderness Tavern. With their more compact interior lines and better knowledge of the countryside, the Confederates won the race to Spotsylvania and threw up an imposing line of breastworks, trenches, and abatis. For the next two weeks Grant tried unsuccessfully to dislodge the Rebel defenders with a desperate combination of flanking maneuvers, massed column assaults, and headlong frontal attacks. George's regiment saw severe fighting on the twelfth and the eighteenth, losing another forty-two men, including three of George's closest companions, who were shot dead beside him. His own uniform coat was riddled by grapeshot, and half his canteen was blown away, but George as usual escaped without a scratch. Not for nothing did one of his comrades tell Walt a year later that his brother was "just the luckiest man in the American army."[26]

As the fighting wore on, almost without pause, an unbroken line of ambulances rumbled into the capital. "The arrivals, the numbers, and the severity of the wounds, outvied anything that we had seen before," Whitman noted. "For days and weeks the melancholy tide set in upon us. The weather was very hot; the wounded had been delayed in coming, and much neglected. Very many of the wounds had worms in them. An unusual portion mortified." Each day in the hospitals held a special grief. On May 21, Whitman witnessed the death of Stewart C. Glover of Company E, 5th Wisconsin Infantry. Glover, barely twenty, had been shot in the knee by a Rebel sharpshooter while attempting to help bring in the wounded on the first day of fighting in the Wilderness. He had already served for nearly three years and was within a few days of his discharge when he received his fatal wound. Following the amputation of his leg, Glover wasted away, and on the day of his death he jotted down in his diary: "To-day the doctor says I must die—all is over with me—ah, so young to die." What particularly troubled Whitman when he read the diary was the addendum Glover had penned on the back of the page: "Dear brother Thomas, I have been brave but wicked—pray for me."[27]

The day after Glover died, Whitman spent the better part of an afternoon sitting with seventeen-year-old Charles Cutter of Lawrence, Massachusetts, who had been mortally wounded in the abdomen. "Well, I thought to myself, as I sat looking at him, it ought to be a relief to his folks if they could see how little he suffer'd," Whitman remembered. "He lay very placid, in a half lethargy, with his eyes closed. As it was extremely hot, and I sat a good while silently fanning him, and wiping the sweat, at length he open'd his eyes quite wide and clear, and look'd inquiringly around. I said, 'What is it, my boy? Do you want anything?' He answer'd quietly, with a good-natured smile, 'Oh, nothing; I was only looking around to see who was with me.'" Soon Whitman was called away on another case. Cutter, he heard later, had died "without any special agitation."[28]

Another patient whose long decline Whitman monitored helplessly was Oscar H. Cunningham of Delaware, Ohio, a member of the 82nd Ohio Regiment, who had languished in a bed at Armory Square for nearly a year after being wounded in the thigh at Chancellorsville. "When he was brought here I thought he ought to have been taken to a sculptor to model for an emblematic figure of the west," Whitman wrote, "he was such a handsome giant over 6 feet high, with a great head of brown yellow shining hair thick & longish, & a manly noble manner & talk." Now, after undergoing an amputation and suffering a relapse, Cunningham was "all wasted away to a skeleton, and look[ed] like someone fifty years old." Once again, there was nothing Whitman could do but wait. A surgical fever, probably pyemia, set in, and Cunningham died about 2 A.M. on Sunday, June 5. "It was a blessed relief," Whitman told his mother, "his life has been misery for months. The cause of death at last was the system absorbing the pus, the bad matter, instead of discharging it from [the] wound." Walt felt bad because he had dissuaded the young man's sister, Helen, from coming to visit him in Washington until it was too late. At Armory Square soldiers were dying now at the rate of one an hour.[29]

A few days earlier Whitman somehow had managed to get hold of ten gallons of ice cream, which he personally dispensed to the patients at Carver Hospital. "You would have cried & been amused too," he told Mrs. Whitman, "many of the men had to be fed, several of them I saw cannot probably live, yet they quite enjoyed it, I gave everybody some—quite a number [of] western boys had never tasted ice cream before." All the ice cream in the world, however, could not dam the tidal wave of suffering whose epicenter was located in the smoky woods of eastern Virginia. Grant, despite losing a sickening total of seven thousand men in a mere eight minutes at Cold Harbor on June 3, had no intention of calling off the campaign. Instead, as he told Lincoln, "I propose to fight it out on this line if it takes all summer." At the rate he was going, it was questionable whether he would have anyone left to fight. A staggering sixty-five thousand soldiers had been killed or wounded since crossing the Rapidan River four weeks earlier—a figure that represented fully 60 percent of all Union casualties during the previous three years put together. The number of unburied bodies rotting in the sun caused one Richmond diarist to speculate mordantly that "Grant intends to *stink* Lee out of his position, if nothing else will suffice."[30]

The constant days of combat wore on even the most experienced soldiers. Union general Gouverneur K. Warren, one of the heroes of Gettysburg, burst forth one night: "For thirty days it has been one funeral procession past me, and it has been too much!" Even Lincoln, catching sight of a long line of ambulances groaning through the capital, was moved to exclaim: "Look yonder at those poor fellows. I cannot bear it. This suffering, this loss of life is dreadful." A Northern congressman visiting the hospital wards was so affected by the sights that he burst into tears. One new feature of the hospitals, Whitman observed, was that "many of the poor afflicted young men are crazy. Every ward has some in it that are wandering. They have suffered too much, and it is perhaps a privilege that they are out of their senses."[31]

Whitman was feeling a little odd, himself. "My head begins to trouble me a little with a sort of fullness," he told his mother, "as it often does in hot weather." He was also getting homesick again, something he attributed to having "seen all the horrors of soldiers' life and not been kept up by its excitement. It is awful to see so much, and not be able to relieve it." If he could only come home for two or three days, he thought, he could drink tea, talk to Jeff, and play with Jeff's little daughters, and then "I should be willing to keep on afterward among these sad scenes for the rest of the summer."[32]

As it turned out, he did not last that long. By the middle of

June Walt had become so ill with a sore throat, congestion of the head, and occasional fainting spells that the doctors ordered him to stay away from the hospitals entirely. "The doctor tells me I have continued too long in the hospitals, especially in a bad place, Armory building, where the worst wounds were, and have absorbed too much of the virus in my system," he told Mrs. Whitman. "It is probable that the hospital poison has affected my system." He had moved again, this time to a three-story boardinghouse at 502 Pennsylvania Avenue, two blocks from the Capitol, and his new accommodations, he complained, were "a miserable place, very bad air." He tried to tough it out in order to be on hand if anything should happen to George, but finally, on June 23, he was forced to leave Washington and return to Brooklyn, as much a casualty of the Wilderness campaign as any of the soldiers in Grant's shot-up army.[33]

The exact nature of Whitman's illness has never been satisfactorily diagnosed. His own doctors' explanations were frustratingly vague; they told him he was suffering from "hospital fever," "hospital malaria," "hospital poison," or "virus." Modern biographers have posited everything from malaria to tuberculosis to mercury poisoning. His chief symptoms—dizziness, congestion, ringing in the ears, headaches, insomnia, and general malaise—seem to suggest hypertension, complicated perhaps by a bad cold and a persistent sore throat. Whitman himself admitted that his case was "tenacious, peculiar and somewhat baffling"; and given his close familiarity with the various scourges of the time, the fact that he could not ascribe them to a single cause leads one to infer that his illness was at least partly psychosomatic. His comparatively rapid recovery once he had gotten away from the hospitals reinforces that view. At any rate, the wonder is not that he got sick but that it took him so long to do so. His fastidious personal hygiene no doubt played a part in staving off illness, but given the fact that he was not at all shy about kissing sick and dying soldiers on the lips, it is still remarkable that he avoided contracting a serious disease for as long as he did.[34]

Whatever was ailing him, Whitman arrived home in a bad state. He was housebound for two full weeks before managing to go on a carriage ride with his brother Jeff on July 8. Thereafter his recovery was steady, and by July 24 he was able to report to William O'Connor that his illness had "gradually alleviated, until now I go about pretty much the same as usual. . . . My head feels clear and comfortable & my strength has returned." He was not, however, in a hurry to return to Washington. His doctors had advised him to stay away from the hospitals, and he determined to make the most of his absence by arranging to publish, at long last, his collection of war poems. Even before he was out of bed, he advised O'Connor that "I intend to move heaven & earth to publish my 'Drum-Taps' as soon as I am able to go around." Later that month O'Connor helpfully sent him a copy of the government publication *Report on Armored Vessels*, which O'Connor thought "might yield hints for poems." Whitman politely thanked him for the report, but he never got around to writing any naval poems.[35]

At any rate, the poems to be included in *Drum-Taps* had been largely completed by then. The problem, as always with Whitman's work, was finding a suitable publisher. Except for the third edition of *Leaves of Grass*, which had been published in

Boston by the small firm of Thayer and Eldridge, all of Whitman's works had been self-published. In the 1850s, when Whitman had completed *Leaves of Grass*, conservative, old-line firms
such as Harpers and Appleton had shown no interest in bringing out the odd-looking proselike poems of an unknown poet.
And when Whitman became better known, it was generally for
the wrong reasons—he was deemed too controversial for the
established publishing houses. "I am trying to make arrange-
ments to publish my volume," he told O'Connor. "I shall probably try to bring it out myself, stereotype it, & print an edition
of 500—I could sell that number by my own exertions in Brooklyn and New York in three weeks." O'Connor worried—cor-
rectly, as it turned out—that if Whitman published the book
privately it would not be accessible to a large-scale audience. "I
want it to have a large sell," he said, adding that "such a volume
ought to make your fame secure." For the time being, that fame
would have to wait.[36]

While Whitman was home recuperating, the Confederate
Army made its most serious effort yet to strike at Washington.
With the weary majority of Lee's forces hunkering down for a
long siege at Petersburg, a key railroad junction twenty miles
below Richmond, a smaller force of fourteen thousand men has-
tened through the Shenandoah Valley toward the Northern capital. Led by irascible, high-strung General Jubal Early, the
threadbare Rebels, many of them barefoot, sought to invoke
the sacred memory of their slain warrior-priest, Stonewall Jackson. Passing Jackson's grave at Lexington, the men uncovered
their heads, reversed their arms, and marched in solemn lockstep
to the mournful accompaniment of muffled drums and muted

horns. It almost worked. After brushing aside token opposition at Lynchburg and Harpers Ferry, Early's men rampaged through southern Maryland, demanding tribute of two hundred thousand dollars from the town of Frederick and another twenty thousand dollars from the merchants of Hagerstown, where Confederate general John McCausland inadvertently dropped a digit from his demands. A brave stand at the Monocacy River by a skeleton force of Federals under Major General Lew Wallace (future author of *Ben-Hur*) delayed the Rebels just long enough to allow Union reinforcements to reach the capital scant hours ahead of the invaders. By July 11 Early's men were within five miles of Washington.

To meet the emergency, all able-bodied—and some not so able-bodied—men were called out for service in the trenches and forts around the capital. One-armed convalescents from the Veteran Reserve Corps, middle-aged clerks from government offices, and ambulatory patients from the various hospitals filled the gaps alongside regular soldiers from the 6th Corps of the Army of the Potomac, which had just arrived in Washington from the front. O'Connor and Burroughs were among those called, and even one-legged Lewy Brown manfully hobbled forth on his crutches, only to be outraged when no one in charge would lend him a gun. Lincoln himself climbed the parapet at Fort Stevens to view firsthand the gray-coated menace. As bullets whizzed about his familiar stovepipe hat—one struck an officer three feet away—Lincoln ignored all warnings until a young captain named Oliver Wendell Holmes, Jr., later to become chief justice of the Supreme Court, shouted: "Get down, you damn fool, before you get shot!"[37]

Burroughs, too, came under fire. "I was out at the front during the siege of Washington and lay in the rifle pits with the soldiers," he reported to Whitman. "I got quite a taste of war and learned the song of those modern minstrels—the minie bullets—by heart." After probing the defenses on July 12, Early began withdrawing the next day, unmolested by Union Major General Horatio Wright, who prematurely halted his own tentative pursuit, "for fear," Lincoln scoffed, that "he might come across the Rebels and catch some of them."[38]

Not even the excitement of Early's raid could tempt Whitman back to Washington. As he regained his health, he fell back into his old habits, looking up longtime stage driver acquaintances—one of whom had been in prison for the past two years at Sing Sing—strolling the streets, attending political rallies, and visiting his sisters in Vermont and Long Island. Perhaps because he had been ordered out of Washington for his health, Whitman did not feel the same degree of guilt over his late-night carousing that he had evinced the previous winter. As he reported to O'Connor: "I go out quite regularly, sometimes out on the bay, or to Coney Island—& occasionally a tour through New York life, as of old—last night I was with some of my friends of Fred Gray association, till late wandering the east side of the city first in the lager beer saloons & then elsewhere . . . it was one of those places where the air is full of the scent of low thieves, druggies, foul play, & prostitution gangrened."[39]

When he was not busy patronizing sawdust saloons or Coney Island sideshows, Whitman found time to visit the sick and wounded soldiers at the Brooklyn City Hospital on Raymond Street. The hospital, which was under contract with the government to take in wounded troops, was "the dullest, most low-spirited hospital I have been in," Whitman complained. "The nursing, ventilation, diet are bad & means to amuse the men entirely deficient; no visitors, no sympathetic connection with the outside world." About one hundred patients were housed there in the fall of 1864, and Whitman brought them tobacco, paper, envelopes, stamps, money, fresh fruit, sugar, and cake. One unnamed doctor drew the poet's scorn by walking away from two badly wounded and sick soldiers because one used tobacco and the other one swore. It confirmed his opinion that "this Brooklyn hospital is a bad place for soldiers, or anybody else. Cleanliness, proper nursing, watching, etc., are more deficient than any in any hospital I know . . . this is the poorest hospital I have been in, out of many hundreds."[40]

One of the patients at Brooklyn City Hospital, seventeen-year-old John C. Logan of the 2nd Pennsylvania Heavy Artillery, had been wounded in the leg at Petersburg during the bitter Battle of the Crater, a fight in which George Whitman had also seen action. The crater in question was a hole eighty feet wide and thirty feet deep that former coal miners in the 48th Pennsylvania Regiment from George's own brigade had blasted in the center of the Confederate trench line at Petersburg, after first tunneling forward secretly for nearly six hundred feet beneath the Rebels' very noses. The plan, endorsed by the always unlucky Ambrose Burnside, called for Brigadier General Edward Ferrero — George's old regimental commander — to lead his new, all-black division into the breach and clear the way for other troops.

At the last minute Grant became concerned that the attack

(which he had never favored anyway) would fail and lead to criticism that he had cynically used black men as cannon fodder. He ordered Burnside to use a white division instead, and in the subsequent confusion Brigadier General James H. Ledlie's untrained force mistakenly rushed into the crater instead of going around it, becoming hopelessly trapped inside. Union reinforcements, including George Whitman's 51st New York, joined the fray but were beaten back by a literally furious Confederate counterattack, the Rebels thinking, not without reason, that exploding four tons of gunpowder under their feet was the epitome of bad sportsmanship.

George's luck finally ran out two months later, at the Battle of Poplar Springs Church, on September 30, 1864. There, making yet another assault on the Confederate defenses below Petersburg, he and his entire regiment were cut off, surrounded, and overrun by a Confederate force commanded by Major General Cadmus Marcellus Wilcox. The operation was a classic example of military bungling: the 51st New York and the rest of the First Brigade were left unsupported on either flank as they moved across an open field to attack the Confederate rear. The ensuing Rebel counterattack caught the Federals by complete surprise, and George Whitman and his comrades—some six hundred in all—were enveloped on all sides by hard-charging infantry and cavalry. With no way to escape and no apparent support from their own lines, George's brigade surrendered en masse. Writing from a Confederate prison a few weeks later, George evinced a bitter pride "to think that we stood and fought until we were entirely surrounded."[41]

Walt and the rest of the family got their first inkling that something had happened to George when they read accounts of the fighting in the *Brooklyn Daily Union* on October 3 and 4, 1864. The initial report gave only a brief account of the losses incurred by the 5th and 9th Corps, which had made the assault at Poplar Springs Church. The second report, however, raised alarms within the Whitman household when it placed the total number of battle casualties at nearly two thousand, "more than half of whom were taken prisoner." Several days passed before the family learned anything concrete about George's fate. Two days after his capture, he had managed to dash off a few lines to Mrs. Whitman from the Confederate prison at Petersburg, but owing to the vagaries of mail service between the warring regions, its delivery was delayed for more than a week. On October 8 Whitman wrote to Charles Eldridge that "we are deprest in spirits home here about my brother George . . . if not killed, he is a prisoner—he was in the engagement of Sept 30 on the extreme left."[42]

After several days of tormenting uncertainty, the family finally received George's letter, which assured everyone that "I am perfectly well and unhurt, but a prisoner. . . . I am in tip top health and Spirits, and am as tough as a mule and shall get along first rate. Mother please dont worry and all will be right in time." He asked her to have Walt write to Lieutenant William E. Babcock of the 51st New York and ask him to send George's personal belongings home to Brooklyn. It was the only message they would receive from George for the next three months.[43]

Off and on for the past two years Whitman had toyed with the idea of writing a history of the 51st New York, and the recent disaster at Poplar Springs Church moved him to publish an

article, "Fifty-First New York City Veterans," in the October
29, 1864, issue of the *New York Times*. The article, gleaned from
sketchy notes he had made at Falmouth two years before,
praised the regiment for its "three years of genuine service" and
noted that the men had marched twelve thousand miles across
fifteen states. It enumerated the honor roll of engagements in
which the unit had fought—"Roanoke, Newburn [New Bern],
Bull Run, Chantilly, South Mountain, Antietam, Fredericksburg, Vicksburg, Jackson, Wilderness, Spotsylvania, Cold
Harbor and Petersburg." After taking pains to mention several
of the other regimental officers by name, Whitman informed
readers that "Capt. Whitman has been heard from since by his
relatives in Brooklyn, by a letter written in a rebel prison at
Petersburg by him a few days after the capture."[44]

Five days after the article appeared in the *Times*, Whitman
joined the rest of the nation in going to the polls to reelect
Abraham Lincoln. With his usual political acuity, Whitman had
assured O'Connor several weeks earlier that "the Republicans
are going to make a stout fight after all, as there is confusion
in the opposition camp." Lincoln's Democratic opponent, erstwhile Army of the Potomac commander George B. McClellan,
had run on a platform calling for an immediate ceasefire with
the South and a convention of states "or other peaceable means"
to end the war. McClellan, typically, had tried to straddle the
fence on the issue of a negotiated settlement, publicly repudi-
ating his own party's peace plank while at the same time promising "a spirit of conciliation and compromise" with the same
Confederates his men had slain by the thousands at Mechanics-
ville, Gaines' Mill, Malvern Hill, and Antietam. Ignoring

entirely the Emancipation Proclamation—Democratic campaign literature called it the Miscegenation Proclamation—McClellan declared that "the Union is the one condition of peace—we ask no more."[45]

Unfortunately for McClellan, timely Union victories at Atlanta and in the Shenandoah Valley convinced many previously doubtful Northerners that the war was finally being won, and an avalanche of absentee ballots from soldiers at the front helped turn the tide in several closely contested states. Lincoln won an easy electoral victory, 212 to 21, and the concomitant landslide of triumphant Republican congressional candidates ensured that he would have all the backing he needed to prosecute the war to an unconditional end. Southern leaders, who had hoped against hope for a McClellan victory, were forced to agree with the grim assessment of the *Daily News* (London) that the North was now "silently, calmly, but desperately in earnest" about winning the war.[46]

On one issue, however, there was still an angry divergence of public opinion, and Whitman for once found himself breaking ranks with the Lincoln administration. This was the issue of prisoner exchanges, which George's recent capture had brought home to Whitman personally and painfully. The trading of prisoners back and forth between the two sides had been standard procedure earlier in the war—there was even a fixed rate of exchange: officers were worth between four and sixty times their number in privates, based on an upward-sliding scale of rank. But prisoner exchanges had foundered on the ever troublesome rock of racism. Union authorities insisted that captured black soldiers be treated as legitimate prisoners of war, while

Confederates maintained that they be treated as recovered property. Lincoln's steely secretary of war, Edwin Stanton, took advantage of the impasse by unilaterally suspending all future prisoner exchanges, and Grant supported him wholeheartedly, declaring that "no distinction whatever will be made in the exchange between white and colored prisoners."[47]

This sounded fair enough, but in fact the actions of Grant and Stanton masked a more cold-blooded mathematical calculation: with its much larger pool of prospective soldiers, the North could afford to let some of its men languish in prisoner of war camps if it meant denying the South a fresh influx of returned troops. "It is hard on our men held in Southern prisons not to exchange them," Grant said in one of his typical understatements, "but it is humanity to those left in the ranks to fight our battles. Every man we hold, when released on parole or otherwise, becomes an active soldier against us. . . . If we commence a system of exchange which liberates all prisoners taken, we will have to fight on until the whole South is exterminated."[48]

Northern families like the Whitmans, with relatives trapped in Rebel prisons, understandably disagreed with Grant's heartless, if logical, reasoning. A delegation of concerned clergymen and physicians visited the White House in September 1864 to implore Lincoln to rescind the order. "For God's sake, interpose!" they urged. "We know you can have them exchanged if you give your attention to it. It is simple murder to neglect it longer." Lincoln refused. Meanwhile, Union soldiers at Andersonville, Georgia, the worst Confederate prison camp, were dying at the rate of one man every eleven minutes.[49]

Weeks passed without hearing further word from George; the Whitmans naturally feared the worst. Meanwhile, there were other problems in the Whitman household. Forty-eight-year-old Jesse, after years of progressively worsening mental illness, had finally become completely unmanageable. After his emotional eruption following the death of Andrew, Jesse had been given a wide berth by other members of the family. Mrs. Whitman, with a mother's habitual loyalty, had reassured Walt that although "Jessy is a very great trouble to me to be sure and dont appreceate what i doo for him . . . he is no more deranged than he has been for the last three years[.] i think it would be very bad for him to be put in the lunatic assiliym . . . as long as i can get any thing for him to eat i would rather work and take care of him that is as long as i see no danger of harm." At length, however, even she could see that Jesse was no longer safe to be around, and on December 5, 1864, Walt had Jesse committed to the Kings County Lunatic Asylum in Brooklyn. The cause of his brother's incapacity, Walt told hospital officials, was a fall from a ship's mast, a polite if understandable fiction, given Jesse's syphilitic condition.[50]

Jesse lived in confinement for another five years before dying of a ruptured aneurism. He was buried in a potter's field at the institution on March 22, 1870. Mrs. Whitman, loyal to the last, lamented to Walt: "aint it sad to think the poor sould hadent a friend near him in his last moments and to think he had a paupers grave. . . . i feel very sad of course walt if he has done ever so wrong he was my first born." Walt, who had never much cared for his older brother—Jesse was said to be their father's favorite—did not respond. Years earlier, in *Leaves of Grass*, he had already foreseen his brother's end, comparing it oddly to an urban renewal project:

> I saw the face of the most smear'd and slobbering idiot
>   they had at the asylum,
> And I knew for my consolation what they knew not,
> I knew of the agents that emptied and broke my brother,
> The same wait to clear the rubbish from the fallen
>   tenement,
> And I shall look again in a score or two of ages,
> And I shall meet the real landlord perfect and unharm'd,
>   every inch as good as myself.[51]

What was no doubt a solemn Christmas in the Whitman household was made sadder still by the arrival on December 26 of George's trunk of belongings. The weather itself conspired to dampen the mood. "We have had a wet day with fog, mud, slush, and the yet unmelted hard polished ice liberally left in the streets," Walt confided to his diary. "All sluggish and damp, with a prevailing leaden vapor. Yesterday, Christmas, about the same." The trunk sat unopened for several hours before the family could bring themselves to touch it. "One could not help feeling depressed," Whitman noted. "There were his uniform coat, pants, sash, &c. There were many things reminded us of him. Papers, memoranda, books, nick-nacks, a revolver, a small diary, roll of his company, a case of photographs of his comrades (several of them I knew as killed in battle) with other stuff such as a soldier accumulates. Mother looked everything over, laid out the shirts to be washed, the coats and pants to hang up, & all the rest were carefully put back. It made us feel pretty solemn."[52]

Gloom was quickly replaced by anger when Whitman thought of the plight of all Union prisoners. A special exchange of gravely ill prisoners earlier in the year had first brought to light the horrible conditions in Southern prisoner of war camps, and Whitman as always followed the news accounts closely. Now George was among them, and Walt could not keep silent any longer. "Their situation, as of all men in prison, is indescribably horrible," Whitman wrote. "Hard, ghastly starvation is the rule. Rags, filth, despair in large open stockades, no shelter, no cooking—such the condition of masses of men, in some places two or three thousand, & in the largest prison as high as thirty thousand confined. The guards are insufficient in numbers, & they make it up by treble severity, shooting the prisoners literally just to keep them under terrorism."[53]

The day after the arrival of George's trunk, Walt published a long, angry letter in the *New York Times* and the *Brooklyn Daily Eagle* asserting that "the public mind is deeply excited, and most righteously so, at the starvation of the United States prisoners of war in the hands of the Secessionists." While condemning the Rebel captors for their "dogged sullenness and scoundrelism," the letter placed the chief blame for the men's continued suffering squarely on the head of Secretary of War Stanton. "In my opinion," Whitman wrote, "the Secretary has taken and obstinately held a position of cold-blooded policy . . . more cruel than anything done by the Secessionists. . . . [S]aying he will not exchange at all, unless the Secession leaders will give us, on average terms, all the blacks they capture in military action, the

Secretary has also said . . . that it is not for the benefit of the Government of the United States that the power of the Secessionists should be repleted by some 50,000 men in good condition now in our hands, besides getting relieved of the support of nearly the same number of human wrecks and ruins, of no advantage to us, now in theirs."[54]

The letter also denounced Generals Benjamin Butler and Ethan Allan Hitchcock, the government's acting—or nonacting—prisoner exchange commissioners. Earlier in the war Butler had enjoyed a controversial reign as military governor of Louisiana, during which time he had infuriated the citizens of New Orleans by ordering that any woman found guilty of verbally abusing a Union soldier be publicly branded a prostitute. He was also suspected of widespread financial shenanigans, even to the point of stealing the household silver from the home where he was staying, a charge that earned him the lifelong nickname of "Spoons." Whitman, who had fond memories of his own time in New Orleans, charged that Butler had "incorporated in the question of exchange a needless amount of personal pique, and an unbecoming obstinacy. He, too, has taken his stand on the exchange of all black soldiers, has persisted in it without regard to consequences, and has made the whole of the large and complicated question of general exchange turn upon that one item alone, while it is but a drop in the bucket." As for Hitchcock, the grandson of Revolutionary War hero Ethan Allen, Whitman observed scathingly: "The public may judge what a valuable contribution he brings to this matter of exchange, from a remark he has made not long since, that 'none but cowards are ever taken prisoners in war.' "[55]

Whitman charged that fully one-fourth of the estimated fifty thousand Union soldiers then in confinement had already died after "they were abandoned by their Government, and left to their fate." He concluded: "In my opinion, the anguish and death of these ten to fifteen thousand American young men, with all the added and incalculable sorrow, long drawn out, amid families at home, rests mainly upon the heads of members of our own government; and if they persist, the death of the remainder of the Union prisoners and often worse than death, will be added." If anything, Whitman was too conservative in his estimate: thirteen thousand Union prisoners died at Andersonville alone (out of a total of forty-five thousand), and more than thirty thousand Northerners in all—some 15.5 percent—perished in Rebel prisons during the war.[56]

The angry but perceptive letter had no effect on the government's policy, but it did earn Whitman a commendatory note from William O'Connor, who managed again to overlook his friend's unenlightened racial views. "I saw your letter about the prisoners," O'Connor wrote. "It was as just as powerful. I have been hearing for a fortnight past that it is the Secretary of War's 'policy' which prevents exchange, and if this is true, I pray from my heart of hearts that it never may be forgotten against him. Reddest murder is white to an act like this and its folly is equal to its crime."[57]

That said, O'Connor came to the gist of his letter, which contained the first good news Whitman had received in quite some time. O'Connor, along with their mutual friend Assistant Attorney General J. Hubley Ashton, had interceded in Walt's behalf with W. T. Otto, assistant secretary of the interior, to obtain a berth for him in Otto's department. All Otto required was a formal application written in Whitman's own hand. "Now, dear Walt, do this without delay," O'Connor urged. "Do this as soon as you can. We shall fetch it this time. I have every confidence that you will get a good and easy berth, a regular income, &c, leaving you time to attend to the soldiers, to your poems, &c.—in a word, what Archimedes wanted, a place on which to rest the lever."[58]

After six long months at home recuperating from a mysterious malady, dealing with one brother's mental illness and another's captivity, and attempting all the while to publish his long-delayed book of war poems, Whitman was ready to return to Washington. "I am well but need to leave here—need a change," he admitted to O'Connor. As requested, he sent Otto a formal application, along with a ghostwritten letter of recommendation he had devised from former Brooklyn mayor George Hall that praised (or self-praised) Whitman's "benevolence, righteousness and ardent patriotism," as well as his steadfast Republican voting record. The letter concluded with the statement that Whitman had two brothers in the U.S. Army, which was false, and that the family was poor, which was only too true. Otto quickly replied that Whitman, upon passing a cursory examination, would be appointed to the post of clerk (first-class), with an annual salary of twelve hundred dollars. For someone who had been subsisting for several years on a few dollars a week, it was a fabulous sum, and Whitman felt sufficiently flush to ask O'Connor to find him a new place to live, "irrespective of price."[59]

In a way, that was how he had been living for the past two

years, bravely disregarding the price his hospital service was exacting on his body and mind. With the war now nearing the end, Whitman was eager once more to enter the fray. Much had changed in the six months he had been gone; the balance of power had tilted inexorably toward the North. In the death-haunted trenches at Petersburg, Robert E. Lee's dwindling army shivered and starved in a pitiless siege that now was entering its seventh month, while farther south, in the enemy heartland, William Tecumseh Sherman had just completed his march to the sea, burning and looting like a latter-day Tartar. Victory for the Union was now a mere matter of time. In the skies over Washington, Venus had begun reappearing nightly, unusually bright and clear, while down below Abraham Lincoln was hard at work on his second inaugural address, crafting a promise "to bind up the nation's wounds" through a large-hearted policy of "malice toward none; with charity for all." In dooryards throughout the ravaged land, lilacs would be blooming soon.

CHAPTER SIX

Retrievements
Out of the Night

W hitman returned to Washington on January 23 and immediately assumed his new duties as clerk in the Bureau
of Indian Affairs. Reflecting perhaps the low priority that the
government now placed on its relations with Native Americans,
the bureau was housed in a dusty basement in the northeast
corner of the U.S. Patent Office at 7th and G streets. Exactly
two years earlier, Whitman had first visited the Patent Office
when it was serving as an ad hoc military hospital. Then he had
found it "a strange, solemn and . . . fascinating sight," with
rows of sick and wounded soldiers lying incongruously between
glass display cases "crowded with models in miniature of every
kind of utensil, machine or invention, it ever enter'd into the
mind of man to conceive." Now the soldiers were gone; they
had been replaced by painted delegations of Plains Indians,
buckskin-wearing braves who had come east to parley with

Indian Commissioner William P. Dole over the latest broken treaty or nonarriving annuity. Whitman, styling himself somewhat grandly "the poet-chief," occasionally interrupted his duties to reassure his fellow chiefs that "we are really all the same man and brethren together . . . however different our places, and dress and language." The Indians responded with vague smiles.[1]

Most of his duties were less Olympian in scope. "All I have hitherto employed myself about," he reported to Jeff, "has been making copies of reports & Bids, &c for the office to send up to the Congressional Committee on Indian Affairs." He was taking it easy, he reassured his always fretful younger brother: "The rule is to come at 9 and go at 4—but I don't come at 9, and only stay till 4 when I want, as at present to finish a letter for the mail." Still, after only six days on the job, Whitman had already received his first paycheck. O'Connor had been right—the job was a plum.[2]

Taking a room in the home of an obliging Southern woman named Grayson whose husband and son were off serving in the Confederate Army, the poet resumed his visits to the hospitals. With the stalemate continuing at Petersburg and no major battles being fought between the two armies elsewhere in Virginia, there were fewer casualties arriving from the front; as of December 17, 1864, a total of 9,265 patients remained in seventeen hospitals in the capital. Whitman was determined to go slow—or so he told Jeff on January 30. "I spent yesterday afternoon in Armory Square Hospital," he wrote, "and had a real good time, and the boys had too. Jeff you need not be afraid about my overdoing the matter. I shall go regularly enough, but I shall be on my guard against trouble."³

A week later, however, Whitman advised his friend Abby Price that he was spending most of his Sundays at the hospitals, as well as "a few hours from time to time, & occasionally in the evening" during the week. It was about the same schedule he had always maintained, although now he was perhaps less willing to commit himself emotionally to the men. "It seemed as if a fellow had to be cautious," he told Horace Traubel years later, "not break his nerves down by a too insistent habit: by devotion, days and nights of unutterable anxiety: sitting there by some poor devil destined to go: always in the presence of death." Still, old habits were hard to break, and "what the government didn't get from me in the office it got from me in the hospitals. If there is any balance in that matter I don't imagine it's on my side."⁴

Through it all Walt was distracted by continued worries over George's well-being. In late January the Union and Confederate governments resumed prisoner exchanges after the Rebels agreed to count black soldiers as legitimate prisoners of war, and a few days later Jeff urged Walt to get his friend John Swinton, managing editor of the *New York Times*, to use his influence with General Grant to secure George's release. Swinton was agreeable, although he pointed out that under the new exchange policy "your brother will be at once exchanged in the general mode." Whitman, however, was not so sure. When the first batch of prisoners began arriving by boat at Annapolis from Danville, Virginia, and Salisbury, North Carolina (George's two known places of detention), George was nowhere to be seen. Nearly frantic, Whitman twice went to see General Hitchcock—whom he had savaged in print a few weeks earlier—demanding to know why George was not among those released. Hitchcock, who either had not seen the poet's December 27 letter in the *Times* or else was remarkably tolerant of criticism, agreed to issue a special memorandum for George's release; he summoned an aide to handle the request.[5]

In a fever of uncertainty, Whitman confided to his diary that "these four days have put me through all the changes of hope and dismay about getting George exchanged." Nor was his state of mind notably improved when he went down to Annapolis to see for himself the condition of the arriving prisoners. "Can those be men—those little livid brown, ash-streak'd, monkey-looking dwarfs?" he marvelled; "are they really not mummied, dwindled corpses? They lay there, most of them, quite still, but with a horrible look in their eyes and skinny lips (often with not enough flesh on the lips to cover their teeth). Probably no more appalling sight was ever seen on this earth."[6]

Finally, after weeks of suspense, Walt learned a little anticlimactically that George had indeed been released on February 22 and had been in Annapolis at the same time that Walt was there. The confusion over his release stemmed from the fact that George had been transferred from Danville to Libby Prison in Richmond three days before he was due to be exchanged. George immediately sent word to Mrs. Whitman in Brooklyn, writing with uncharacteristic but understandable high spirits, "I arrived here from the Hotel de Libby, and if ever a poor devil was glad to get in a Christian Country it was me."[7]

Even then, Walt was the last to hear. Mrs. Whitman, apparently assuming that Walt would see George's name in the long list of exchanged prisoners published in the *New York Times* on February 28, neglected to send him word of his brother's return for another week. Then, in her usual morose, uninflected way, she reported: "George has come home came this morning he looks quite thin and shows his prison life but feels pretty well considering what he suffered he was very sick at one time i think it was in january with lung fever he was six weeks in the hospital so bad that the doctor thought he would die."[8]

The day Whitman learned of his brother's release, March 4, 1865, was also the date of Lincoln's second inauguration. Whitman caught sight of the president at various times throughout the day, although he apparently did not attend the inauguration itself. That morning he was sitting in the visitors' gallery in the House of Representatives when a freak thunderstorm startled the sleepy members, who had been up all night concluding the current legislative session. "The slumberers awaked with fear," Whitman reported with some relish; "some started for the doors, some look'd up with blanch'd cheeks and lips to the roof, and little pages began to cry. . . . [T]he storm raged on, beating, dashing, and with loud noises at times. But the House went ahead with its business . . . as calmly and with as much deliberation as at any time in its career. Perhaps the shock did it good."[9]

About noon Whitman went outside—the weather had cleared—to watch the final preparations for a giant pre-inauguration parade, complete with festooned floats and marching troops. He was surprised to see the president come riding alone down Pennsylvania Avenue in his carriage, en route to Capitol Hill to sign some last-minute bills. Unaware of the political motive, Whitman thought Lincoln was simply coming early to his inauguration to avoid "marching in line with the absurd procession, the muslin temple of liberty and pasteboard monitor." At three o'clock, Whitman again saw Lincoln riding down the street; he looked "very much worn and tired; the lines, indeed, of vast responsibilities, intricate questions, and demands of life and death, cut deeper than ever upon his dark brown face; yet all the old goodness, tenderness, sadness, and canny shrewdness, underneath the furrows." By the president's side sat his eleven-year-old son, Tad.[10]

That night Whitman went to the White House and joined the large crush of people clamoring to see the president. The crowd swept Walt along through the Blue Room and the East Room as the Marine Band sawed away at various airs, until at length he caught sight of Lincoln and the First Lady working the receiving line. "I saw Mr. Lincoln, drest all in black, with white gloves and a claw-hammer coat," he reported, "looking very disconsolate, and as if he would give anything to be somewhere else." As always, Whitman did not impose on the president but remained discreetly in the background. He had no way of knowing that this was the last time he would ever see Lincoln.[11]

The streets of Washington thronged with soldiers as the fifth and final spring of the war began. Whitman, passing restlessly from Patent Office to hospital to Burroughs's red-brick home near the Capitol, saw it all. "This city, its suburbs, the capitol, the front of the White House, the places of amusement, the

Avenue, and all the main streets, swarm with soldiers . . . more than ever before," he wrote. "Some are out from the hospitals, some from the neighboring camps, &c. One source or another, they pour plenteously, and make, I should say, the mark'd feature in the human movement and costume-appearance of our national city. Their blue pants and overcoats are everywhere."[12]

The steady erosion of Southern morale was evident in the number of Confederate deserters who were flocking to the city in ever growing numbers. Walt, with his special affinity for Southerners, mingled freely with the deserters, most of whom were poorly clothed and worse fed. "I saw a large procession of young men from the rebel army, (deserters they are call'd, but the usual meaning of the word does not apply to them,) passing along the Avenue today," he wrote. "There were nearly 200 of them, coming up yesterday by boat from James River. I stood and watch'd them as they pass'd along in a slow, tired, worn sort of way. There was a curiously large proportion of light-hair'd, blonde, light gray-eyed young men among them. Their costumes had a dirty-stain'd uniformity; most had been originally gray; some of them had articles of our uniform, pants on one, vest or coat on another . . . As I stood quite close to them, several good looking enough youths, (but O what a tale of misery their appearance told,) nodded or just spoke to me, without doubt divining pity and fatherliness out of my face, for my heart was full enough of it."[13]

Two young brothers from North Carolina, aged seventeen and twenty-five, told him that they were on their way to Missouri; Whitman advised them to seek work on a Northern farm instead. They had been conscripted into the Confederacy along with their four other brothers, three of whom had since died in the war. Now they were down to their last six dollars, which they had raised by selling their tobacco to Union soldiers on the boat ride to Washington; Whitman gave them each "a trifle" to tide them over. He also met a Tennessee boy named John Wormley who had served in the 9th Alabama Regiment. The youth was an orphan who "had the look of one for a long time on a short allowance—said very little—chew'd tobacco at a fearful rate, spitting in proportion—large clear dark-brown eyes, very fine—didn't know what to make of me." Putting aside his misgivings, Wormley told the poet that he wanted some clean underwear and "a chance to wash himself well." Perhaps Whitman took him home; at any rate, "I had the very great pleasure of helping him to accomplish all those wholesome designs."[14]

The hospitals, too, were full of Confederates. Whitman spent many long hours attending the sick Rebels, most of whom were suffering from scurvy and diarrhea. "Pass'd this afternoon among a collection of unusually bad cases, wounded and sick Secession soldiers, left upon our hands," he confided to his diary. "I spent the previous Sunday afternoon there also. At that time two were dying. Two others have died during the week. Several of them are partly deranged. . . . Poor boys, they all needed to be cheer'd up." Like their Northern counterparts, they asked him mainly for postage stamps, paper, and tobacco; one called him over and asked in a whisper what religious denomination he was (the man himself was a Catholic). As usual Whitman finessed the question. "I gave him something to read, and sat down by him for a few minutes. Moved around with a word for each. They were hardly any of them personally attractive cases, and no visitors come here."[15]

A middle-aged Mississippi soldier emaciated by diarrhea caught Whitman's eye "as he lay with his eyes turn'd up, looking like death. His weakness was so extreme that it took a minute or so . . . for him to talk with anything like consecutive meaning; yet he was evidently a man of good intelligence and education. As I said anything, he would lie a moment perfectly still, then, with closed eyes, answer in a low, very slow voice, quite correct and sensible, but in a way and tone that wrung my heart." Gently, Whitman asked him if he had sent home a letter since arriving in Washington. The man could not remember— everything lately seemed like a dream. "Two or three great tears silently flow'd out from the eyes, and roll'd down his temples," Whitman recalled, "he was doubtless unused to be spoken to as I was speaking to him. Sickness, imprisonment, exhaustion, &c., had conquer'd the body, yet the mind held mastery still, and call'd even wandering remembrance back." Whitman wrote letters for two other young Confederates, Thomas J. Byrd of Russell County, Alabama, and John W. Morgan of Brunswick County, North Carolina. Morgan, "a gentle, affectionate boy . . . wish'd me to put in the letter for his mother to kiss his little brother and sister for him." Whitman personally dropped off the letters at the post office the next morning.[16]

Despite the all too familiar scenes of suffering, Whitman felt a new easefulness in the air, symbolized by the brightly looming Venus. The evening star, he said, "seems as if it told something, as if it held rapport indulgent with humanity, with us

Americans. Five or six nights since, it hung close by the moon, then a little past its first quarter. The star was wonderful, the moon like a young mother. The sky, dark blue, the transparent night, the planets, the moderate west wind, the elastic temperature, the miracle of that great star, and the young and swelling moon swimming in the west suffused the soul." A change had come over Whitman as well. Simply put, he had met someone.[17]

The young man's name was Peter Doyle—Pete the Great, he styled himself—and he and Whitman met sometime in the winter of 1865. For the next five years the two would be inseparable. Like most of Whitman's romantic attachments, his relationship with the twenty-one-year-old Doyle began simply and off-handedly. One stormy night the poet was returning from a visit to Burroughs. He had thrown a blanket around his shoulders to ward off the cold, and he clambered aboard a Washington and Georgetown Railroad horsecar for the forty-five-minute ride down Pennsylvania Avenue to his room at 468 M Street. It was late, he was the only passenger, and the young, red-haired conductor immediately noticed his solitary fare—"he seemed like an old sea-captain." Years later Doyle described his first meeting with Whitman as almost an irresistible urge. "We felt [drawn] to each other at once," he recalled. "He was the only passenger, it was a lonely night, so I thought I would go in and talk with him. Something in me made me do it and something in him drew me that way. He used to say there was something in me had the same effect on him. Anyway, I went into the car. We were familiar at once—I put my hand on his knee—we understood." Whitman did not get off at his stop but rode all the way back to the Capitol with Doyle, and "from that time on we were the biggest sort of friends."[18]

Friends quickly noticed the change in Whitman. "A change had come upon him," noted William O'Connor. "The rosy color had died from his face in a clear splendor, and his form, regnant and masculine, was clothed with inspiration, as with a dazzling aureole." Whitman happily explained the difference: "Love, love, love! That includes all. There is nothing in the world but that—nothing in all the world. Better than all is love. Love is better than all." John Burroughs saw Whitman and Doyle riding side by side at the front of the streetcar and immediately formed an impression that "the young conductor [was] evidently his intimate friend." Washington physician William Tindall, who also liked to ride on the front platform of the car, remembered sharing rides with the two. "During the rides with them in which I participated, their conversation, so far as I can remember, consisted of less than fifty words," he recalled. "It was the most taciturn mutual admiration society I ever attended; perhaps because the young Apollo was generally as uninformed as he was handsome, and Whitman's intellectual altitude was too far beyond his understanding to be reached by his apprehension or expressed in his vocabulary. The fellowship was a typical manifestation of the unconscious deference which mediocrity pays to genius, and of the restfulness which genius sometimes finds in the companionship of an opposite type of mentality."[19]

Like so many of the rootless young men in Washington that spring, Doyle was a Confederate deserter—although in his case he had been in the capital for two years by then. A native of Limerick, Ireland, he had immigrated to America with his parents in 1852, settling first in Alexandria, Virginia. His father, Peter Doyle, Sr., was a blacksmith, and the family relocated to Richmond a few years before the Civil War. Young Doyle enlisted in the Richmond Fayette Artillery (named in honor of the Marquis de Lafayette) on April 25, 1861, eight days after Virginia voted to secede from the Union. It was his first tenuous connection to Whitman, who cherished his own childhood memory of being lifted out of the crowd by Lafayette during the Frenchman's 1825 visit to Brooklyn.[20]

Doyle was one of 108 enlisted men in the company, and one of ten Irish nationals. The men, serving four six-pounder cannons, two ten-pounder Parrot guns and one twelve-pounder howitzer, saw a good of action during Union general George McClellan's Peninsula campaign in the spring of 1862, fighting at Yorktown, Williamsburg, Seven Pines, Gaines' Mill, Frayser's Farm, and Malvern Hill. Forty-eight members of the company were killed, wounded, missing, or hospitalized during the campaign. Two months later the company was transferred to the division of Major General Lafayette McLaws and subsequently fought at South Mountain, Harpers Ferry, and Antietam during Lee's ill-advised invasion of Maryland. At the latter battle Doyle was wounded and sent to a hospital in Richmond to recuperate. While there he formally petitioned the Confederate secretary of war to be released from his military duties, on the somewhat dubious grounds that he planned to return to Ireland "as soon as an opportunity will afford his doing so." Doyle was granted the discharge on November 7, 1862.[21]

Instead of returning to Ireland, which he never intended to do in the first place, Doyle hung around Richmond for several months before being arrested for desertion in March 1863 and ordered to return to his company. It is unclear whether the arrest was a simple clerical error or part of an official crackdown on foreign-born residents illegally claiming exemption from Confederate service, but at any rate Doyle did not report to his old unit. Instead, he was arrested by Union authorities while attempting to cross Federal lines at Petersburg, where he had gone to receive further medical treatment, and on April 18 he was confined in the Old Capitol Prison at Washington. While he languished there his relatives appealed to the British foreign minister, Lord Lyons, in Doyle's behalf, and Secretary of State William Henry Seward personally looked into the case and found somewhat charitably that Doyle was one of several "poor Irishmen who fled from Richmond to avoid starvation." On May 11 Doyle was released from prison after taking an oath—in his case no doubt superfluous—not to rejoin the Confederacy, and he began working as a smith's helper at the Washington Navy Yard. He was moonlighting as a streetcar conductor when he first met Walt Whitman.[22]

Sunny, good-natured Peter Doyle was a welcome change from the tight-lipped, suffering soldiers in the hospitals, and Whitman took to him immediately. The pair rode up and down Pennsylvania Avenue on Doyle's streetcar, went for long walks in the woods outside the city, and prowled the waterfront in Alexandria. At night, after Doyle was through with his run, they would retire to the bar at the Union Hotel, which had reverted to its prewar status as a popular watering hole after serving for two years as a hospital. "It was our practice to go to a hotel on Washington Avenue after I was done with my car," Doyle recollected. "Like as not I would go to sleep—lay my head on my hands on the table. Walt would sit there, wait, watch, keep me undisturbed—would wake me up when the hour of closing came."[23]

Years later, autographing a copy of his book *Specimen Days* for Doyle, Whitman remembered warmly their days together: "Pete do you remember—(of course you do—I do well)—those great long jovial walks we had . . . out of Washington City—often moonlight nights, 'way to 'Good Hope'; or, Sundays, up and down the Potomac shores, one side or the other, sometimes ten miles at a stretch? Or when you work'd on the horse-cars, and I waited for you, coming home late together—or resting chatting at the Market, corner 7th Street and the Avenue, and eating those nice musk or watermelons?"[24]

Pete did remember, telling Horace Traubel thirty years later that he and Whitman "were awful close together. In the afternoon I would go up to the Treasury building and wait for him to get through if he was busy, then we'd stroll out together, often without any plan, going where we happened to get. . . . We took great walks together—off towards or to Alexandria, often. We went plodding along the road, Walt always whistling or singing. We would talk of ordinary matters. He would recite poetry, especially Shakespeare—he would hum airs or shout in the woods. He was always active, happy, cheerful, good-natured. . . . We would tackle the farmers who came into town, buy a water-melon, sit down on the cellar door of Bacon's grocery, Seventh and Pennsylvania Avenue, halve it and eat it. Peo-

ple would go by and laugh. Walt would only smile and say,
'They can have the laugh—we have the melon.' "25

In mid-March 1865 Whitman left Doyle behind and went
home to Brooklyn on furlough from the Bureau of Indian
Affairs. He intended to use his visit to reunite with George,
who was still recuperating from his harrowing imprisonment,
and also to arrange for the publication, at long last, of *Drum-
Taps*. George was in "fair condition," Walt reported to the
O'Connors, but "his legs are affected—it seems to me it is rheumatism, following the fever he had." George was also exhibiting
all the signs of post-traumatic stress disorder. "He goes to bed
quite sleepy & falls to sleep," Walt noted, "but then soon wakes,
& frequently little or no sleep that night—he most always leaves
the bed, & comes downstairs, & passes the night on the sofa."26

Perhaps to buoy his brother's spirits, Whitman wrote a long,
complimentary account of George's war experience for the
Brooklyn Daily Union. Published on March 16, 1865, under the
heading, "Return of a Brooklyn Veteran," the piece celebrated
George's service from his first battle at Roanoke, North Carolina, in February 1862 to his capture at Poplar Grove Church in
September 1864, after which "he had now to endure that worst
part of a soldier's experience of life—if that can be called life,
which is worse than death—in one after another of the Confederate States military prisons; a series of many weary months
of starvation, humiliation, and every pressure on body and
spirit, of which the world knows too well." If George was
suffering from survivor's guilt, it is no wonder: of all the regiment's officers who began the war, Walt said, "not a single one
remains; and not a dozen out over a thousand of the rank and

file. Most of his comrades have fallen by death." George's own return, said his brother, was nothing short of a miracle.[27]

While Whitman was home in Brooklyn, the war in Virginia played out its hand. On the first day of April Major General Phil Sheridan's dismounted cavalry, supported by Gouverneur K. Warren's 5th Corps infantry, overwhelmed the Confederate right at Five Forks, capturing more than five thousand prisoners and paving the way for an all-out assault on Petersburg the next morning. As Grant's emboldened soldiers poured over the Rebel trenches, sending Lee and his surviving forces fleeing westward in a desperate attempt to escape to North Carolina and link up with General Joseph E. Johnston's equally harried army, Jefferson Davis and his cabinet caught the last train leaving the Confederate capital. Two days later Abraham Lincoln, guarded by a skeleton crew of ten rifle-bearing Union sailors, sailed into Richmond aboard a humble barge and walked the streets in quiet triumph. "Thank God I have lived to see this," he exclaimed. "It seems to me that I have been dreaming a horrid dream for four years, and now the nightmare is gone."[28]

Five days later Lee surrendered to Grant at Appomattox, and the war for all intents and purposes was over. Surprisingly, Whitman did not take special note of the war's end, although he did allow to O'Connor that "the grand culminations of last week" had impressed him with a renewed sense of national destiny. Off in Brooklyn, he missed the nine hundred-gun salute that rang out in Washington following the fall of Richmond and the five hundred-gun salute that signaled Lee's surrender a week later and smashed windows all over Lafayette Square. Nor did he take part in — or at any rate memorialize in writing — the raucous celebration that emptied the stores and houses in New York and sent the brokers on Wall Street falling into each other's arms on the confetti-strewn floor of the Stock Exchange. Perhaps, like George, he was simply worn out by the war; more likely he was preoccupied with his ongoing efforts to shepherd *Drum-Taps* into final printed form.[29]

On April 1, the same day that Phil Sheridan was driving the last nail into the coffin of George Pickett's military reputation at Five Forks, Whitman signed a contract with New York printer Peter Eckler to produce five hundred copies of *Drum-Taps*. He had already drafted an advertising flyer for the volume listing forty-seven new poems and promising a revised edition of *Leaves of Grass* sometime in the near future. *Drum-Taps*, he told O'Connor with authorial pride, was "in my opinion superior to Leaves of Grass—certainly more perfect as a work of art." The ordinary reader, he said, might think the poems "let loose with wildest abandon, [but] the true artist can see it is yet under control." The new poems, he felt, delivered on his ambition "to express in a poem (& in the way I like, which is not at all by directly stating it) the pending action of this *Time & Land we swim in*, with all their large conflicting fluctuations of despair & hope, the shiftings, masses, & the whirl & deafening din . . . the unprecedented anguish of wounded & suffering, the beautiful young men, in wholesale death & agony, everything sometimes as if in blood color, & dripping blood. The book is therefore unprecedentedly sad, (as these days are, are they not?)—but it also has the blast of the trumpet, & the drum pounds & whirrs in it, & then an undertone of sweetest comradeship & human love, threading its steady thread inside the chaos, & heard at every lull & interstice thereof . . . clear notes of faith & triumph."[30]

The triumph, if not the faith, was short lived. Whitman had wheedled from Otto an extra two weeks of furlough, and he was home with his mother on Portland Avenue when the early editions of the day's newspapers landed on their doorstep on the morning of April 15, 1865. Almost simultaneously church bells began tolling all across the city—Abraham Lincoln was dead. The Whitmans, like millions of other Americans, received the news in stunned silence. "Mother prepared breakfast—and other meals afterwards," Whitman recalled, "but not a mouthful was eaten all day by either of us. We each drank half a cup of coffee; that was all. Little was said. We got every newspaper morning and evening, and the frequent extras of that period, and pass'd them silently to each other."[31]

Back in Washington Peter Doyle had been among those in attendance at Ford's Theatre that fatal night and had seen the assassin, John Wilkes Booth, jump down from the presidential box, catch his foot on the red-white-and-blue bunting, and crash heavily to the stage. Doyle had not been able to make out what Booth shouted—"*Sic semper tyrannis!*"—over the general hub-bub, but he had lingered in the theater in a sort of daze until a furious Union soldier accosted him with the warning, "Get out of here! we're going to burn this damned building down!" "If that is so I'll get out," Doyle responded sensibly.[32]

Years later, preparing an account of the assassination for a series of lectures on Lincoln, Whitman drew freely from Doyle's eyewitness account of the tragedy. He also drew on a lengthy, if vicarious, association of his own with the celebrated first family of American drama. He had long admired John Wilkes Booth's father, Junius Brutus Booth, whose acting genius, Whitman said, "was to me one of the grandest revelations of my life, a lesson of artistic expression." The elder Booth, a certified madman, appealed to Whitman as an intuitive artist who dared to break the formalized tradition of stage acting that Americans had inherited secondhand from the British. "He stood out 'himself alone' in many respects beyond any of his kind on record," Whitman wrote of Booth, "and with effects and ways that broke through all rules and all traditions"—which is to say, he acted the same way that Whitman wrote. The son too had scattered moments of inspiration but failed to match his father's towering genius. Often considered the handsomest man in America, John Wilkes Booth shared Whitman's taste in Shakespeare—each man's favorite play was *Richard III*—and the actor used a line from the play to advertise his performances, "I am myself alone," which might well have served as a four-word synopsis of *Leaves of Grass*.[33]

With his lifelong love of theatrics, Whitman found the assassination fascinating on a number of levels. Not only was the president himself "the leading actor in the greatest and stormiest drama known to real history's stage," but his ebony-eyed assassin had become in life what he had been only fitfully in his art, a romantic villain of Shakespearean proportions: "And so the figure, Booth, the murderer, dress'd in plain black broadcloth, bare-headed, with a full head of glossy, raven hair, and his eyes like some mad animal's flashing with light and resolution, yet with a certain strange calmness, holds aloft in one hand a large knife . . . turns fully toward the audience his face of statuesque beauty, lit by those basilisk eyes, flashing with desperation, per-haps insanity—launches out in a firm and steady voice the words, *Sic semper tyrannis*—and then walks with neither slow nor very rapid pace across to the back of the stage, and disappears."[34]

The sense of Lincoln's murder as a dramatic set piece came later; at the time Whitman was as shocked and depressed as everyone else. He rose from his untouched breakfast that after-noon and caught the Brooklyn ferry into Manhattan, where he walked up and down a nearly deserted Broadway in a dripping rainstorm past shuttered storefronts draped in mourning. Thousands of sodden American flags, which the day before had flown in triumph from porches and rooftops, had been lowered to half-mast, and the boats crossing the East River trailed be-hind them long black pennants. Everywhere Whitman sensed a "strange mixture of horror, fury, tenderness, & a stirring of wonder." Nature herself, in pathetic fallacy, mirrored the mood of the populace, showing "long broad black clouds like great serpents slowly undulating in every direction."[35]

The next day Whitman began putting Lincoln's death into perspective. The dead president, he noted, "leaves for America's history and biography . . . not only its most dramatic reminis-cence—he leaves, in my opinion, the greatest, best, most char-acteristic, artistic, moral personality. . . . The tragic splendor of his death, purging, illuminating all, throws round his form, his head, an aureole that will remain and will grow brighter through time, while history lives, and love of country lives. By many has this Union been help'd; but if one name, one man, must be pick'd out, he, most of all, is the conservator of it, to

the future. He was assassinated—but the Union is not assassinated. . . . [T]he Nation is immortal."³⁶

Following the murderous events of Good Friday, Walt remained in New York for another week, probably to watch over
George, whom he had persuaded with some difficulty—George
was being "sulky" again—to ask for an extension of his medical
furlough. Then, too, Walt was unsure what to do about *Drum-
Taps* in the wake of the assassination. He dashed off a short,
rather uninspired poem, "Hush'd Be the Camps To-day," which
he took to the printer's on April 19 for insertion into the book.
But it was a poor stopgap, as even Whitman must have sensed,
for after giving Bradstreet's Bindery another twenty dollars on
April 21 in partial payment, he apparently decided to shelve the
book until he could complete a more suitable tribute to the
president. The next day he returned to Washington, thus managing to miss not only the public funeral service at the White
House and the ceremonial lying in state at the Capitol rotunda
on April 19 but also the passage of the president's funeral train
through New York City on April 24. Henceforth, Walt would
do his mourning alone.

The weather in Washington was almost insupportably beautiful. Venus still loomed brightly over the capital, and the soft,
cloying scent of lilacs filled the air. "The season being advanced,
there were many lilacs in full bloom," Whitman noted. "By one
of those caprices that enter and give tinge to events without
being at all a part of them, I find myself always reminded of
the great tragedy of that day by the sight and odor of these
blossoms. It never fails." The national press, in its nonstop cov-
erage of Lincoln's funeral cortege back to Springfield, Illinois,

also made much of the fact that great sprays of lilac covered the president's coffin as it sat side-by-side with the exhumed coffin of his favorite son, Willie, who had died in the White House of typhoid fever three years earlier. In Whitman's mind the ubiquitous flower became inextricably linked with Lincoln's death.[37]

There were other, less celebrated deaths that spring. Despite the end of the shooting war, the hospitals were more crowded than ever, with the sick outnumbering the wounded two-to-one. On May 1, at Armory Square, Whitman witnessed the death of Corporal Frank H. Irwin of the 93rd Pennsylvania Infantry. Irwin had been wounded in the left knee in a skirmish near Fort Fisher, Virginia, on March 25. Two weeks later his leg was amputated. At first the young man seemed to be doing well. Then, in the usual, depressing way of so many cases, Irwin suddenly sickened and died of pyemia. His death occasioned one of the last, and most poignant, of Whitman's wartime letters of condolence.

"Frank," he wrote to Mrs. Irwin, "was so good and well-behaved, and affectionate, I myself liked him very much. I was in the habit of coming in the afternoons and sitting by him, and soothing him, and he liked to have me—liked to put his arm out and lay his hand on my knee—would keep it so a long while. Toward the last he was more restless and flighty at night—often fancied himself with his regiment—by his talk sometimes seem'd as if his feelings were hurt by being blamed by his officers for something he was entirely innocent of—said, 'I never in my life was thought capable of such a thing, and never was.' At other times he would fancy himself talking as it seem'd to children or such like, his relatives I suppose, and giving them good advice; would talk to them a long while. All the time he was out of his head not one single bad word or thought or idea escaped him. It was remark'd that many a man's conversation in his senses was not half as good as Frank's delirium.

"He was perfectly willing to die—he had become very weak and had suffer'd a good deal, and was perfectly resign'd, poor boy. I do not know his past life, but I feel as if it must have been good. At any rate what I saw of him here, under the most trying circumstances, with a painful wound, and among strangers, I can say that he behaved so brave, so composed, and so sweet and affectionate, it could not be surpass'd. And now like many other noble and good men, after serving his country as a soldier, he has yielded up his young life at the very outset in her service. . . . I thought perhaps a few words, though from a stranger, about your son, from one who was with him at the last, might be worthwhile, for I loved the young man, though I but saw him immediately to lose him. I am merely a friend visiting the Hospitals to cheer the wounded and sick."[38]

Another dead young man, another stranger loved and lost—it put Whitman in mind of all "the unknown dead . . . the unrecorded, the heroes so sweet & tender . . . the unreturned, the sons of the mothers." His own mother's son had returned from the war more or less in one piece, and now George had rejoined his regiment as it camped outside of Washington preparatory to the Grand Review of the victorious Union armies through the capital on May 23 and 24. Once again, and for the last time, Washington was awash in troops. "The city is full of soldiers, running around loose," Whitman reported. "Officers everywhere, of all grades. All have the weather-beaten look of practical service. It is a sight I never tire of. . . . You see them swarming like bees everywhere."[39]

Upwards of two hundred thousand soldiers in the Armies of the Potomac and the Tennessee had gathered to march triumphantly past their new commander in chief, Andrew Johnson, and a packed reviewing stand of generals, politicians, diplomats, bureaucrats, socialites, family members, and assorted hangers-on. The parade route stretched the length of Pennsylvania Avenue from the Capitol to the presidential box betweeen 15th and 17th streets. Across the street in Lafayette Square three other stands were reserved for less exalted dignitaries, including one that was specially set aside for wounded soldiers from the various hospitals.

The Army of the Potomac, having doggedly protected the capital and striven with Robert E. Lee and his legion of accomplished man-killers for four long and grueling years, opened the review on May 23. Major General George Gordon Meade, its vinegary commander, led the way, followed by a seven-mile-long procession of the Cavalry Corps. George Armstrong Custer, at the head of the 3rd Division, stole the show, galloping bareheaded past the reviewing stand, his long blond hair streaming behind him, atop a suspiciously "runaway" horse. The 51st New York, with the newly promoted Major George Whitman back in its ranks, marched in a place of honor alongside the rest of the 9th Corps. Behind each infantry brigade came six mule-drawn army ambulances, their bloodstained stretchers strapped to their sides in graphic, if mute, recognition of the human cost underlying the triumph being celebrated that day.[40]

The next day belonged to Major General William Sherman and his western army. The ever touchy Sherman, his nerves further exacerbated by the recent controversy surrounding his supposedly too generous surrender terms to General Joseph Johnston's Confederate army in North Carolina, worried aloud that his "tatterdemalion" troops would make a poor showing after the spit-and-polish grandeur of Meade's Potomac veterans. He needn't have worried. The tanned and rangy westerners stole the show, marching along with easy grace behind bullet-shredded banners bearing the names of their already legendary battles: Shiloh, Stones River, Vicksburg, Chickamauga, Chattanooga, Missionary Ridge, Kennesaw Mountain, Peachtree Creek. A particular highlight was the antic performance of the regimental bummers who accompanied each unit with a squawking menagerie of chickens, ducks, pigs, and cows "borrowed" from local farms in shameless emulation of their less fraternal borrowings from Georgia civilians a few months before.[41]

Whitman, as usual, was in the forefront of the crowd. For once, mere words almost failed him; the Grand Review, he told his mother, "was too much & too impressive to be described." Nevertheless he tried, recalling for her the "solid rank of soldiers, 20 or 25 abreast, just marching steadily all day long for two days without intermission, one regiment after another, real war-worn soldiers, that have been marching & fighting for years . . . mostly all good-looking hardy young men . . . all sunburnt — nearly every one with some old tatter all in shreds (that *had been* a costly and beautiful *flag*)." Apparently he had taken a position near the presidential reviewing stand, since he reported seeing

Johnson, Grant, Meade, Stanton and "lots of other celebrated government officers & generals" during the review. But the poet of the people did not forget his roots—"the *rank & file* was the greatest sight of all." Walt also caught a glimpse of George as he marched by, but did not have a chance to speak to him.[42]

In all, some 342 infantry regiments, 27 cavalry regiments, and 44 artillery batteries, together with assorted engineers, signal corpsmen, ambulance drivers, provost marshals, and black civilian pioneers, tramped past the reviewing stands in a remarkable show of military might. Such an army, marveled the Prussian ambassador to Washington, could whip the world. Indeed, it was a testament to the individual fighting prowess and sheer Rebel cussedness of their Confederate opponents that it had taken these proud Union soldiers four long years to whip the South. But whip it they had, and soon they would be going home, demobilized from an army that, as Sherman told his troops in parting, had "done all that men could do" to ensure that "our Government stands vindicated before the world."[43]

With its formal sense of closure, the Grand Review appealed to Whitman on an artistic as well as a patriotic level. He quickly wrote two new poems commemorating the event, "How Solemn as One by One" and "Spirit Whose Work Is Done," each of which was subtitled, "Washington City, 1865." The poems, although not truly companion pieces, show similar signs of the conflicting emotions that whipsawed their author at the end of the war. The first reveals the intense psychic connection that Whitman felt to the men in the ranks as he watched them file past:

How solemn the thought of my whispering soul to each in
the ranks, and to you,
I see behind each mask that wonder a kindred soul,
O the bullet could never kill what you really are, dear
friend,
Nor the bayonet stab what you really are;
The soul! yourself I see, great as any, good as the best,
Waiting secure and content, which the bullet could never
kill,
Nor the bayonet stab O friend.[44]

Bullets and bayonets may not have killed the souls of the
men, but the poet had seen enough suffering in the hospitals to
know what the war could do to a person's psyche. Mindful
perhaps of his brother's difficult readjustment to civilian life after his months in a Rebel prison, Whitman invoked the "spirit
of dreadful hours" that still flitted "like a tireless phantom"
above the ranks of the returning veterans. As the soldiers passed
on, leaving him to watch them receding into the distance, Whitman offered himself as a sort of surrogate sacrifice to the malign
gods of war:

Spirit of hours I knew, all hectic red one day, but pale as
death next day,
Touch my mouth ere you depart, press my lips close,
Leave me your pulses of rage—bequeath them to me—fill
me with currents convulsive,

Let them scorch and blister out of my chants when you are
gone,
Let them identify you to the future in these songs.[45]

By assuming the spirit of the "war now closed," the poet also
assumed the responsibility of perpetuating its hideous truths,
even if talking of those "dreadful hours" might "scorch and blister" his own mouth. Whitman soon undertook to speak of, and
for, the martyred president as well. In the quickening heat of
early summer, walking the woods with Peter Doyle, John Burroughs, or Thomas Proctor, a fellow New Yorker who kept a
room in the same Tenth Street boardinghouse where Lincoln
had been carried from Ford's Theatre to die, the poet rehearsed
the lines of a slowly forming elegy. As he had done throughout
his career, he took his cues from nature, trusting in the common
forms of earth for his inspiration. In Venus, the western star,
he found the physical objectification of Lincoln the man of the
West. The heart-shaped leaves of the lilac bush, so prominent
that spring when Lincoln died, symbolized the love the poet
felt for the fallen president. And in the quicksilver song of the
hermit thrush, a solitary singer whose lonely ways Whitman had
learned firsthand from Burroughs, he began to make out the
subtle notes of a murmuring chant that was at once sorrowful,
ecstatic, consoling, and welcoming: the high holy song of death.

All summer long he worked on the poem, which he planned
to include in a short sequel to *Drum-Taps* that he could append
to the unbound sheets already stored at the printer's. The
poem's title was also its first line: "When Lilacs Last in the
Dooryard Bloom'd." It came together slowly but easily in the

unforced rhythms of the natural world, a threnody not just for
Abraham Lincoln but for all the bruised and broken young men
who over the past four years had given their lives to the Union
cause. It was also, in a way, an elegy for the poet himself. Like
Lincoln, Whitman too had come a long way from that distant
afternoon in February 1861 when he first had seen the president-
elect emerge from his carriage at the Astor House. Together
they had suffered through "the foulest crime in history known
in any land or age," a heartbreaking civil war that filled the
hospitals of the capital with the ruined bodies of beautiful
young soldiers. In the end the war had claimed Lincoln as well,
on Easter eve, and it had also taken away a fundamental part of
the poet himself, the part that believed in the blissful love
of comrades as a working model for the American republic.
That republic, he had come to understand, had been purchased
with the dearest coin of the realm: the very lifeblood of its
sons.[46]

The poem was saturated with death. It found its voice in the
song of the thrush, "song of the bleeding throat/Death's outlet
song of life," which carried from the swamp down the winding
way that the president's funeral procession followed on its journey home:

Coffin that passes through lanes and streets,
Through day and night with the great cloud darkening the
    land,
With the pomp of the inloop'd flags with the cities draped
    in black,

With the show of the States themselves as of crape-veil'd
    women standing,
With processions long and winding and the flambeaus of
    the night,
With the countless torches lit, with the silent sea of faces
    and the unbared heads,
With the waiting depot, the arriving coffin, and the sombre
    faces,
With dirges through the night, with the thousand voices
    rising strong and solemn,
With all the mournful voices of the dirges pour'd around
    the coffin,
The dim-lit churches and the shuddering organs—where
    amid these you journey,
With the tolling tolling bells' perpetual clang,
Here, coffin that slowly passes,
I give you my sprig of lilac.[47]

The humble gift, like the poet's heart, was given not just to
the president, but to all the dead young men whose hands he
had held during the past three years as they waited so calmly
and courageously for death:

(Nor for you, for one alone,
Blossoms and branches green to coffins all I bring

     . . .

All over bouquets of roses,
O death, I cover you over with roses and early lilies,

But mostly and now the lilac that blooms the first,
Copious I break, I break the sprigs from the bushes,
With loaded arms I come, pouring for you,
For you and the coffins all of you O death.)[48]

Even in the midst of returning spring, at a time when the soldiers were marching home to resume—as well as they could—their former lives, the poet cannot escape "death, its thought, and the sacred knowledge of death." He has seen too much to be content, as he previously was content in *Leaves of Grass*, with the joyous cataloging of life in all its variegated forms. Instead, he must wait in "the hiding receiving night" to hear once more the "carol of death":

Come lovely and soothing death,
Undulate round the world, serenely arriving, arriving,
In the day, in the night, to all, to each,
Sooner or later delicate death.

Prais'd be the fathomless universe,
For life and joy, and for objects and knowledge curious,
And for love, sweet love—but praise! praise! praise!
For the sure-enwinding arms of cool-enfolding death.[49]

In the bird's song the poet relives the many deaths he has witnessed personally and the battle scenes he has known vicariously:

And I saw askant the armies,
I saw as in noiseless dreams hundreds of battle-flags,

Borne through the smoke of the battles and pierc'd with
   missiles I saw them,
And carried hither and yon through the smoke, and torn
   and bloody,
And at last but a few shreds left on the staffs, (and all in
   silence,)
And the staffs all splinter'd and broken.

I saw battle-corpses, myriads of them,
And the white skeletons of young men, I saw them,
I saw the debris and debris of all the slain soldiers of the
   war.[50]

Ultimately, however, it is not the dead he is seeing, in all
their familiar agony, but a new vision of peace and calm:

I saw they were not as was thought,
They themselves were fully at rest, they suffer'd not.[51]

And it is this reassuring vision that enables the poet at last
to let go of his grief, to "unloos[e] the hold of my comrades'
hands" and leave the death-haunted woods forever, taking with
him only his "retrievements out of the night," the memories of
the dead soldiers and their dead commander, "the sweetest, wisest soul of all my days and lands."[52]

"When Lilacs Last in the Dooryard Bloom'd" was a triumph,
the last great poem of Whitman's career, and it was with a sense
of proud accomplishment that he sent it off to New York for

inclusion in *Drum-Taps*, which was finally released with a twenty-four-page insert, "Sequel to Drum-Taps," in October 1865. The book now totaled seventy-one poems, tracing the war as Whitman had seen it, from the first brief flush of patriotic optimism on the streets of New York, through the strangely solemn soldiers' camps in Virginia, to the pain-wracked hospitals of the faithful but sorrowing "Wound-Dresser" in Washington. It had indeed been, as one poem put it, "A March in the Ranks Hard-Prest, and the Road Unknown." Now the war was over, and all that remained for the poet to do was to whisper at last the "word over all, beautiful as the sky"—reconciliation. The man who had known "many a soldier's kiss . . . on these bearded lips," had one kiss left to bestow:

> For my enemy is dead, a man divine as myself is dead,
> I look where he lies white-faced and still in the coffin—I
> draw near,
> Bend down and touch lightly with my lips the white face
> in the coffin.[53]

With the publication of *Drum-Taps*, Whitman closed the book, so to speak, on his Civil War career, although, faithful to the end, he continued visiting Harewood, the last remaining wartime hospital, until it closed in April 1866. By then he had been sacked from his job in the Bureau of Indian Affairs by an overzealous new secretary of the interior, James Harlan, for allegedly setting a poor example—morally, physically, and politically—for the other clerks. His sudden firing was scarcely more than an inconvenience to Whitman (his friend J. Hubley Ashton found him another job, in the attorney general's office, within a day), but it occasioned an impassioned defense by his self-appointed champion, William O'Connor. *The Good Gray Poet*, a forty-six-page panegyric to Whitman's selfless Civil War service, came out in January 1866, and although it did not create quite the sense of public outrage that its author intended at the time, it did serve to fix in place a favorable image of Whitman that endures unchanged to the present day.

With its catchy title and fervid, overheated prose, O'Connor's pamphlet was the opening shot in a decades-long battle by Whitman's supporters to enshrine the poet in the pantheon of spotless American heroes. Saluting Whitman as "one of the greatest of the sons of men," O'Connor painted a highly sub-jective portrait of his friend. Ignoring the fact that Harlan had fired a number of other Indian Bureau employees at the same time that he fired Whitman, including Commissioner James Dole, O'Connor portrayed the firing as a "peculiar wrong" com-mitted against Whitman alone. In O'Connor's imaginative re-telling, Harlan becomes Whitman's Pontius Pilate, cruelly de-livering the poet into the hands of those who would judge him "a brute, a scallawag, and a criminal." Against these harsh judg-ments O'Connor set his own view: "For solid nobleness of char-acter, for native elegance and delicacy of soul, for a courtesy which is the very passion of thoughtful kindness and forbear-ance, for his tender and paternal respect and manly honor for woman, for love and heroism carried into the pettiest details of life, and for a large and homely beauty of manners, which makes the civilities of parlors fantastic and puerile in comparison, Walt

Whitman deserves to be considered the grandest gentleman that treads this continent."⁵⁴

The Good Gray Poet—particularly its title—defined Whitman for an entire generation of American readers. In a larger sense, however, Whitman did not need O'Connor's special pleading to cement his place in the history of the war or the affections of the soldiers he encountered during its course. The soldiers themselves, those who survived, kept his memory evergreen within them. They were his truest legacy. In letter after letter they addressed him variously as "dear friend," "dear comrade," "kind uncle," "dear brother," "dear father," "esteemed friend," or simply "dear Walt." They wrote to tell him the progress of their lives—their wives and children, their successes and failures, their travels and travails, their health, their politics, their dreams. But mostly they wrote to tell him their love. One-legged Lewy Brown, embarked on his own fifty-year career with the paymaster's division of the Treasury Department, spoke for them all when he told Whitman: "There is many a soldier now that never thinks of you but with emotions of the greatest gratitude & I know that the soldiers that you have bin so kind to have a great big warm place in their heart for you. I never think of you but it makes my heart glad to think that I have bin permitted to know one so good."⁵⁵

Whitman received dozens of such letters in the decades following the Civil War. The letters he probably treasured most were those from soldiers he had not known so intimately as he knew Lewy Brown, but who nevertheless still remembered him fondly and had taken steps to ensure that others would remember him as well. "You stated in your [letter] that you hoped that I had not forgotten you," William H. Millis wrote to Whitman on January 12, 1865, from Ward M of Armory Square Hospital, where he was recovering from a bullet wound to the chest. "I never will forget you so long as life should last. . . . May god bless you forever I cant find words to tell you the love their is in me for you. I hope you & I may live to meet again on this earth if not I hope will shall meet in the world where there is no more parting." Ten years later Millis wrote again, this time from his home in Dover, Delaware: "Again I take the time & privilege of droping a few lines to tell you that we have not forgotten you & want to hear from you. We have had a son borned since we heard from you & We call him Walter Whitman Millis in honer to you for Love for you."[56]

A series of letters also arrived from Benton H. Wilson, a Syracuse, New York, piano maker who, like Millis, had met Whitman while confined to Armory Square Hospital. Wilson, a former color-bearer for the 185th New York, wanted to tell Whitman about "our Baby Walt." At regular intervals during the baby's first three years Wilson kept the poet up-to-date with his namesake's modest but steady progress. "My little baby Walt is well & Bright as a dollar," he reported proudly in October 1868. Other letters described the child variously as "a fine boy . . . full of fun & rather quick tempered . . . quite a big Boy . . . full of mischief, he can walk all around the house & yard & talk very little." By December 1869, his father said, little Walt was "just getting interesting he runs all around and is beginning to talk quite plainly." Wilson offered to send Whitman a photograph of the child "& then you can judge for yourself. I wish you could see him."[57]

Whitman never did make it up to Syracuse for a visit, but one likes to imagine that somehow, if only in his mind's eye, he did catch a glimpse of towheaded little Walt Whitman Wilson, happily playing in his father's backyard, as far away from "war's hell-scenes" as it was possible to get. He had seen such a child many years before—the child was him—and perhaps for one last time he saw him again:

> There was a child went forth every day,
> And the first object he look'd upon, that object he became,
> And that object became part of him for the day or a certain
> part of the day,
> Or for many years or stretching cycles of years.
>
> The early lilacs became part of this child,
> And grass and white and red morning-glories . . .
> . . .
> These became part of that child who went forth every day,
> and who now goes, and will always go forth every day.[58]

Now the child had many names—Oscar and Stewart, Erastus and Frank, Johnny and Thomas and Frederick and Lorenzo and Charles. They were all there with him, at the end of his life, as he had been there with them at the end of theirs, a great mothering sort of man, a bearded stranger hovering near, at peace in a country that was once more at peace with itself.

Lose Not My Sons

Whitman never forgot his soldier boys, but as the war receded into the past, he sometimes despaired that the nation as a whole had already forgotten them. These were the years of the Gilded Age, when the courage and compassion engendered by the war gave way to a scarcely less savage — if considerably less noble — fight for money, power, and social position. Like other thoughtful Americans, Whitman watched with a sort of wondering disgust "the almost maniacal appetitite for wealth prevalent in the United States." Taking his cue from the Scottish writer Thomas Carlyle, who savagely mocked the descent of democratic Britain into "blockheadism, gullibility, bribeability, amenability to beer and balderdash," Whitman saw a similar decline at work in America. "Society in these States is canker'd, crude, superstitious, and rotten," he declared. "The spectacle is appalling. We live in an atmosphere of hypocrisy throughout. . . . The depravity of the business classes of our country is not less than has been supposed, but infinitely greater. The official services of America, national, state, and municipal . . . are saturated in corruption, bribery, falsehood, maladministration. . . . The best class we show, is but a mob of fashionably dress'd speculators and vulgarians. . . . It is as if we were somehow being endow'd with a vast and more and more thoroughly appointed body, and then left with little or no soul."[1]

In his poetry, too, Whitman attacked the postwar climate of graft and malaise. In a telling addition to his 1856 jeremiad, "Respondez!", he thundered:

> Stifled, O days! O lands! in every public and private
> corruption!
> Smother'd in thievery, impotence, shamelessness, mountain-
> high;
> Brazen effrontery, scheming, rolling like ocean's waves
> around and upon you, O my days! my lands!
> For not even those thunderstorms, nor fiercest lightnings
> of the war, have purified the atmosphere.[2]

And in another poem of the same period, he could scarcely bring himself to read the morning newspaper, filled as it was with lurid accounts of governmental misbehavior:

> Nay, tell me not to-day the publish'd shame,
> Read not to-day the journal's crowded page,

The merciless reports still branding forehead after forehead.
The guilty column following guilty column.[3]

For Whitman himself, the postwar years were a time of sudden, then steady, physical decline. On January 23, 1873, while
working late at his office in the Treasury Building, he suffered
a devastating stroke that left him partially paralyzed. With the
help of such old friends as Nelly O'Connor, Peter Doyle, John
Burroughs, and Charlie Eldridge, he struggled slowly to get
better, only to be staggered anew by the death of his beloved
mother four months later. Once more he rallied, getting out of
his sickbed to attend her funeral, but after the twin shocks of
1873 he was never again entirely well. He moved into his brother
George's home in Camden, New Jersey, across the Delaware
River from Philadelphia, and there in a little upstairs room he
kept watch on an increasingly heedless nation. In the short space
of a single decade, the war and its heroes seemed virtually
forgotten.

"Future years will never know the seething hell and the black
infernal background . . . of the Secession War," he fretted in his
long-promised reminiscence, *Memoranda During the War*, published finally in 1875. "In the mushy influences of current times
the fervid atmosphere and typical events of those years are in
danger of being totally forgotten." Already the events of the
war had lost their direct personal connection to the people, he
complained, "and the living heat and excitement of their own
times are being marshalled for casting . . . into the cold and
bloodless electrotype plates of History. . . . [T]he embers of
them are already dying embers, and a few more winters and

summers, a few more rains and snows, will surely quench their fires, and leave them only as a far off memory."[4]

For the poet himself, the war and its memories were never far away. As his health declined and he rapidly fell into a somewhat premature old age, Whitman could still take heart in the unsurpassed example of the common soldiers of the Civil War, the ardent young men who "sprang at the first tap of the drum, to arms—not for gain, nor even glory, nor to repel invasion— but for an emblem, a mere abstraction—for the life, the safety of the flag." Looking again at the bloodstained notebooks he had kept at his side in the hospitals, he marveled anew at their undiminished hold over his emotions. "Even these days, at the lapse of so many years, I can never turn their tiny leaves, or even take one in my hand, without the actual army sights and hot emotions of the time rushing like a river in full tide through me," he said. "Each line, each scrawl, each memorandum, has its history. Some pang of anguish—some tragedy, profounder than ever poet wrote."[5]

He worried, perhaps presciently, that "the real war will never get in the books," and yet he continued writing about it to the end of his days. Books, poems, essays, letters, newspaper articles all sprang unstoppably from his pen. Like the mystical "Mother of All" whom he invoked in the poem "Pensive on Her Dead Gazing," he implored his forgetful fellow citizens: "Lose not my sons, lose not an atom." He willed himself to perform a lifelong act of memory; his paper-strewn room was filled with ghosts. One of his last poems, written when he was seventy-one, depicts him sitting alone at twilight in front of a fire:

Musing on long-pass'd war-scenes — of the countless buried
   unknown soldiers,
Of the vacant names, as unindented air's and sea's — the un-
   return'd . . .

                     . . .

(Even here in my room-shadows and half-lights in the
   noiseless flickering flames,
Again I see the stalwart ranks on-filing, rising — I hear the
   rhythmic tramp of the armies;)
You million unwrit names all, all — you dark bequest from
   all the war,
A special verse for you — a flash of duty long neglected —
   your mystic roll strangely gather'd here,
Each name recall'd by me from out the darkness and
   death's ashes,
Henceforth to be, deep, deep within my heart recording,
   for many a future year,
Your mystic roll entire of unknown names, or North or
   South,
Embalm'd with love in this twilight song.[6]

Each April 15, when he was able, he made it a point
to deliver a memorial lecture on the anniversary of Abraham
Lincoln's death. His last such appearance came in 1890, less than
two years before his own demise. Still weakened by a lengthy
bout of influenza, the poet had to be helped up the stairs to the
second-floor meeting hall of the Philadelphia Art Gallery, where
a crowd of some four hundred onlookers awaited his arrival.

The audience, which included his longtime critic Thomas Wentworth Higginson, listened patiently as he read from a sheaf of crumpled papers while sitting at a tiny roundtop table decorated, appropriately enough, with a spray of lilacs. It was his standard talk, ranging from his first brief glimpse of Lincoln in New York City in February 1861 to the president's assassination, based largely on Peter Doyle's eyewitness account, at Ford's Theatre in April 1865. He closed, as always, with an emotional recitation of his most popular, if personally his least favorite, poem, "O Captain! My Captain!". And perhaps at this last performance, with his own death settling slowly upon him like the fraying shawl he wore draped across his shoulders, the poem's opening lines spoke to him with particular poignancy:

> O Captain! my Captain! our fearful trip is done,
> The ship has weather'd every rack, the prize we sought is
>   won.[7]

Afterward he confided to Horace Traubel: "We got home *trim*: it was a good ride, both ways. . . . We held our chin up very well. The thing we ought to felicitate ourselves on, is, that we didn't give out altogether—that we came out of it alive! It was a good trip: I enjoyed it: it was a full breath—a new aroma." The same could have been said of his time in Washington, when compelled by a strange unspoken need he had enlisted vicariously in the great army of the sick and so discovered, almost by accident, a new vocation: "I am he bringing help for the sick as they pant on their backs." He had promised once to write "the evangel-poem of comrades and of love," and true to his calling he had kept his word, down all the sad declining years that followed. The Civil War, he insisted, "proved Humanity, and proved America." It also proved him. His service in the hospitals tested him physically, mentally, spiritually, and artistically. He did not give out. And now, back home in the lengthening Camden twilight, a quarter of a century removed from the suffering and sorrow of the hospitals, he could truly say to his familiar ghosts:

> The moon gives you light,
> And the bugles and the drums give you music,
> And my heart, O my soldiers, my veterans,
> My heart gives you love.[8]

NOTES

Introduction: The Medicine of Daily Affection

1 Horace Traubel, *With Walt Whitman in Camden*, 9 vols. (New York: D. Appleton, 1908), 2:402.

2 T. W. Higginson, "Unmanly Manhood," *The Woman's Journal* 12 (February 1882): 33. Traubel, *With Walt Whitman*, 2:46–47. Clara Barrus, *Whitman and Burroughs, Comrades* (Boston: Houghton Mifflin, 1931), 339.

3 Traubel, *With Walt Whitman*, 3:582.

4 Justin Kaplan, *Walt Whitman: A Life* (New York: Simon and Schuster, 1980), 275.

5 Edwin Haviland Miller, ed., *Walt Whitman: The Correspondence*, 6 vols. (New York: New York University Press, 1961–77), 1:111, 159. Hereafter cited as *Correspondence*.

6 Floyd Stovall, ed., *Walt Whitman: Prose Works 1892*, 2 vols. (New York: New York University Press, 1963–64), 1:81, 114–15. Hereafter cited as *Prose Works*. Sculley Bradley and Harold W. Blodgett, eds., *Leaves of Grass* (New York: W. W. Norton, 1973), 66. Hereafter cited as *Leaves*.

Chapter One: New York Stagnation

1 David S. Reynolds, *Walt Whitman's America: A Cultural Biography* (New York: Alfred A. Knopf, 1995), 405.

2 James M. McPherson, *Battle Cry of Freedom: The Civil War Era* (New York: Oxford University Press, 1988), 247.

3 *Correspondence*, 1:61, 41. *Leaves*, 448.

4 *Leaves*, 608–609.

5 *Leaves*, 609. Roy P. Basler, ed., *The Collected Works of Abraham Lincoln*, 8 vols. (New Brunswick, N.J.: Rutgers University Press, 1953), 4:271.

6 Kaplan, *Walt Whitman*, 55. Reynolds, *Walt Whitman's America*, 14–15.

7 *Leaves*, 741, 52, 28, 17.

8 David Herbert Donald, *Lincoln* (New York: Simon and Schuster, 1995), 273–78. *Prose Works*, 2:499.

9 *Prose Works*, 2:499–501.

10 Edward F. Grier, ed., *Walt Whitman: Notebooks and Unpublished Prose Manuscripts*, 6 vols. (New York: New York University Press, 1984), 6:2121–26. Hereafter cited as *Notebooks*.

11 *Notebooks*, 6:2121.

12 *Leaves*, 591–93.

13 Albert Parry, *Garrets and Pretenders: A History of Bohemia in America* (New York: Covici, Friede, 1933), 22–23. See also Christine Stansell, "Whitman at Pfaff's: Commercial Culture, Literary Life and New York Bohemia at Mid-Century," *Walt Whitman Quarterly Review* 10 (Winter 1993): 107–23.

14 Parry, *Garrets and Pretenders*, 44–46.

15 Traubel, *With Walt Whitman*, 3:118.

16 *Saturday Press*, November 12, 1859. Traubel, *With Walt Whitman*, 1:236.

17 Parry, *Garrets and Pretenders*, 16, 28.

18 Kaplan, *Walt Whitman*, 243–44.

19 Quoted in Kaplan, *Walt Whitman*, 244. Traubel, *With Walt Whitman*, 3:117. Parry, *Garrets and Pretenders*, 35–37.

20 Kaplan, *Walt Whitman*, 243, 246. Parry, *Garrets and Pretenders*, 41. Traubel, *With Walt Whitman*, 3:116–17.

21 *Leaves*, 660–61.

22 Parry, *Garrets and Pretenders*, 54.

23 Parry, *Garrets and Pretenders*, 47, 55.

24 Traubel, *With Walt Whitman*, 1:56. Kaplan, *Walt Whitman*, 293–95.

25 Reynolds, *Walt Whitman's America*, 409.

26 *Notebooks*, 1:405.

27 Reynolds, *Walt Whitman's America*, 69–76. Quoted in Kaplan, *Walt Whitman*, 236. *Leaves*, 132.

28 *Leaves*, 386.

29 *Leaves*, 596.

30 *Leaves*, 134. For Fred Vaughan, see Charley Shively, ed., *Calamus Lovers:*

Walt Whitman's Working-Class Camerados (San Francisco: Gay Sunshine Press, 1987), 36–50.

31 Charles I. Glicksberg, "Walt Whitman in 1862," *American Literature* 6 (November 1934): 275–80.

32 *Leaves*, 126–27

33 *Leaves*, 133.

34 John H. Johnston, *Diary Notes of a Visit to Walt Whitman and Some of His Friends, in 1890* (Boston: T. Brimelow, 1890), 99–100.

35 *Prose Works*, 2:180. Kaplan, *Walt Whitman*, 266. Glicksberg, "Walt Whitman in 1862," 278.

36 Reynolds, *Walt Whitman's America*, 106.

37 Charles I. Glicksberg, ed., *Walt Whitman and the Civil War* (Philadelphia: University of Pennsylvania Press, 1933), 24, 44–45.

38 Glicksberg, *Walt Whitman*, 27–29.

39 Glicksberg, *Walt Whitman*, 41.

40 Glicksberg, *Walt Whitman*, 42–43. Jerome Loving, *Walt Whitman: The Song of Himself* (Berkeley: University of California Press, 1999), 260–61.

41 Emory Holloway, "Whitman Pursued," *American Literature* 27 (March 1955): 6. See also Edwin Haviland Miller, "Walt Whitman and Ellen Eyre," *American Literature* 33 (March 1961): 64–65.

42 Holloway, "Whitman Pursued," 6.

43 Glicksberg, "Walt Whitman in 1862," 276.

44 D. B. St. John Roosa, "Walt Whitman," *New York Mail and Express*, June 10, 1896.

45 Glicksberg, *Walt Whitman*, 30, 44–45.

46 Roosa, "Walt Whitman."

47 John Townsend Trowbridge, *My Own Story* (Boston: Houghton Mifflin, 1903), 362.

48 John Burroughs, *Whitman: A Study* (Boston: Houghton Mifflin, 1896), 27. Edward Carpenter, *Days with Walt Whitman* (London: George Allen, 1906), 42–43. *Correspondence*, 3:266. *Leaves*, 32.

49 Walt Whitman, *Memoranda During the War* (Old Saybrook, Conn.: Globe Pequot Press, reprinted 1993), 60. Hereafter cited as *Memoranda*.

50 Quoted in Kaplan, *Walt Whitman*, 262. *Memoranda*, 60.

51 Memoranda, 60. *Correspondence* 1:57. Jerome M. Loving, ed., *Civil War Letters of George Washington Whitman* (Durham, N.C.: Duke University Press, 1975), 40. Hereafter cited as *Civil War Letters*.

52 *Memoranda*, 61–62.

53 *Leaves*, 283.

54 *Leaves*, 282.

55 *Leaves*, 280.

56 *Leaves*, 281.

57 *Leaves*, 309.

58 Glicksberg, *Walt Whitman*, 18, 42.

59 Kaplan, *Walt Whitman*, 268. *Civil War Letters*, 67.

60 *Civil War Letters*, 74.

61 Kaplan, *Walt Whitman*, 268. *Correspondence*, 1:61.

Chapter Two: A Sight in Camp

1 *Correspondence*, 1:58. Quoted in Reynolds, *Walt Whitman's America*, 411.

2 *Correspondence*, 1:58.

3 Kaplan, *Walt Whitman*, 268.

4 *Civil War Letters*, 77, 152. *Correspondence*, 1:58.

5 *Civil War Letters*, xii, 137.

6 *Correspondence*, 1:58. *Memoranda*, 6.

7 Moncure D. Conway, *Autobiography: Memories and Experiences*, 2 vols. (Boston: Houghton Mifflin, 1904), 1:356. Stephen B. Oates, *A Woman of Valor: Clara Barton and the Civil War* (New York: Free Press, 1994), 103, 110–11.

8 Oates, *Woman of Valor*, 3, 7, 25. The married colonel was John J. Elwell of Cleveland, Ohio. For his affair with Barton, see Oates, 148–154.

9 Oates, *Woman of Valor*, 11, 32.

10 *Correspondence*, 1:58.

11 *Civil War Letters*, 75, 77.

12 *Correspondence*, 1:58. Glicksberg, *Walt Whitman*, 68.

13 Glicksberg, *Walt Whitman*, 68–71. The Forbes drawing is reproduced in Charley Shively, ed., *Drum Beats: Walt Whitman's Civil War Boy Lovers* (San Francisco: Gay Sunshine Press, 1989), 15.

14 Quoted in Shelby Foote, *The Civil War: A Narrative*, 3 vols. (New York: Random House, 1958–74), 2:44.

15 Edward J. Stackpole, *The Fredericksburg Campaign* (Harrisburg, Pa.: Stackpole Books, 1957), 239. *Civil War Letters*, 152. *Correspondence*, 1:68, 81. Quoted in McPherson, *Battle Cry of Freedom*, 574.

16 Glicksberg, *Walt Whitman*, 69, 74–75.

17 Quoted in Oates, *Woman of Valor*, 114.

18 Glicksberg, *Walt Whitman*, 73–74, 79.
19 *Leaves*, 306–307.
20 Robert B. Sweet, "A Writer Looks at Whitman's 'A Sight in Camp in the Daybreak Gray and Dim,' " *Walt Whitman Review* 17 (June 1971): 58.
21 Patricia L. Faust, ed., *Historical Times Illustrated History of the Civil War* (New York: Harper & Row, 1986), 599. Glicksberg, *Walt Whitman*, 68.
22 Glicksberg, *Walt Whitman*, 70.
23 *Memoranda*, 6.
24 Quoted in Robert E. Denney, *Civil War Medicine: Care & Comfort of the Wounded* (New York: Sterling Publishing, 1995), 180–81.
25 Glicksberg, *Walt Whitman*, 67, 69–70.
26 *Memoranda*, 6–7.
27 George Worthington Adams, *Doctors in Blue: The Medical History of the Union Army in the Civil War* (Baton Rouge: Louisiana State University Press, 1971), 75–76.
28 Adams, *Doctors in Blue*, 76–77, 86–87.
29 Glicksberg, *Walt Whitman*, 73.
30 Glicksberg, *Walt Whitman*, 81. *Leaves*, 300.
31 Glicksberg, *Walt Whitman*, 68, 73–75.
32 *Leaves*, 667–68.
33 Glicksberg, *Walt Whitman*, 70, 80–81.
34 Glicksberg, *Walt Whitman*, 81.
35 Traubel, *With Walt Whitman*, 2:157, 279. *Memoranda*, 7.
36 *Memoranda*, 7.
37 Ellen M. Calder, "Personal Recollections of Walt Whitman," *Atlantic Monthly* 99 (June 1907): 825.
38 Calder, "Personal Recollections," 826.
39 Calder, "Personal Recollections," 825. *Correspondence*, 1:60.
40 Florence B. Freedman, "W. D. O'Connor: Whitman's 'Chosen Knight,' " *Walt Whitman Review* 27 (September 1981): 100. For O'Connor, see Jerome Loving, *Walt Whitman's Champion: William Douglas O'Connor* (College Station, Tex.: Texas A&M University Press, 1978).
41 Florence B. Freedman, "New Light on an Old Quarrel: Walt Whitman and William Douglas O'Connor 1872," *Walt Whitman Review* 11 (June 1965): 28, 30.
42 Kaplan, *Walt Whitman*, 288.
43 Kaplan, *Walt Whitman*, 287. Freedman, "New Light on an Old Quarrel," 29–30, 39.

44 Quoted in Reynolds, *Walt Whitman's America*, 232. Loving, *Walt Whitman's Champion*, 144.

45 Traubel, *With Walt Whitman*, 3:525–26. *Leaves*, 67.

Chapter Three: The Great Army of the Sick

1 *Correspondence*, 1:59.

2 *Correspondence*, 1:61.

3 *Correspondence*, 1:65–66.

4 Quoted in Barrus, *Whitman and Burroughs*, 10.

5 Basler, *Collected Works of Abraham Lincoln*, 5:318–19. Donald, *Lincoln*, 362–65.

6 Basler, *Collected Works of Abraham Lincoln*, 5:529. *Civil War Letters*, 71.

7 Quoted in Loving, *Walt Whitman's Champion*, 38.

8 *Prose Works*, 2:580. *Leaves*, 145. Emory Holloway and Vernolian Schwartz, eds., *I Sit and Look Out: Editorials from the Brooklyn Daily Times* (New York: AMS Press, 1966), 90.

9 Traubel, *With Walt Whitman*, 6:323. Quoted in Reynolds, *Walt Whitman's America*, 470.

10 Freedman, "New Light on an Old Quarrel," 30. Thomas L. Brasher, *Whitman as Editor of the Brooklyn Daily Eagle* (Detroit: Wayne State University Press, 1970), 164. *Notebooks*, 1:69.

11 Traubel, *With Walt Whitman*, 3:43, 7:158. *Leaves*, 173.

12 *Correspondence*, 1:61.

13 *Correspondence*, 1:61. *Massachusetts Soldiers, Sailors, and Marines in the Civil War* (Norwood, Mass.: Norwood Press, 1932), 291–93.

14 Walt Whitman, "The Great Army of the Sick," *New York Times*, February 26, 1863, reprinted in Richard M. Bucke, ed., *The Wound Dresser: A Series of Letters Written in Washington During the War of Rebellion* (Boston: Small, Maynard, 1898), 5–6.

15 Whitman, "The Great Army of the Sick," 6.

16 Whitman, "The Great Army of the Sick," 7.

17 Whitman, "The Great Army of the Sick," 7–8.

18 Calder, "Personal Recollections," 828.

19 Kaplan, *Walt Whitman*, 273.

20 Calder, "Personal Recollections," 828–29.

21 Calder, "Personal Recollections," 829. Traubel, *With Walt Whitman*, 7:189, 3:77–78.

22 *Medical and Surgical History of the War of the Rebellion*, 6 vols. (Washington, D.C.: Government Printing Office, 1875–85), 1:98. Adams, *Doctors in Blue*, 154.

23 Adams, *Doctors in Blue*, 194–203.

24 Adams, *Doctors in Blue*, 49–51, 224. See also Frank R. Freemon, *Gangrene and Glory: Medical Care during the American Civil War* (Cranbury, N.J.: Associated University Presses, 1998), 19–26.

25 Adams, *Doctors in Blue*, 203, 226–28. See also Stewart Brooks, *Civil War Medicine* (Springfield, Ill.: Charles C. Thomas, 1966), 106–21.

26 Adams, *Doctors in Blue*, 38–39.

27 Adams, *Doctors in Blue*, 38. Martha Saxton, *Louisa May: A Modern Biography of Louisa May Alcott* (Boston: Houghton Mifflin, 1977), 251–68.

28 Adams, *Doctors in Blue*, 112–14. Brooks, *Civil War Medicine*, 74–75.

29 Brooks, *Civil War Medicine*, 75. Adams, *Doctors in Blue*, 117.

30 W. W. Keen, "Military Surgery in 1861 and 1918," *Annals of the American Academy of Political and Social Science* 80 (1918): 14–15.

31 Adams, *Doctors in Blue*, 138–39.

32 Quoted in Adams, *Doctors in Blue*, 139.

33 Adams, *Doctors in Blue*, 141–42. H. H. Cunningham, *Doctors in Gray* (Baton Rouge: Louisiana State University Press, 1958), 237–38.

34 Cunningham, *Doctors in Gray*, 238–41. Brooks, *Civil War Medicine*, 83–84.

35 Cunningham, *Doctors in Gray*, 240.

36 *Correspondence*, 1:69.

37 *Correspondence*, 1:69. Traubel, *With Walt Whitman*, 1:332–33.

38 Traubel, *With Walt Whitman*, 6:194. *Correspondence*, 1:77.

39 Traubel, *With Walt Whitman*, 4:195. For the modern gay perspective, see Shively, *Drum Beats*, 50–70, and Shively, *Calamus Lovers*, 63–70.

40 *Leaves*, 73–74.

41 *Leaves*, 310.

42 *Leaves*, 34–35.

43 *Memoranda*, 18.

44 *Correspondence*, 1:89.

45 Walt Whitman, "Life Among Fifty Thousand Soldiers," reprinted in Bucke, *The Wound Dresser*, 14–15. *Memoranda*, 12.

46 *Correspondence*, 1:81.

47 Whitman, "The Great Army of the Sick," 2–3.

48 Whitman, "The Great Army of the Sick," 8–9.

49 Quoted in Bell Irvin Wiley, *The Life of Billy Yank: The Common Soldier*

of the Union (Baton Rouge: Louisiana State University Press, 1952), 149–50.

50 Glicksberg, *Walt Whitman*, 171–72. Quoted in Kaplan, *Walt Whitman*, 275.

51 Richard Hinton, "Washington Letter," *Cincinnati Commercial*, August 26, 1871.

52 George Frederickson, *The Inner Civil War: Northern Intellectuals and the Crisis of the Union* (New York: Harper & Row, 1965), 90. *Correspondence*, 1:110–11.

53 Quoted in Kaplan, *Walt Whitman*, 276. Whitman, "Life Among Fifty Thousand Soldiers," 12–13.

54 *Correspondence*, 1:73–74.

55 Traubel, *With Walt Whitman*, 1:416, 3:77.

56 Whitman, "Life Among Fifty Thousand Soldiers," 17.

57 Whitman, "Life Among Fifty Thousand Soldiers," 17–18.

58 Adams, *Doctors in Blue*, 184–85.

59 Adams, *Doctors in Blue*, 187–88. Brooks, *Civil War Medicine*, 61–62. Gary L. Todd, "An Invalid Corps," *Civil War Times Illustrated* (December 1985): 10–19.

60 Glicksberg, *Walt Whitman*, 82, 168.

61 *Memoranda*, 16–17.

62 *Memoranda*, 37.

63 Mark H. Dunkelman, "Oscar Wilber," *America's Civil War* (November 1996): 8–18, 86–88.

64 *Memoranda*, 21.

65 *Memoranda*, 13.

66 *Correspondence*, 1:97–98.

67 *Correspondence*, 1:100.

68 Calder, "Personal Recollections," 832. William Sloane Kennedy, *Reminiscences of Walt Whitman* (Paisley, Scotland: Alexander Gardner, 1896), 34–35. Traubel, *With Walt Whitman*, 3:293.

69 *Correspondence*, 1:105–106, 111, 115.

70 *Correspondence*, 1:81–82.

71 *Leaves*, 310–11.

Chapter Four: The Real Precious & Royal Ones of This Land

1 *Memoranda*, 16–18.

2 Calder, "Personal Recollections," 831. *Correspondence*, 1:105.

3 *Correspondence*, 1:111–12.

4 *Correspondence*, 1:112. Quoted in Shively, *Drum Beats*, 115–16.

5 *Prose Works*, 1:155.

6 *Prose Works*, 1:155. *Correspondence*, 1:119.

7 *Correspondence*, 1:127–28.

8 *Correspondence*, 1:128–29.

9 *Leaves*, 451.

10 *Leaves*, 536.

11 *Correspondence*, 1:118n.

12 Glicksberg, *Walt Whitman*, 132. *Correspondence*, 1:90–91.

13 *Correspondence*, 1:93.

14 *Correspondence*, 1:90–91n.

15 *Correspondence*, 1:93.

16 *Correspondence*, 1:106, 107, 139.

17 *Correspondence*, 1:181, 186.

18 *Correspondence*, 1:110, 114. *Memoranda*, 18.

19 *Correspondence*, 1:113.

20 McPherson, *Battle Cry of Freedom*, 609–11. Faust, *Illustrated Encyclopedia of the Civil War*, 225–26.

21 *Leaves*, 9. *Correspondence*, 1:117, 136.

22 Dennis Berthold and Kenneth M. Price, eds., *Dear Brother Walt: Letters of Thomas Jefferson Whitman* (Kent, Ohio: Kent State University Press, 1984), 65–66. *Civil War Letters*, 102. Kaplan, *Walt Whitman*, 292.

23 *Prose Works*, 2:587–89.

24 *Correspondence*, 1:212.

25 Quoted in Shively, *Drum Beats*, 120. *Correspondence*, 1:121, 134.

26 *Correspondence*, 1:112, 136, 137, 141, 173.

27 *Correspondence*, 1:130, 137, 169.

28 *Prose Works*, 2:617.

29 *Prose Works*, 2:618.

30 Bucke, *The Wound Dresser*, 111. *Correspondence*, 1:157.

31 Traubel, *With Walt Whitman*, 2:137.

32 *Correspondence*, 1:143.

33 *Correspondence*, 1:69.

34 *Correspondence*, 1:171.

35 *Correspondence*, 1:171–72.

36 *Memoranda*, 27. Glicksberg, *Walt Whitman*, 138.

37 *Memoranda*, 34.

38 *Correspondence*, 1:142, 168.

39 Traubel, *With Walt Whitman*, 2:397. John Townsend Trowbridge, "Reminiscences of Walt Whitman," *Atlantic Monthly* 89 (February 1902): 170–71.

40 *Correspondence*, 1:80. Glicksberg, *Walt Whitman*, 138.

41 Edward J. Renehan, Jr., *John Burroughs: An American Naturalist* (Post Mills, Vt.: Chelsea Green, 1992), 51, 57.

42 Barrus, *Whitman and Burroughs*, 7. Quoted in Kaplan, *Walt Whitman*, 307. Clara Barrus, *The Life and Letters of John Burroughs*, 2 vols. (Boston: Houghton Mifflin, 1925), 1:107.

43 John Burroughs, *Notes on Walt Whitman as Poet and Person* (New York: American Book Company, 1867), 13. Barrus, *Life and Letters*, 108.

44 Barrus, *Life and Letters*, 108–109.

45 Renehan, *John Burroughs*, 77.

46 Quoted in Barrus, *Whitman and Burroughs*, 110.

47 Barrus, *Life and Letters*, 109–110.

48 *Correspondence*, 1:179, 183.

49 *Correspondence*, 1:184. Kaplan, *Walt Whitman*, 236.

50 *Correspondence*, 1:181, 185.

51 *Correspondence*, 1:187.

52 *Correspondence*, 1:187.

53 Quoted in Shively, *Calamus Lovers*, 79, 84.

54 Clarence Gohdes and Rollo G. Silver, eds., *Faint Clews & Indirections: Manuscripts of Walt Whitman and His Family* (Durham, N.C.: Duke University Press, 1949), 187–90. Berthold and Price, *Dear Brother Walt*, 85.

55 Berthold and Price, *Dear Brother Walt*, 85. Randall H. Waldron, ed., *Letters of Martha Mitchell Whitman* (New York: New York University Press, 1977), 32–36. *Correspondence*, 1:189.

56 Calder, "Personal Recollections," 830.

57 Calder, "Personal Recollections," 831.

Chapter Five: The Melancholy Tide

1 *Notebooks*, 2:669.

2 *Notebooks*, 2:669.

3 Glicksberg, *Walt Whitman*, 156–57. *Correspondence*, 1:194.

4 John M. Taylor, *Garfield of Ohio: The Available Man* (New York: W. W. Norton, 1970), 275–78. *Leaves*, 500. Traubel, *With Walt Whitman*, 3:130.

5 Renehan, *John Burroughs*, 77.

6 Renehan, *John Burroughs*, 78–79.

7 *Correspondence*, 1:234n. See also Freedman, "New Light on An Old Quarrel," 44–47.

8 *Correspondence*, 1:193.

9 Quoted in Bruce Catton, *A Stillness at Appomattox* (New York: Washington Square Press, 1958), 28–29. McPherson, *Battle Cry of Freedom*, 719–20.

10 *Correspondence*, 1:196.

11 *Correspondence*, 1:196.

12 *Memoranda*, 29.

13 *Leaves*, 301.

14 *Correspondence*, 1:197. *Leaves*, 317.

15 *Correspondence*, 1:197–98.

16 *Correspondence*, 1:197–98. Traubel, *With Walt Whitman*, 3:293.

17 *Correspondence*, 1:205.

18 *Correspondence*, 1:204.

19 *Correspondence*, 1:205.

20 *Correspondence*, 1:206.

21 McPherson, *Battle Cry of Freedom*, 722.

22 *Correspondence*, 1:211–12.

23 Noah Andre Trudeau, *Bloody Roads South* (Boston: Little, Brown, 1989), 116. See also Roy Morris, Jr., "Titans Clash in the Wilderness," *Military History* (April 1997): 43–56.

24 *Correspondence*, 1:219–21.

25 *Correspondence*, 1:223–24. *Leaves*, 484.

26 *Civil War Letters*, 119n.

27 Walt Whitman, "Visits Among Army Hospitals," *New York Times*, December 11, 1864, reprinted in Bucke, *The Wound Dresser*, 37. *Memoranda*, 32.

28 *Correspondence*, 1:225.

29 *Correspondence*, 1:218n, 229, 231.

30 *Correspondence*, 1:230. Trudeau, *Bloody Roads South*, 304, 322.

31 Catton, *Stillness at Appomattox*, 192. Donald, *Lincoln*, 513. *Correspondence*, 1:231.

32 *Correspondence*, 1:228, 230, 232.

33 *Correspondence*, 1:233.

34 Kaplan, *Walt Whitman*, 295–96. *Correspondence*, 1:324.

35 *Correspondence*, 1:236, 238, 239n.

36 Reynolds, *Walt Whitman's America*, 310, 457. *Correspondence*, 1:239. Traubel, *With Walt Whitman*, 3:338–39.

37 Shively, *Calamus Lovers*, 86. McPherson, *Battle Cry of Freedom*, 756–57.

38 Barrus, *Whitman and Burroughs*, 19. Donald, *Lincoln*, 519.

39 *Correspondence*, 1:240–41.

40 Whitman, "Visits Among Army Hospitals," 41.

41 *Civil War Letters*, 133.

42 *Civil War Letters*, 18. *Correspondence*, 1:243.

43 *Correspondence*, 1:243n.

44 Walt Whitman, "The Fifty-First New York City Veterans," *New York Times*, October 29, 1864, reprinted in Emory Holloway, ed., *The Uncollected Poetry and Prose of Walt Whitman*. 2 vols. (New York: Peter Smith Press, 1921), 2:37–41.

45 *Correspondence*, 1:241. Stephen W. Sears, *George McClellan: The Young Napoleon* (New York: Ticknor & Fields, 1988), 372–76.

46 Sears, *George McClellan*, 385. McPherson, *Battle Cry of Freedom*, 806.

47 McPherson, *Battle Cry of Freedom*, 793.

48 McPherson, *Battle Cry of Freedom*, 799.

49 McPherson, *Battle Cry of Freedom*, 798.

50 Gay Wilson Allen, *The Solitary Singer: A Critical Biography of Walt Whitman* (New York: New York University Press, 1955), 308, 318.

51 Allen, *The Solitary Singer*, 419. *Leaves*, 465–66.

52 Allen, *The Solitary Singer*, 318–19.

53 *Civil War Letters*, 20.

54 Glicksberg, *Walt Whitman*, 178–79.

55 Glicksberg, *Walt Whitman*, 180.

56 Glicksberg, *Walt Whitman*, 180. McPherson, *Battle Cry of Freedom*, 803.

57 Traubel, *With Walt Whitman*, 2:402.

58 Traubel, *With Walt Whitman*, 2:401.

59 Traubel, *With Walt Whitman*, 2:399. *Correspondence*, 1:247, 249.

Chapter Six: Retrievements Out of the Night

1 *Memoranda*, 10. Kaplan, *Walt Whitman*, 298. See also Dixon Wecter, "Walt Whitman as Civil Servant," *PMLA* 58 (December 1943): 1094–97.

2 *Correspondence*, 1:250.

3 *Correspondence*, 1:250.

4 *Correspondence*, 1:253. Traubel, *With Walt Whitman*, 3:538, 541–42.

5 Traubel, *With Walt Whitman*, 2:426–27. Glicksberg, *Walt Whitman*, 180–81.

6 *Civil War Letters*, 23. *Memoranda*, 50.

7 *Civil War Letters*, 134.

8 *Civil War Letters*, 24.

9 *Memoranda*, 45.

10 *Memoranda*, 42.

11 *Memoranda*, 43.

12 *Memoranda*, 38.

13 *Memoranda*, 40.

14 *Memoranda*, 41–42.

15 *Prose Works*, 2:622–23.

16 *Prose Works*, 2:623–24.

17 *Memoranda*, 44.

18 Martin G. Murray, " 'Pete the Great': A Biography of Peter Doyle," *Walt Whitman Quarterly Review* 12 (Summer 1994): 12–13.

19 Quoted in Shively, *Calamus Lovers*, 101. Murray, " 'Pete the Great,' " 17–18.

20 Murray, " 'Pete the Great,' " 1–4.

21 Murray, " 'Pete the Great,' " 4–7.

22 Murray, " 'Pete the Great,' " 9–10.

23 Murray, " 'Pete the Great,' " 18.

24 Murray, " 'Pete the Great,' " 35.

25 Shively, *Calamus Lovers*, 117–20.

26 *Correspondence*, 1:256.

27 Walt Whitman, "Return of a Brooklyn Veteran," *Brooklyn Eagle*, March 19, 1865, reprinted in Glicksberg, *Walt Whitman*, 88–89.

28 Foote, *The Civil War*, 3:896.

29 *Correspondence*, 1:257.

30 *Correspondence*, 1: 246–47, 260n.

31 *Notebooks*, 2:764.

32 Murray, " 'Pete the Great,' " 15.

33 *Prose Works*, 2:592, 593, 597. Reynolds, *Walt Whitman's America*, 158–60, 441.

34 *Memoranda*, 46–48.

35 Glicksberg, *Walt Whitman*, 174–75.

36 *Memoranda*, 49.

37 *Leaves*, 329n.

38 *Correspondence*, 1:259.
39 *Memoranda*, 52.
40 Jack Rudolph, "The Grand Review," *Civil War Times Illustrated* (November 1980), 38.
41 John F. Marszalek, *Sherman: A Soldier's Passion for Order* (New York: Free Press, 1993), 355. Rudolph, "The Grand Review," 39–42.
42 *Correspondence*, 1:260–62.
43 Rudolph, "The Grand Review," 43. Marszalek, *Sherman*, 358.
44 *Leaves*, 322.
45 *Leaves*, 324–25.
46 *Leaves*, 339.
47 *Leaves*, 330–31.
48 *Leaves*, 331.
49 *Leaves*, 335.
50 *Leaves*, 336.
51 *Leaves*, 336.
52 *Leaves*, 336–37.
53 *Leaves*, 321.
54 Loving, *Walt Whitman's Champion*, 158, 159, 162.
55 Shively, *Calamus Lovers*, 85.
56 Shively, *Drum Beats*, 159, 161.
57 Shively, *Drum Beats*, 222–24.
58 *Leaves*, 364, 366.

Epilogue: Lose Not My Sons

1 *Prose Works*, 2:384–85. Kaplan, *Walt Whitman*, 335. *Prose Works*, 2:369–70.
2 *Leaves*, 591–92.
3 *Leaves*, 578.
4 *Memoranda*, 5, 65.
5 *Prose Works*, 2:466. *Memoranda*, 3.
6 *Prose Works*, 1:81. *Leaves*, 498, 549.
7 Traubel, *With Walt Whitman*, 6:362–65. *Leaves*, 337.
8 Traubel, *With Walt Whitman*, 6:366. *Leaves*, 19, 74, 315. *Memoranda*, 59.

BIBLIOGRAPHY

Adams, George Worthington. *Doctors in Blue: The Medical History of the Union Army in the Civil War*. Baton Rouge: Louisiana State University Press, 1952.

Allen, Gay Wilson. *The Solitary Singer: A Critical Biography of Walt Whitman*. New York: New York University Press, 1955.

Barrus, Clara. *The Life and Letters of John Burroughs*. 2 vols. Boston: Houghton Mifflin, 1925.

———. *Whitman and Burroughs, Comrades*. Boston: Houghton Mifflin, 1931.

Basler, Roy P., ed. *The Collected Works of Abraham Lincoln*. 8 vols. New Brunswick, N.J.: Rutgers University Press, 1953.

Berthold, Dennis, and Kenneth M. Price, eds. *Dear Brother Walt: Letters of Thomas Jefferson Whitman*. Kent, Ohio: Kent State University Press, 1984.

Bradley, Sculley, and Harold W. Blodgett, eds. *Leaves of Grass*. New York: W. W. Norton, 1973.

Brasler, Thomas L. *Whitman as Editor of the Brooklyn Daily Eagle*. Detroit: Wayne State University Press, 1970.

Brooks, Stewart. *Civil War Medicine*. Springfield, Ill.: Charles C. Thomas, 1966.

Bucke, Richard M., ed. *The Wound Dresser: A Series of Letters Written in Washington During the War of Rebellion*. Boston: Small, Maynard, 1898.

Burroughs, John. *Notes on Walt Whitman as Poet and Person*. New York: American Book Company, 1867.

———. *Walt Whitman: A Study*. Boston: Houghton Mifflin, 1896.

Calder, Ellen M. "Personal Recollections of Walt Whitman." *Atlantic Monthly* 99 (June 1907), 825–34.

Carpenter, Edward. *Days with Walt Whitman*. London: George Allen, 1906.

Catton, Bruce. *A Stillness at Appomattox*. New York: Washington Square Press, 1958.

Conway, Moncure D. *Autobiography: Memories and Experiences*. 2 vols. Boston: Houghton Mifflin, 1904.

Cunningham, H. H. *Doctors in Gray: The Confederate Medical Service*. Baton Rouge: Louisiana State University Press, 1958.

Denny, Robert E. *Civil War Medicine: Care & Comfort of the Wounded*. New York: Sterling, 1995.

Donald, David Herbert. *Lincoln*. New York: Simon and Schuster, 1995.

Dunkelman, Mark H. "Oscar Wilber." *America's Civil War* (November 1996): 8–18, 86–88.

Faust, Patricia L., ed. *Historical Times Illustrated Encyclopedia of the Civil War*. New York: Harper & Row, 1986.

Frederickson, George. *The Inner Civil War: Northern Intellectuals and the Crisis of the Union*. New York: Harper & Row, 1965.

Freedman, Florence B. "New Light on an Old Quarrel: Walt Whitman and William Douglas O'Connor 1872." *Walt Whitman Review* 11 (June 1965): 27– 52.

———. "W. D. O'Connor: Whitman's 'Chosen Knight.' " *Walt Whitman Review* 27 (September 1981): 95–101.

Freemon, Frank R. *Gangrene and Glory: Medical Care during the American Civil War*. Cranbury, N.J.: Associated University Presses, 1998.

Foote, Shelby. *The Civil War: A Narrative*. 3 vols. New York: Random House, 1958–74.

Glicksberg, Charles I. *Walt Whitman and the Civil War*. Philadelphia: University of Pennsylvania Press, 1933.

———. "Walt Whitman in 1862." *American Literature* 6 (November 1934): 264–82.

Gohdes, Clarence, and Rollo G. Silver, eds. *Faint Clews & Indirections: Manuscripts of Walt Whitman and His Family*. Durham, N.C.: Duke University Press, 1949.

Grier, Edward F., ed. *Walt Whitman: Notebooks and Unpublished Prose Manuscripts*. 6 vols. New York: New York University Press, 1984.

Higginson, T. W. "Unmanly Manhood." *The Woman's Journal* 12 (February 1882): 33–37.

Hinton, Richard. "Washington Letter." *Cincinnati Commercial*, August 26, 1871.

Holloway, Emory. "Whitman Pursued." *American Literature* 27 (March 1955): 6–7.

———, ed. *The Uncollected Poetry and Prose of Walt Whitman*. 2 vols. New York: Peter Smith Press, 1921.

———, and Vernolian Schwartz, eds. *I Sit and Look Out: Editorials from the Brooklyn Daily Times*. New York: AMS Press, 1966.

Johnston, John H. *Diary Notes of a Visit to Walt Whitman and Some of His Friends, in 1890.* Boston: T. Brimelow, 1890.

Kaplan, Justin. *Walt Whitman: A Life.* New York: Simon and Schuster, 1980.

Keen, W. W. "Military Surgery in 1861 and 1918." *Annals of the American Academy of Political and Social Science* 80 (1918): 14–15.

Kennedy, William Sloane. *Reminiscences of Walt Whitman.* Paisley, Scotland: Alexander Gardner, 1896.

Loving, Jerome. *Walt Whitman: The Song of Himself.* Berkeley: University of California Press, 1999.

———. *Walt Whitman's Champion: William Douglas O'Connor.* College Station: Texas A&M University Press, 1978.

———, ed. *Civil War Letters of George Washington Whitman.* Durham, N.C.: Duke University Press, 1975.

Marszalek, John F. *Sherman: A Soldier's Passion for Order.* New York: Free Press, 1993.

Massachusetts Soldiers, Sailors, and Marines in the Civil War. Norwood, Mass.: Norwood Press, 1932.

McPherson, James M. *Battle Cry of Freedom: The Civil War Era.* New York: Oxford University Press, 1988.

Medical and Surgical History of the War of the Rebellion. 6 vols. Washington, D.C.: Government Printing Office, 1875–85.

Miller, Edwin Haviland. "Walt Whitman and Ellen Eyre." *American Literature* 33 (March 1961): 64–65.

———. ed. *Walt Whitman: The Correspondence.* 6 vols. New York: New York University Press, 1961–77.

Morris, Roy, Jr. "Titans Clash in the Wilderness." *Military History* (April 1997): 43–56.

Murray, Martin G. " 'Pete the Great': A Biography of Peter Doyle." *Walt Whitman Quarterly Review* (Summer 1994): 1–51.

Oates, Stephen B. *A Woman of Valor: Clara Barton and the Civil War.* New York: Free Press, 1994.

Parry, Albert. *Garrets and Pretenders: A History of Bohemia in America.* New York: Covici, Friede, 1933.

Renehan, Edward J., Jr. *John Burroughs: An American Naturalist.* Post Mills, Vt.: Chelsea Green Publishing Company, 1992.

Reynolds, David S. *Walt Whitman's America: A Cultural Biography.* New York: Alfred A. Knopf, 1995.

Roosa, D. B. St. John. "Walt Whitman." *New York Mail and Express*, June 10, 1896.

Saxton, Martha. *Louisa May: A Modern Biography of Louisa May Alcott*. Boston: Houghton Mifflin, 1977.

Sears, Stephen W. *George McClellan: The Young Napoleon*. New York: Ticknor & Fields, 1988.

Shively, Charley, ed. *Calamus Lovers: Walt Whitman's Working-Class Camerados*. San Francisco: Gay Sunshine Press, 1987.

———. *Drum Beats: Walt Whitman's Civil War Boy Lovers*. San Francisco: Gay Sunshine Press, 1989.

Sixbey, George L. "Walt Whitman's Middle Years: 1860–1867." Ph.D. diss., Yale University, 1940.

Stackpole, Edward J. *The Fredericksburg Campaign*. Harrisburg, Pa.: Stackpole Books, 1957.

Stansell, Christine. "Whitman at Pfaff's: Commercial Culture, Literary Life and New York Bohemia at Mid-Century." *Walt Whitman Quarterly Review* 10 (Winter 1993): 107–23.

Stovall, Floyd, ed. *Walt Whitman: Prose Works 1892*. 2 vols. New York: New York University Press, 1963–64.

Sweet, Robert B. "A Writer Looks at Whitman's 'A Sight in Camp in the Daybreak Gray and Dim.'" *Walt Whitman Review* 17 (June 1971): 58–62.

Taylor, John M. *Garfield of Ohio: The Available Man*. New York: W. W. Norton, 1970.

Todd, Gary L. "An Invalid Corps." *Civil War Times Illustrated* (December 1985): 10–19.

Traubel, *With Walt Whitman in Camden*. 9 vols. New York: D. Appleton, 1908.

Trowbridge, John Townsend. *My Own Story*. Boston: Houghton Mifflin, 1903.

———. "Reminiscences of Walt Whitman." *Atlantic Monthly* 89 (February 1902): 163–71.

Trudeau, Noah Andre. *Bloody Roads South*. Boston: Little Brown, 1989.

Waldron, Randall H. *Letters of Martha Mitchell Jefferson*. New York: New York University Press, 1977.

Wecter, Dixon. "Walt Whitman as Civil Servant." *PMLA* 58 (December 1943): 1094–97.

Whitman, Walt. *Memoranda During the War*. Saybrook, Conn.: Globe Pequot Press, 1993.

Wiley, Bell Irvin. *The Life of Billy Yank: The Common Soldier of the Union*. Baton Rouge: Louisiana State University Press, 1952.

INDEX

Abolitionism, Whitman on, 81–82
Affection
    hospital visits and, 132–36
    and integrity of Union, 12
    letters of, 133–34, 235–36
    medicine of, 6
    same-sex, 133
    for Whitman, 157, 235–36
"After the Supper and Talk" (poem),
    132
Alcott, Louisa May, 93–94, 146
Aldrich, Thomas Bailey, 21, 22, 24
Allen, Elijah, 104, 150
Ambulance Corps, 65
Amputations
    during Civil War, 94, 95–96
    Whitman's attendance of, 37, 118,
    161–62
Andersonville prison camp, 193, 198
Antietam, Battle of, 46, 62, 65
    aftermath of, 97–98
Arnold, George, 21, 23, 24
"The Artilleryman's Vision" (poem),
    170
Ashby, Mrs., 167–68
Ashby, Turner, 24, 167
Ashton, J. Hubley, 87, 198, 234
Attendants, hospital, 112–14

Babcock, William E., 190
Baker, Mrs. E. S., 148
Baker, Frank, 87
Barton, Clara, 53–54, 63
Bauldsir, John Y., 31
"Beat! Beat! Drums!" (poem), 42–
    43
Benton, Myron, 153
Bliss, Willard, 163
Bloom, Nat, 120, 148
Boardman, Henry, 105–6
Bohemians, New York, 18–25
Booth, John Wilkes, 218, 219
Booth, Junius Brutus, 219
Brooks, Livingston, 126
Brown, Lewis, 132–34
    gratitude to Whitman, 235
    leg amputation of, 161–62
    letters to, 135, 140–41, 156
    siege of Washington and, 186
Buchanan, James, 16
Bucke, Richard, 39
Bull Run, Battle of, 41–42
Bullet wounds, 95
Bureau of Indian Affairs, 201–2, 233–
    34
Burnside, Ambrose, 46, 57, 66–67, 175,
    188